6/30/15

To My
Thanks for all you do for JAK.

[signature]

©2014 by Southwest Historic Press, San Antonio, TX

All rights reserved. 1st paperback printing 2015

Library of Congress Cataloging-in-Publication Data

Butler, Judge Ed

Galvez!

SPAIN -- OUR FORGOTTEN ALLY IN THE AMERICAN REVOLUTIONARY WAR: A CONCISE SUMMARY OF SPAIN'S ASSISTANCE

Judge Ed Butler - 1st ed.

Includes bibliographical references and index

ISBN NO: 978-0-692-03088-2

Published by

Southwest Historic Press

San Antonio, TX

1. United States - History - Revolution, 1775-1783 - Participation, Spanish. 2. United States - Foreign relations - 1774-1783. 3. United States - Foreign relations - Spain. 4. Spain - Foreign relations - Spain. 4. Spain - Foreign relations - United States.

# DEDICATION

## To Robin

JUDGE EDWARD F. BUTLER, SR.

## OTHER BOOKS BY THE AUTHOR

*Wanderlust*, Butler Family Limited Partnership, San Antonio 2012 (Covers travel between 2005-2012).

*Pacifica*, Butler Family Limited Partnership, San Antonio 2005 (covers a series of travel articles from January–August 1998 through Hawaii, the islands of the South Pacific, Australia, New Zealand, Indonesia, Singapore, China, Taiwan, Philippines, Korea and Japan).

*1997 Around-The-World Adventure*, Butler Family Limited Partnership, San Antonio 2004 (covers a series of travel articles from July - December 1997 through Western Europe, Eastern Europe, Scandinavia, the Baltics, Russia, Belarus, Oman, The United Arab Emirates, India, Nepal, Singapore, Myanmar, Malaysia, and Thailand).

Contributing editor, *Colonial America: An Encyclopedia of Social, Political, Cultural, and Economic History*, East River Books, Santa Barbara, CA.

*Travels With the Judge*, Butler Family Limited Partnership, San Antonio 2003 (covers travels around the world from 1963 – 1997).

*The Texas Genealogist's Handbook*, Butler Family Limited Partnership, San Antonio, January 2001.

*The Descendants of Private Philip Nicholas Myers, American Revolutionary War Patriot,* jointly with Robin Myers Butler, Butler Family Limited Partnership, San Antonio, December 2000.

*The Ancestors and Descendants of Diana Parker Martin, of Lane, DeWitt County, Illinois*, jointly with Robin Myers Butler, Butler Family Limited Partnership, San Antonio, December 2000.

*The Descendants of Thomas Pincerna, Progenitor of the Butler Family*, Gen Pub, Dallas, 1997 **(First Prize, Best Family History Book, Dallas Genealogical Soc., 1997).**

*Texas Litigator's Handbook*, Butterworth, Austin, 1989 (ISBN 040925432-0).

*Family Law in Texas*, co-author, Legal Education Institute, Naples, FL, 1988.

*Cultural Behavior Handbook: Australia/A Guide For Defense Attaches*, U.S. State Dept., Washington, November, 1986.

## ABOUT THE AUTHOR

Judge Edward F. Butler, Sr. is a retired U.S. Administrative Law Judge. Before serving in that position he served as Presiding Municipal Judge for South Padre Island, Texas. He is an honor graduate of Vanderbilt University School of Law, which he attended as a Ford Foundation Scholar. He was a board certified civil trial lawyer before assuming full time duties on the bench. He is the author of eleven books, three of which are on family history.

Judge Butler is a frequent seminar and after dinner speaker on historical and genealogical topics, and is a regular contributor to national and state historical and genealogical society journals and magazines. Since his retirement in 1997, he has devoted a considerable amount of his time and energy to the National

Society Sons of the American Revolution, where he served as President General, and Chairman of the Board of the SAR Foundation.

In March 2001, then SAR President General Larry D. McClanahan, appointed Judge Butler as the SAR Ambassador to México and Latin America. Judge Butler's interest in Spain's assistance to the colonists in the American Revolutionary War stems from his participation with the SAR in México for which he was the founder and Charter President. In 2010 he also founded the SAR Society in Spain.

Judge Butler previously served as Genealogist General of the national SAR before which he served as Genealogist for the Texas Society, SAR. He served for seven years as a member of the National SAR genealogy committee. He served for two years as genealogical editor of *The Texas Compatriot*, magazine of the Texas Society of SAR. He also published a monthly column for SAR chapter newsletters, entitled "The Genealogy Corner". He was the author of the monthly historical column, "Remembering Yesterday", carried in many Texas newspapers.

Judge Ed Butler was the 2009-2010 President General, National Society Sons of the American Revolution. In July 2011 he was made an Honorary Member of the Order of the Granaderos y Damas de Gálvez. In July 2012 he was the founder and Charter Grand Viscount General of the Order of the Founders of North America 1492-1692. His accomplishments have earned him inclusion in *Whós Who in the World* (Marquis 2011), *Whós Who in America* (2010)**,** *Whós Who in American Law, Whós Who in the South and Southwest, Whós Who in Practicing Attorneys (1989), Whós Who in Texas, Dictionary of International Biographees,* and *2000 Notable Americans*. He has been honored as an Admiral in the Texas Navy, Tennessee Colonel, Kentucky Colonel, and as an Arkansas Traveler. He had been the recipient of Keys to the Cities of Memphis, TN and Birmingham, AL.

Other groups in which he has actively participated include:

México Society, Sons of the American Revolution (Founder, Charter President)

Spain Society, Sons of the American Revolution (Founder, Charter Chancellor)

France Society, Sons of the American Revolution - Honorary President General (2010)

Children of the American Revolution - Honorary Vice President General (2009-2010)

SAR Conference on the American Revolution - Founding Board Member

Military Order of the Knights of the Temple of Jerusalem (Deputy Grand Prior; Grand Croix)

Raymond J. Davis Foundation of the Knights Templar - Board Member 2003-present

General Society of the Colonial Wars (Deputy Governor General 2012-2014)

Society of the Descendants of Washington's Army at Valley Forge (Judge Advocate General)

Order of the First Families of Maryland, President, Texas Society (2013-2014); Chancellor General (2014- present).

George Washington Foundation - Fellow (2001-present)

General Society of the War of 1812 (Judge Advocate General)

Military Order of the Stars and Bars (Deputy Judge Advocate General)

General Society Sons of Revolution (President of the Texas Society; Vice President General)

Order of the Founder and Patriots of America (Governor of the Texas Society)

Magna Charta Dames and Barons (Vice Regent of the Texas Society; Regent of the San Antonio Colony)

Reserve Officers Association (Navy Vice President Tennessee and Texas)

Navy Reserve Association (President of Mississippi Valley Chapter)

Military Order of Foreign Wars (President of Memphis, TN Chapter)

Sons of Confederate Veterans (Texas Division Parliamentarian; Camp Commander)

Texas Chapter, Royal Society of St. George (Founding Secretary)

Judge Butler is also a member of the following groups:

Sons of the Republic of Texas (Honorary Member, Tyler, TX Chapter)

Order of the *Granaderos y Damas de Gálvez* (Honorary Member)

*Los Bexarenos* Genealogical and Historical Society.

Sovereign Colonial Society Americans of Royal Descent

Colonial Order of the Crown

Plantagenet Society

Order of Americans of Armorial Ancestry

Military Order of the World Wars

Society of Descendants of Knights of the Most Noble Order of the Garter

Military Order of the Crusades

Order of the Crown of Charlemagne in the United States of America

National Huguenot Society

Sons and Daughters of the Colonial and Antebellum Bench and Bar

Gavel Club

Boonesboro Society

Alamo Defenders Descendants Soc.

Order of the First Families of North Carolina

Travelers Century Club (Silver level member, for those who have traveled to 150 countries or more). The author has visited 180 countries accepted by TCC.

# PROLOGUE

The horizontal rain peppering his face stung like a thousand needles. The salt water burned his eyes and blurred his vision. The violent storm had scattered his armada. He could see none of his ships. His hands were bloody from holding on dearly to the jack line[1] made out of coarse sisal rope. When the hurricane winds cracked the mizzenmast, his nose was broken by wind driven debris. The noise of the last sail exploding was ear splitting. Pitching, rolling and yawing, his ship was unable to make headway. The tempestuous winds rushing thought the ship's rigging created an eerie wailing sound.

General Bernardo de Gálvez[2] had no way of knowing when he led his sixty-four ship armada out of Havana bound for Pensacola to attack the final British stronghold in the Gulf of México, that he would encounter a hurricane.[3] His armada

---

[1] A jackline is a rope or wire strung from a ship's bow to its stern to which a safety harness can be clipped, allowing a crewmember to move about the deck safely when there is risk of falling or being swept overboard during heavy weather.

[2] For whom Galveston, TX is named.

[3] The third important hurricane of October 1780 arose in the western Caribbean south of Cuba near Jamaica on 15 October. It became known as "Solanós Hurricane", after the commander of the 64 vessel Spanish war fleet, Admiral Jose Solano. This hurricane caught the Spanish armada on its way from Havana, Cuba to Pensacola, Florida, to capture the capital of British West Florida. The fleet transported an army of 4,000 under the command of General Bernardo de Gálvez, commander of New Orleans.

included about 7,800 soldiers and sailors[4]. His flagship was the *San Juan Nepomuceno*[5], a 7,400 ton, sixty-six gun ship of the line, under the command of Admiral Jose Solano. The night before gale winds brought heavy rains and blew up monster waves. As the night wore on the storm intensified, making it almost impossible to hold the 181 foot three master on course. As a precaution, Admiral Solano had ordered that all sails be furled except the jib - an order that sadly came too late.

Gálvez, normally a snappy dresser, even with his oil slicker on, was soaked to the bone and his uniform underneath was drenched and shapeless. He had left his hat in his quarters. As he braced himself on the wheel deck, his raven black hair fell over his eyes. His handsome face looked bedraggled after enduring the tempest for several hours.

*San Juan Nepomuceno*

Solono was a comical looking man. His body was pear shaped, and his legs were short for his 5 foot 6 inch frame. When he walked, he appeared to waddle. The folds of fat on his stomach and abdomen were so large that he must have had to hold up the folds to

---

[4] At this time General George Washington commanded only about 6,000 troops of the continental line.

[5] Generally referred to as the "San Juan".

urinate. His long double chin was exaggerated by a narrow handlebar mustache. It had taken Gálvez a while to take anything he said seriously - yet Solano was an extraordinary ship captain, and an accomplished navigator. The two men worked well together.

Even without full sails, the wind snapped the main mast. As it plummeted to the deck it crushed three deckhands. Green water swept away a junior officer and three 24 pounders. As the *San Juan* careened into a thirty foot wave, the ship was slammed violently to starboard. The wheel spun wildly, breaking the jaw of the helmsman.

Before the injured helmsman could be replaced, the bow of the ship plowed into another enormous wave, with such force that the stern of the ship abruptly rose out of the water, as if it intended to become perpendicular. While the stern was above the sea, a rogue wave swept away the tiller, leaving the ship totally at the mercy of the sea. This violent action unleashed six more 24 pounders from their safety lines.

Before the day was over all three masts had been destroyed. Four crewmen had been crushed by loose cannon awash on the quarterdeck. In addition to the bodies of dead crewmen, masts, rigging, debris and loose cannon cluttered the quarterdeck. Few things are as dangerous as a loose cannon in high seas.

His plan to capture Pensacola from the English was dashed for the time being. Over half his gunships and troop transports were sent to the bottom of the Gulf of México. At least 2,000 men had been lost. The remainder of his fleet with their crews was cast upon the shores of the Gulf from the Yucatan of México to the shore of Alabama.

As the remains of his ship were being towed back to Havana he had plenty of time to think - and to plan. How would this catastrophe be viewed by King Carlos III? Would Gálvez obtain a second chance to attack Pensacola? Would he be provided with replacement ships? How would he acquire additional troops? As the wheels in his brain continued to spin, his thoughts drifted back to the beginning - his appointment as Governor of Spanish West Florida - his involvement in the war against England - the battles of Baton Rouge, Manchac, Natchez[6] and Mobile - and the war for American Independence. His story and the saga of Spain's involvement in the American Revolution begins:

Prime Minister, José Moñino y Redondo, Count of Floridablanca, wrote in March 1777:

"The fate of the colonies interests us very much, and we shall do for them everything that circumstances permit".

---

[6] Natchez was actually surrendered by the British without a shot being fired.

# TABLE OF CONTENTS

| | |
|---|---|
| Dedication | v |
| Photo of the author | vi |
| Other Books by the Author | vi |
| About The Author | ix |
| Prologue | xv |
| Table of Contents | xix |
| List of Important Individuals in the Book | xxv |
| Introduction | xxix |
| Preface | xxxv |
| Scope of This Book | xxxvii |
| List of Illustrations | xliii |
| List of Appendices | xlvii |
| Foreword | xlix |
| Acknowledgments | liv |
| The Beginning | 1 |
| Historical Relationship Between Spain and England | 3 |
| Spain's Goals | 7 |

| | |
|---|---|
| Spanish Assistance | 9 |
| Aid by Spain Prior to the Declaration of Independence | 11 |
| Spain Continued to Send Supplies to The Americans Up The Mississippi River and on the East Coast | 29 |
| Spain Throughout the American Revolutionary War Continued to Enlarge Its Fleet And Military In The Caribbean and Feigned an Attack on Great Britain Which Kept a Large Part of its Fleet at Home | 39 |
| The American Revolutionary War Was Part of a Global War | 43 |
| Don Bernardo de Gálvez y Madrid | 53 |
| Oliver Pollock | 63 |
| Gálvez Captures Manchac | 67 |
| Gálvez Captures Ft. New Richmond at Baton Rouge and Ft. Panmure at Natchez | 69 |
| Gálvez Attacks Ft. Charlotte at Mobile: | 71 |
| The Spanish Armada Heading to Pensacola was Destroyed in a Hurricane | 75 |

| | |
|---|---|
| Spanish Siege of Ft. George at Pensacola Took Two Months: *The Most Decisive Battle Of The American Revolutionary War*[7] | 79 |
| Gálvez Takes the Bahamas | 89 |
| Gálvez Defeats the British in the Upper Mississippi Valley | 91 |
| Spain's Assistance in the Midwest: General George Rogers Clark[8] | 93 |
| Fort Kaskaskia, Illinois | 101 |
| Fort Vincennes, Indiana | 105 |
| Fort Cahokia, Illinois | 111 |
| Fort Jefferson, Kentucky | 113 |
| Fort San Carlos, Missouri (Saint Louis) | 115 |
| Spanish Attack British Fort St. Joseph, Michigan | 125 |

---

[7] For an in depth account of the Battle of Pensacola, see *The Longest Siege of the American Revolution: Pensacola*, by Wesley S. Odom, self published, 2009.

[8] For an excellent review of the extensive activities of General Clark during the American Revolutionary War, see *George Rogers Clark and the War in the West*, by Lowell H. Harrison, Univ. Press of Kentucky, Louisville, 1976.

| | |
|---|---|
| Fort Nelson, KY | 129 |
| Arkansas Post | 133 |
| Spanish Soldiers Were at the Ready at California Presidios | 135 |
| Spanish Fleet Captures 55 Ships of the English Fleet | 139 |
| The Texas Connection to the American Revolutionary War | 143 |
| Spain and France Prepare to Attack the British at Jamaica | 151 |
| Current Descendants of Spanish Patriots are Eligible For Membership in Patriotic Lineage Societies: | 155 |
| Descendants Of Spanish Royalty are Eligible for Membership in Patriotic Organizations: | 157 |
| The *Donativo* | 159 |
| Chronological Summary of Spain's Assistance to the Americans | 161 |
| Diego de Gardoqui | 179 |
| Don Juan De Miralles | 183 |
| Official Thanks to Spain and to General Bernardo de Gálvez | 185 |
| Bernardo de Gálvez is on the way to being Declared a U.S. Citizen | 189 |

| | |
|---|---|
| Gálvez Portrait | 195 |
| The First American Dollar was A Spanish Coin | 201 |
| SAR Trip to Spain and Gibraltar | 207 |
| Conclusion | 221 |
| Bibliography | 225 |
| Appendices | 247 |
| Index | 287 |

# LIST OF IMPORTANT INDIVIDUALS IN THE BOOK

To assist the reader in understanding the interaction among the military and governmental representatives of England, Spain, France and the United States, the following list is provided.

**From Spain**

| | |
|---|---|
| Carlos III de Borbón | King of Spain (1716 to 1788) |
| Juan Carlos de Borbón | King of Spain (1975 to 2014) |
| Felipe VI de Borbón | King of Spain (2014 to present) |
| Don José Moñino y Redondo, Count of Floridablanca | Prime Minister of Spain |
| General Bernardo de Gálvez | Governor of Spanish Louisiana |
| Jose' de Gálvez | Spanish Minister of the West Indies. |
| Matias de Gálvez | Spanish Viceroy of the Americas and Father of Bernardo de Gálvez. |
| Luis De Unzaga y Amezaga | Spanish Governor of Louisiana immediately |

| | |
|---|---|
| | before Bernardo De Gálvez arrived in late 1776. |
| Don Fernando de Leyba | Commandant of Fort San Carlos, MO |
| Joseph Gardoqui & Sons in Balbao, Spain | Spanish Merchants who supplied the colonists |
| Don Francisco de Saavedra | Special Emissary to represent the Crown of Spain, giving him authority to make decisions regarding transfer of funds from the Royal Treasury in Havana. |
| Don Juan de Miralles | A wealthy Spanish merchant from Havana, Cuba, who King Carlos III appointed as a Royal Envoy of King Carlos to the United States in 1778. |

**From England:**

Thomas Robinson, 2nd Baron Grantham — British Ambassador to Spain, 1771 to 1779.

**From America:**

General George Rogers Clark — American Commander, North West Territories

Robert Morris — American representative in New Orleans empowered to purchase and ship military supplies acquired from Spain and France.

Captain George Gibson — Trilengual frontiersman who in July, 1776 headed a trip from Ft. Pitt to New Orleans to obtain arms, gunpowder and supplies from the Spanish.

Lieutenant William Linn — Second in Command to Captain George Gibson. He captured a British schooner on Lake Pontchatrain, LA; renamed it the

| | |
|---|---|
| Gibson's Lambs | *Gálveztown*, and presented it to Bernardo de Gálvez.<br><br>The crew of Captain George Gibson, most of whom were Irish. |
| Antonio Gil Ybarbo | Lieutenant Governor of Texas, 1775-1781 |

**From France:**

| | |
|---|---|
| François-Joseph-Paul, Count de Grasse | Admiral of the French fleet in North America and the Caribbean. |
| Charles Gravier de Vergennes, Count de Vergennes | French Secretary for Foreign Affairs. |
| Pierre Beaumarchais | Manager of *Rodrique Hortalez et Cie,* which distributed the funds from Spain and France. |

# INTRODUCTION

I became interested in Spain's involvement in the American Revolutionary War when in 2001, I was appointed the Sons of the American Revolution (SAR) Ambassador to México and Latin America. Both the SAR and the Daughters of the American Revolution (DAR) have recognized Spain's assistance for many years, and many members of both societies are descendants of Spanish soldiers who participated in the conflict.

It soon became apparent to me that Spain and Gálvez had both been short changed in recognition for their efforts in our cause for freedom. In the next few years I researched Spain's involvement and wrote several articles which were published in the *National Genealogical Society's Magazine* and in the *SAR Magazine*. I wanted the public to know that Spaniards living in what is now Texas participated in the cause by herding long horn cattle from the San Antonio area to feed General Bernardo de Gálvez' troops in Louisiana.

On Columbus Day each October, US citizens honor Christopher Columbus, but the Italians have hijacked the holiday. Discovery of the New World would not have been possible at that time without the financial support of Ferdinand and Isabella, joint monarchs of Spain. They were a great couple, who defeated the Moors and drove them from Spain. During their reign they united Spain and centralized power in the crown. They insured that the peoples of the New World became Christians. Through their wisdom Spain became the first world power, and a vast, wealthy empire. Their vast military dominated the world for the next 150 years. I have a slight prejudice in favor of Ferdinand and Isabella, as they are my 23$^{rd}$ great grandparents.

Since my research has proved that Spain was just as important an alley as France, I started examining the reasons that could have precipitated the oversight of Spain's support.

I suspect that most Americans believed that Spain started the Spanish American War by sinking the *USS Maine* in Havana harbor. Recently, evidence has come forth that the explosion on the *Maine* was accidental, but there has never been an apology issued to Spain, nor any attempt made to adjust the results of that war.

Some may resent Spain's position of neutrality in the First and Second World Wars. Some historians look down on Ferdinand and Isabella because of the Inquisition. The insidious "Black Legend" criticized Spain for the Inquisition, yet this was a function of the Catholic Church, and not the Crown.

Also the Black Legend contended that Spain was crueler to American natives than other colonial powers. To the contrary, Spain was the only colonial power to pass laws for the protection of Native Americans. In 1512, the Laws of Burgos forbad the mistreating of indigenous people and it also limited the powers of landowners. In 1542, Spain passed a new law to further protect the natives. Even though there were Spaniards in America who mistreated the natives, these two laws reflected the intent of the Spanish colonial government of the time to protect the rights of the native population.

**Ed Butler and wife, Robin, meet Crown Prince Felipe**

No matter the reason for this historical slight, hopefully after reading this book, readers will understand the extent of Spain's assistance and give credit where credit is due.

After my first article about Spain's involvement in the American Revolutionary War, I received a letter of thanks from His Royal Majesty Juan Carlos I de Borbón, King of Spain. A copy of the letter from the king is attached as Appendix A. Subsequent letters from the royal family are attached as Appendix B, C, and D.

In May 2010, my wife Robin and I led a group of SAR members and their wives, many of whom were members of DAR on a tour of Spain.

We were granted a private audience with Crown Prince Felipe The SAR and DAR chapters of Spain; and a large group of the Order of the Granaderos y Damas de Gálvez joined us. At that time I presented Crown Prince Felipe with the SAR International Medal.

Following the formal ceremonies, Crown Prince Felipe called me aside. He said:

"I want you to write a book about Spain in the American Revolutionary War. Then, I want you to write a screen play and make a movie. I would like to see Antonio Banderas play the part of Gálvez".

I told the prince that I could write the book, but I had no experience with writing a screen play, and that it would be up to Hollywood to make a movie and they would select the stars.

## Participants at Private Audience with Crown Prince Felipe de Borbón

This book fulfills my obligation to King Felipe. For a thorough coverage of Spain's contributions, see *Spain And the Independence of the United States: An Intrinsic Gift*, Thomas E. Chavez, Univ. of NM Press, Albuquerque (2002), ISBN 0-8263-2794-x.

In prior discussions with some of my friends and associates, they claim that calling Spain an "ally" is incorrect because Spain never signed any treaty with the colonists. The *Webster Dictionary* definition of *"Ally": 2. To associate or connect by some mutual relationship as resemblance or friendship; 3. To enter into an alliance, join, unite; Synonyms: partner, confederate, friend, aide, accomplice, accessory, assistant, abettor, colleague, coadjutor, auxiliary, and helper.*[9] Under that definition of "ally", I hope you will agree with me after reading this book that Spain was in fact a very important ally.

---

[9] *Webster New Universal Unabridged Dictionary*, 1996.

# PREFACE

This book starts with the premise that France was an important ally and benefactor to the Americans seeking independence. Clearly, France provided the colonists with money, arms, ammunition, troops, and supplies. Great leadership was afforded by Lafayette, Rochambeau and DeGrasse. Thousands of French troops fought on our shores, and we are eternally grateful.

I consider myself a Francophile. For many years I have been a dual member of the France Society, Sons of the American Revolution. My wife and I participated in the NSSAR Congresses in Paris in 2003, 2008, and 2010. We led the American delegation to the NSSAR Congress in Paris in 2010, where I penned the new charter to the France Society, thereby elevating its status above state societies.

As a Texan I was saddened that few people were aware of the Texas connection to the American Revolution. The SAR, DAR and CAR for years have acknowledged service by Spain during the American Revolutionary War, but few historians have written about Spain's participation. I felt that appropriate credit should be given to Spain without in any way lessening the credit to our French Allies. *VIVE LA FRANCE!*

In this book the punctuation and capitalization standard used is that of the current Spanish and French languages. The surname "Borbón" is used throughout, and is the Spanish spelling. The French use "Bourbon".

# SCOPE OF THIS BOOK

I have attempted to gather from many sources the documents and literature concerning Spain's participation in the American Revolutionary War. My hope is that it will be a comfortable read for the amateur historian and classroom student.

An important reason for writing this book is to educate the educators. Lamentably, many highly respected historians and biographers are not aware of the facts about Spain's tremendous assistance to the American Revolutionary cause. For instance, James Srodes in his book about Benjamin Franklin[10] misstated:

> *France knew not to expect much from Spain because Charles III's ambassador to Paris had told him so.* **Madrid's only real military contribution was to join its navy with that of the French, resulting in a combined force that in theory rivaled Britain's Royal Navy.** *Beyond that, however, Charles III was even less inclined to aid rebels than his nephew Louis was. All Charles wanted to do was seize Gibraltar from the British and to protect his holdings in the Caribbean and North America.*[11]

---

[10] *Franklin, The Essential Founding Father*, James Srodes, Regnery Pub. Co., Washington (2002).

[11] *Id* at p. 338.

It is hard to understand Srodes in making such a blatantly incorrect statement.[12] A journalist by profession, he at least admitted that Spain and France initially committed equal 1,000,000 Livres deposits to the fictitious French company, Roderigue Hortalez & Cie,[13] and that Arthur Lee was able to secure an addition 1,000,000 Livres from King Charles.[14] This book will clearly reflect the unsurpassed military support by Spain to assist our American forefathers.

During the American Revolutionary War, the Spanish fleet attacked the English navy around the world. Spain opened its ports to American ships everywhere. Spanish privateers attacked the English navy, primarily in the Caribbean and Atlantic Ocean. Spanish merchants provided military supplies to Captain John Paul Jones for his frequent attacks on the English mainland, and to American colonists as early as 1775.

The threat of a Franco-Spanish attack on Great Britain resulted in hundreds of British fighting ships and thousands of soldiers being withheld in England to defend the homeland, if necessary. Through the heroic efforts of General Bernardo de Gálvez, the British were expelled from the Mississippi River Valley. General George Rogers Clark depended upon supplies from Spain to defeat the British in the Northwest Territory. Gálvez went on to remove the British from well established fortresses in Baton Rouge, Manchac, Natchez, Mobile, Pensacola and the Bahamas. The western and southern fronts fought by Spain

---

[12] Shown in bold lettering.

[13] *Id* at p. 298.

[14] *Id* at p. 317.

caused the British to allocate ships, soldiers, arms, ammunition and supplies away from their battles with the colonists in the eastern 13 colonies.

Although George Washington and Thomas Jefferson both applauded the efforts of Bernardo de Gálvez and the contributions of Spain, noted biographers did not see fit to even mention Spain's efforts in their respective works.[15]

At the time of the American Revolutionary War, accepted International Law prohibited neutral governments from providing money, arms or ammunition to a belligerent country. However, there was no prohibition of private citizens of neutral countries from making those gifts. This was the reason for France and Spain forming a secret corporation for the purpose of funneling money, arms and ammunition to the American colonists.

When discussing the relative involvement and importance of Carlos III of Spain and Louis XVI of France, the reader should understand that King Carlos was clearly the head of the Borbón family at the time of the war. Carlos was 38 years older than Louis. As his uncle, Louis owed Carlos family respect. Carlos had already served as King of Naples and Sicily[16] for 19 years

---

[15] See *Thomas Jefferson, A Strange Case of Mistaken Identity*, Alf J. Mapp, Jr., Madison Books, New York (1987, and *The First of Men: A Life of George Washington*, John E. Ferling, Univ. of Tennessee Press, Knoxville, (1988).

[16] Carlos III became Duke of Parma in 1731. As the Duke of Parma he conquered Naples and Sicily, and was crowned King of Naples and Sicily on 3 July 1735, at age 19.

when Louis was born. Carlos had been a king for 39 years when Louis finally became King of France on 10 May 1774.

When Louis became King of France, Spain was already supplying the colonists with arms and ammunition through Gardoqui & Sons in Bilbao, Spain. When Louis was crowned, Spain controlled all of North America west of the Mississippi, together with most of Central and South America. By the 1762 Treaty ending the Seven Years War[17], France had lost all of its land in the Western Hemisphere, except a few small islands in the Caribbean. Not only did Spain control vastly more land mass than France in 1774, but Spain controlled much more wealth than France, with its oriental treasures coming through the Philippines, and the seemingly unending supply of gold and silver from Spain's colonies in México and Peru.

I have attempted to bring forth heretofore unknown or not well known events which helped shape the outcome of the war. The archives in England, South Carolina and Spain were researched about the exploits of two Spanish sea captains who ran the British blockade at Charleston. Repositories in Missouri, Illinois, Michigan and Ohio were researched to illuminate the exploits of Spanish soldiers and militia from Fort San Carlos who attacked and secured the British storage depot at Ft. Saint Joseph, near present day Niles, Michigan.

It can be said that this one successful battle prevented the British from fulfilling their plan to sweep down the Mississippi River Valley and take all Spanish forts and settlements including New

---

[17] Known as the "French and Indian War" in the United States.

Orleans. It may well have been the most significant battle in the war. This Spanish victory stopped the English in their tracks!

Another purpose of this book is to note that the American Revolutionary War was part of a global conflict, the main characters of which were England, France and Spain. Spain and France battled with England in the Mediterranean (Gibraltar, Majorca and Minorca); in the English Channel and on the Shores of England; South America, Central America, Gálvez in the lower Mississippi, Gulf Coast, and Caribbean; George Rogers Clark in the upper Mississippi and Ohio River valleys; in far flung India and the Philippines, and the battle with the colonists along the eastern coast of North America.

During this same time, France and Spain plotted an attack on British shores, which caused England to hold back thousands of troops and hundreds of ships that could have been used against the colonists. Spanish merchants outfitted Captain John Paul Jones in his attacks all around the English coast. The far away battles and defenses limited the resources available to the British to fight the colonists. Their supply lines were stretched very thin.

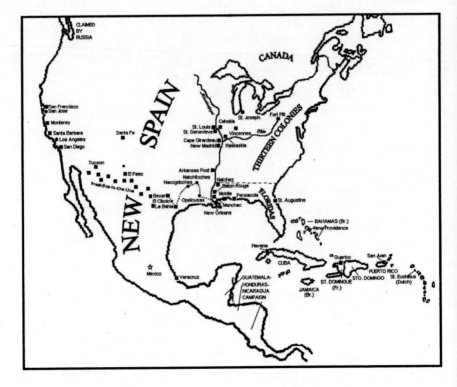

**Map courtesy of Judge Robert H. Thonhoff**

**Map of New Spain during the American Revolutionary War:**

- British, French and Spanish presence in the Gulf and Caribbean

- Spanish Presidios in present day California

- Southwest Sites of Battles involving Spanish troops and Spanish Militia

- Cattle drive from Texas to Louisiana

# LIST OF ILLUSTRATIONS

| | |
|---|---|
| Photo of Edward F. Butler, Sr. in judicial robes | v |
| Photo of Edward F. Butler, Sr. in colonial uniform | viii |
| Photo of Model of Flagship *San Juan Nepomuceno* | xv |
| Photo of Edward F. Butler, Sr. & Robin M. Butler with Crown Prince Felipe | xxxi |
| SAR Group photo with Crown Prince Felipe | xxxiii |
| US Map marking battles in Manchac, Baton Rouge, Natchez, Fort San Carlos, Ft. Ste. Genevieve, Fort St. Joseph, Michigan, Kaskaskia, Cahokia, Vincennes, Ft. Nelson, Texas Connection, Arkansas Post, Mobile, Pensacola, Havana, New Orleans, Ft. Pitt, California Missions, Bahamas & Jamaica | xli |
| Painting of Carlos III | lvii |
| Map of Current U.S. During American Revolution | 2 |
| Painting of Carlos III, King of Spain | 8 |
| Map of Eastern Portion of New Spain Adjoining the Mississippi River | 28 |
| Painting of Typical Mississippi River boat | 31 |
| Painting of General Bernardo de Gálvez | 38 |
| Map including Great Britain, Spain, Majorca & Minorca | 44 |

xliii

| | |
|---|---|
| Portrait of Captain John Paul Jones | 46 |
| Map of Central America | 48 |
| Portrait #2 of Gálvez | 53 |
| Gálvez family arms | 59 |
| Gulf Coast Campaign | 60 |
| Painting of Oliver Pollock | 63 |
| Painting of Spanish Gunship in Hurricane | 76 |
| Map of Pensacola Bay | 79 |
| *Yo Solo* Pensacola Monument | 83 |
| Author at *Yo Solo* Monument in Pensacola | 84 |
| Story of "Yo Solo" | 88 |
| Map of the Bahamas in 1803 | 89 |
| Map of Mississippi River Valley during the American Revolution | 92 |
| Painting of George Rogers Clark | 94 |
| Photos of SAR Presidents General Butler and Sympson at Sycamore Shoals | 96 |
| Map of Forts and Battles in the Northwest Territories | 98 |
| Photo of George Rogers Clark U.S. Commemorative Postage Stamp | 106 |

| | |
|---|---|
| Photo of SAR ceremony at George Rogers Clark Memorial | 109 |
| Photo of Model of Stone Tower at Ft. San Carlos | 118 |
| Map of Spanish Missions and Presidios in California | 136 |
| Map of Texas in 1799 - Thonhoff | 145 |
| The Texas Connection - Cattle Drives | 148 |
| Painting of Washington's Inauguration | 181 |
| Gálvez US Commemorative Postage Stamp | 186 |
| Portrait of Gálvez Hanging in the U.S. Congress | 196 |
| Gálvez Cartoon | 198 |
| Painting of Bernardo de Gálvez | 193 |
| Photos of Spanish Gold and Silver Coins | 199 |
| Photo of Spanish 40 Milled Dollar Certificate | 204 |
| Photo of Wreath Laying Ceremony at Tomb of Carlos III, King of Spain | 209 |
| Photo of Ed Butler pinning medal on lapel of Crown Prince Felipe | 211 |
| Photo of Ed and Robin Butler with Marqui de Legarda and Doña Carmen | 211 |
| Photo of Judge Butler Inducting the Duke of Seville as SAR Spain President | 216 |

# LIST OF APPENDICES

A.   Letter from King Juan Carlos I to
Judge Ed Butler - March 15, 2010     248

B.   Letter from King Juan Carlos I to
Judge Ed Butler - April 5, 2010     249

C.   Letter from King Juan Carlos I to
Judge Ed Butler - April 28, 2010     250

D.   Letter from Crown Prince Felipe to
Judge Ed Butler - May 31, 2010     251

E.   NSSAR Resolution to make
Bernardo de Gálvez a U.S. Citizen     252

F.   Cover Letter from SAR President General
Brock to U.S. Congressmen     255

G.   Texas Ranchers who provided cattle, etc.
to Bernardo de Gálvez     257

H.   *Donativos* made by Spanish Soldiers
at the Presidio de la Bahia, TX     258

I.   *Donativos* made by Spanish Soldiers
at the Presidio de Alta, CA     261

J.   Remarks Of Judge Edward F. Butler, Sr.,
106th President General National Society Sons Of
The American Revolution To His Royal Highness

Crown Prince Felipe de Borbón at The Royal Audience
In The Royal Palace In Madrid - May 14, 2010         263

K.   Money Paid by Spanish Treasury in
Havana to French Officials                             266

L.   Havana Merchants and Military Who
Loaned Money to France                                 267

M.   Letter of Appreciation from King
Juan Carlos                                            268

N.   Chronology Of Events Surrounding Spain's
Participation In The American Revolutionary War;
Noting Other Important Dates Between Spain and
England Leading Up To The War                          269

# FOREWORD

by

Mimi Lozano

Based on select pertinent primary documents, Judge Butler has used his legal skills in writing an easily absorbable and concise history of Spain's involvement in the American Revolution. His purposely brief coverage targets educators, amateur historians, and the classroom student. Facts are presented, laid out clearly for the general public, but with an eye aimed at the heart of descendents of the Spanish soldiers and Spanish families living in the colonial Americas. I am honored to be asked to write the foreword to Judge Butler's book.

*Gálvez / Spain- Our Forgotten Ally in the American Revolutionary War: a Concise Summary of Spain's Assistance* is exactly that: a succinct arrangement of information that facilitates exploring the pages in different ways. In addition to the running history narrative, bibliography and appendixes, is a list of important historical figures with mini-bios, and a list in chronological order of the assistance the colonists received from Spain.

Spain was an important ally, without which, many historians have concluded, the colonists would not have won their freedom from Great Britain. Judge Butler proposes to seek out the descendents of Spanish solders to encourage them to join the National Society of the Sons of the American Revolution, and to internalize their pride. His book honors their ancestors for the important role their ancestors played in the founding, establishment, and development of the United States of America.

I was educated in California, from K-through graduate school, but never once did I get the message that Spain had played an important role in the history of the United States. It was not until the early 1980s when I started pursuing my family history, that I realized the roots of my European heritage in the U.S. went back over 500 years. It was as if a light had been turned on. The history that I had been taught was terribly wrong. I felt betrayed, ignored, and demeaned. I wanted to learn the truth about my heritage. The more I researched, the more I stumbled on examples of misinformation that was being taught as fact.

It was not until 1997 that my heritage had been internalized sufficient to protect the Spanish historic presence, to extol and promote the facts on a national level. It was on my first trip to Washington, D.C., which revealed the need for historic correction on a national level. I was serving as a member of the Senate Task Force for Hispanic Affairs. The Smithsonian had a display with two French colonial soldiers, and a plaque identifying France's support for the American Revolution. No mention of the Spanish contributions.

It was painful watching busloads of students, going in and out of the museums, realizing that hundreds of thousands of students yearly were being taught incorrect history by the federal government - in a government facility. Visiting museums, bookstores, exhibits, etc., in D.C. and surrounding areas, it became clear, the Spanish/Latino historic presence was invisible in Washington, D.C. I started speaking up at our Task Force meetings, criticizing strongly what I observed.

Determined to promote the colonial Spanish presence, in 1998 when I was President of the Society of Hispanic Historical and Ancestral Research, SHHAR, we organized a 2-day conference at the Autry Heritage Museum with historians, genealogists, and Spanish soldier re-enactors. We also began publishing a series of 8 manuals, *Spanish Patriots of the American Revolution* written by Dr. Granville W. Hough and his daughter, N.C. Hough. The books were the records of the Spanish soldiers serving in the Americas during the American Revolution, all of whose descendents, could apply for membership in the Sons and Daughters of the American Revolution.

In the following years, every trip that I made, I learned more about the need, which Judge Butler's *Gálvez / Spain – Our Forgotten Ally in the American Revolutionary War* is helping to fulfill. In 2002, I took 75 copies of Judge Robert Thonhoff's wonderful booklets about *The Texas Connection to the American Revolution,* and distributed them to the Task Force. In 2003, *Somos Primos* was joined by SHHAR and other groups in hosting a 3-day Gálvez Festival with Spanish soldier re-enactors in Long Beach, California. In 2005, members of the Texas Connection to the American Revolution (TCARA) joined me in marching in the July 4th parade in Washington, D.C. .

After the news of our participation in the July 4, 2005 parade became more public, Judge Butler contacted me. He suggested we meet at the George Washington Parade in Laredo, Texas in 2007. We did, and Judge Butler shared his personal interest and history of reaching out to the Spanish for inclusion in the SAR, such as setting up SAR chapters in México and Spain.

Judge Butler explained that in 2009-2010, he would be assuming the responsibility as President General of the National Society of the Sons of the American Revolution, and his intention during his tenure was to honor Spain and increase SAR membership among descendents of those Spanish citizens involved in any aspect of support to the American Revolution as soldiers, ranchers, and *donativo* givers. Judge Butler continues working towards that goal and his new book will be an on-going contribution to that mission.

I hope that every SAR and DAR chapter will have *Gálvez / Spain- Our Forgotten Ally in the American Revolutionary War* in their Chapter library and will place copies of the book for their local libraries and high schools. There are many fine books of recent publication out on General Bernardo de Gálvez, but,

*Gálvez / Spain- Our Forgotten Ally in the American Revolutionary War* is a tidy, quick-read, quick-reference book, handy to have on hand to convince any sincere truth seeker, that in fact, the Spanish did play an important, very major role in winning the American Revolution.

As an added note: through our emails I found that Judge Butler and I are cousins. Both of us descend from King Ferdinand V. Maybe it is not just happenstance that we are both strongly committed to protecting our Grandfather's history . . . maybe it was meant to be.

Mimi Lozano
December 2, 2014

## ABOUT MIMI LOZANO

**Mimi Lozano** was born in San Antonio, TX. Her family moved to Los Angeles, CA when she was an infant. She is an educator and activist for Hispanic rights who co-founded the Society of Hispanic Historical and Ancestral Research and is the editor and publisher of *Somos Primos*, an online monthly publication dedicated to Hispanic heritage.

Lozano attended the University of California, Los Angeles (UCLA) and in 1955, earned her Bachelors of Science degree. She continued her academic education at UCLA where she earned her Masters Degree. In 1970, she earned her Teaching Credentials from the University of California State, Dominguez College.

She became involved in promoting Hispanic heritage, locally and nationally and in 1986, Lozano, co-founded the Society of Hispanic Historical and Ancestral Research (SHHAR) in Orange County, California. SHHAR is a non-profit, all-volunteer organization whose purpose is helping Hispanics and Latinos research their family history. Lozano currently serves as president of the organization which has grown to a national networking status.

In 1990, Lozano founded and has served as the editor and publisher of *Somos Primos*. *Somos Primos*, is an online monthly publication dedicated to Hispanic heritage. Currently, there are over 8,000 subscribers to *Somos Primos*. The web site gets an average of 1.2 million hits per month. That same year, Lozano was named to the US Senate Task Force on Hispanic Affairs.

In 1995, she was involved with a Heritage Subcommittee which formed the nucleus of the Hispanic Heritage Committee of Orange County. The subcommittee's activity attempted to promote more awareness of Hispanic history and culture. In 1999, Lozano became a member of the Pepperdine University's Hispanic Council of Orange County. Lozano was named to the US Senate Republican Conference Task Force on Hispanic Affairs (1997–2003), and has spoken as an invited guest by the U.S. Army at the Pentagon during the celebration of Hispanic Heritage Month.

Lozano, was named California's 68th Assembly District's 2006 Woman of the Year by the California Legislative Women's Caucus. Lozano is credited with pressing the Archives and other federal agencies to acknowledge publicly the significant contributions of Hispanics nationwide. She is quoted in *Weekly Report* as saying:

"There are too many such stories long ignored, but there's still time to add them to the nation's historical record for future generations to integrate our historical contributions into the history and development of the U.S. We have been viewed as separate and apart, when in fact we provided a foundation. These events will reveal that truth of our continual presence and support."

## ACKNOWLEDGEMENTS

I wish to thank:

King Felipe VI de Borbón, King of Spain, who in May 2010 asked me to write this book. He also wanted me to write a movie screen play, and to have Antonio Banderas play the role of Bernardo de Gálvez. I told him I could write the book, but the rest was up to Hollywood.

Professor Thomas E. Chavez, who has contributed significantly in telling the full story about the impact of Spain's assistance to America, both before and after the revolution by his recent research, public speaking and writing.

Judge Robert H. Thonhoff, who was the first to research the Texas Connection to the American Revolution. He has assisted many other researchers and writers about the vital contribution of Spain in the winning of the American Revolution.

Jack Vance Cowan, who founded the "Texas Connection to the American Revolution Association (TCARA). Jack has done more than anybody to promote the involvement of Texas in the American Revolution. He has developed a strong sense of coordination among the efforts of the Sons of the American Revolution, the Order of the Granaderos y Damas de Gálvez, and other groups. His efforts have contributed to many young Hispanics not feeling estranged, and have given them an understanding that their ancestors played an important part in the formation of our nation.

Many of the members of the Sons and Daughters of the American Revolution and the Granaderos y Damas de Gálvez, who have encouraged me during my research and writing of this book.

Lila Guzman, noted author; Judge Robert H. Thonhoff; respected historian; Jack Cowan; respected activist; Mimi Lozano, web master of *Somos Primos*; Joe Perez, Governor General of the Order of the Granaderos y Damas de Gálvez and Larry D. McClanahan, former President General of the National Society Sons of the American Revolution, for taking their time to edit this book and by making suggestions to improve it.

Gerald Burkland of Michigan, and Ann Patten of Pennsylvania both of whom assisted me in research, for which I am very appreciative.

My lovely wife, who allowed me to concentrate on research and writing of this book, and also for her time in proofreading this book.

## Carlos III de Borbón, King of Spain During the American Revolutionary War

# THE BEGINNING[18]

The following was overheard at a platoon roll call during the American Revolutionary War:

"Corporal Rios?" ............................ "Presente!"

"Private de la Garza?" ...................."Presente!"

"Private Marti'nez?" ........................"Aqui'!"

"Private Herna'ndez?" ......................"Presente!"

Possibly you think you are reading about a roll call in another revolutionary war. No mistake. Many Spanish soldiers were directly involved as combatants in the American Revolutionary War. In fact, the list of Spanish patriots extends beyond the military personnel of Spain. Ranchers, vaqueros, the Franciscan priests, members of the New Spain militia, privateers, Canary Islanders and American Indians living in that part of New Spain now known as Texas all contributed to the victory of the American colonists against the English crown.

To better understand these developments, a look into the history and geography of New Spain is beneficial. The following map

---

[18] For an excellent comprehensive book about Spain's efforts during the American Revolutionary War, see *Spain and the Independence of the United States; An Intrinsic Gift*, by Thomas E. Chavez, Univ. of NM Press, Albuquerque, 2002.

shows the areas controlled by England, France and Spain after the 1763 treaty:

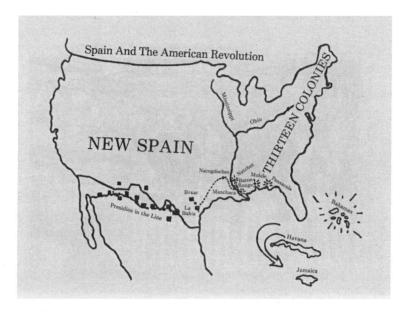

**Map courtesy of Judge Robert H. Thonhoff**

# HISTORICAL RELATIONSHIP
# BETWEEN SPAIN AND ENGLAND

In 1763 Spain occupied much of the New World. New Spain included Louisiana, and all of the continental North America west of the Mississippi River, "to the arctic snows"; and what is now México and Central America. The Spanish colony of Peru included all of its colonies in South America. Additionally, Spain occupied Hispaniola, Puerto Rico and Cuba.

England, in addition to the original 13 American colonies, owned parts of Canada, Bermuda, the Bahamas, Jamaica, East Florida and West Florida, including some forts on the east bank of the Mississippi River as far north as St. Louis (now Missouri). England and Spain were traditional enemies, since at least 1588 when Lord Nelson and Admiral Sir Robert Cross defeated the Spanish Armada; and the following year when Admiral Cross captured Ca'diz, Spain.

Spain had lost Florida to England after a seven-year war, which also cost Spain it's valuable colony in the Philippines. British West Florida included the southern part of what is now Mississippi and Alabama. It resulted from cessions by France and Spain by treaty in 1762. Under the terms of that treaty, Spain regained Havana, a city captured by the British, and Britain obtained Spanish Florida. Under a separate treaty, Spain received Louisiana from France. Pensacola was the capital of British West Florida.

For hundreds of years before the American Revolutionary War, there was bad blood between England and Spain. The two countries were at war with one another more often than not. The following chronological list of wars and battles in which they were adversaries illustrate the point:

| | |
|---|---|
| 1337-1453 | The Hundred Years' War. Aragon, Castile and Majorca were allied with France against England. |
| 1381-1382 | 3rd Ferdinand War. England was allied with Portugal against Castile. |
| 1383-1385 | Crises between England and Castile |
| 1508-1516 | War of the League of Cambrai, a conflict in Italy, also known as the War of the Holy League. |
| 1526-1530 | War of the League of Cognac between England and Spain. |
| 1568-1648 | Eighty Years' War |
| 1579-1583 | Second Desmond Rebellion |
| 1585-1604 | First Anglo Spanish War |
| 1588 | The sinking of the Spanish Armada by the English fleet. |
| 1589 | The destruction of the remainder of the Spanish fleet and the capture of Cádiz by England. |
| 1594-1603 | Nine Years' War |
| 1602-1663 | Dutch-Portuguese War |

| | |
|---|---|
| 1618-1648 | Thirty Years' War |
| 1625-1630 | Second Anglo-Spanish War |
| 1635-1659 | Franco-Spanish War |
| 1640-1668 | Portuguese Restoration War |
| 1654-1660 | Third Anglo-Spanish War. This war was started by Oliver Cromwell's attack on Spanish holdings in the Caribbean, Spanish Netherlands, Canary Islands and Spain. That war was concluded by the 1670 Treaty of Madrid in which Spain lost Jamaica to England. |
| 1672-1678 | Franco-Dutch War |
| 1701-1714 | War of Spanish Succession. Spain was divested of its possessions in Europe outside the Iberian Peninsula. |
| 1702-1713 | Queen Ann's War |
| 1718-1720 | War of Quadruple Alliance |
| 1727-1729 | Third Anglo-Spanish War |
| 1739-1748 | War of Jenkins' Ear |
| 1740-1748 | War of Austrian Succession |
| 1761 | The "Borbón Family Compact" between Carlos III of Spain and his young nephew, Louis LVI of France, provided that if any nation attacked France or Spain, and when one nation was at war, the other member of the compact |

|  |  |
|---|---|
|  | could be called upon to render military or naval aid. |
| 1762-1763 | The fourth Anglo-Spanish War was a part of the Seven Years' War[19]. |
| 1763 | The Seven Years' War was concluded with the Treaty of Paris in which Spain lost Havana and Manila, Philippines to the English. To get these forts back Spain traded East Florida and West Florida to England. Spain received New Orleans from the French. France lost all its possessions in mainland North America. |

From the above we can see that during the 439 years between 1337 and 1776 Spain and England were at war for 264 years and at peace for only 175 years. In addition to these formal wars, there were also the exploits of British pirates and privateers, who constantly captured Spanish ships ladened with silver and gold from México and South America as well as oriental goods from the Philippines. Clearly, there was bad blood between the two nations.

---

[19] Commonly referred to in the United States as the "French and Indian War".

# SPAIN'S GOALS

Spain's original goals in exploring to the west were:

    1)    To find a passage from the Atlantic to the Spice Islands off the east coast of Asia;

    2)    To acquire wealth, including silver, gold and jewels

    3)    To Christianize the native populations[20]

Spain, at the outset of the American Revolutionary War, sought the return of Florida and West Florida, and to keep Louisiana. Spain also desired the return of Gibraltar and the island of Minorca in the Mediterranean from England. It was also to Spain's interest to remove England from its sphere of influence in the New World.

As the rumblings of independence became louder in the American colonies, Spain saw it's opportunity. Spain's original goals continued throughout the period of the war.

---

[20] Queen Isabella and Christopher Columbus were both deeply Christian. Isabella and Ferdinand had just ended 700 years of Moslem rule in Spain, and were thankful for God's help. They felt it was the Lord's will that his word be spread around the world. Many religious scholars believe that spreading Christianity was goal number one.

# King Carlos III of Spain

# SPANISH ASSISTANCE

The courts of Madrid and Paris had agreed, early in the year 1776, upon a plan for giving secret assistance to the rebellious American colonies. It was agreed between them that in order to insure the secrecy of their support, all monies and supplies should be handled by a third party and appear as open business transactions.[21]

Sympathy for the Americans, when they began open hostilities against the mother country, ran high throughout Spain. At that time, however, Spain was not in a position to make her sympathy openly known. She was engaged in a war with Portugal over possessions in Brazil that was costing her vast amounts in money, men, and ships. England, the open ally of Portugal, held the strategic points of Minorca, Mahan, and Gibraltar. England's navy was the most powerful on the seas, with the Spanish fleet being the second in number of ships.

Carlos III was, at this time, diplomatically involved in peace negotiations with Portugal and could not afford to enter into any alliance that might endanger those negotiations. To become openly engaged in the struggle of the American colonists against

---

[21] Why was it feasible on 4 July 1776 for the American Colonies to declare independence? One partial answer is that the framers knew that France and Spain were in support and would presumably be trading partners for the future. Without such support, it would not have made sense to declare independence from one's lifeline, and the war would have taken some other course.

their mother country would certainly lead to a declaration of war by England. It would invite an immediate blockade of all Spanish ports, which would end any possibility of signing the desired treaty with Portugal. This explains the reasons why Spain decided to keep secret her aid to the rebellious colonies.

The two Borbón Courts would initially make an outright gift of two million *"livres"*[22] one million to come from each country. One of the first moves consisted of setting up a fictitious company to direct the aid program, make purchases of supplies, arrange for their shipment to the colonies, contact American agents living in France, and account for the money spent[23]. Even before the signing of the Declaration of Independence, Carlos III began to supply the colonists with guns, ammunition, medical supplies and money.

Spain's assistance will be analyzed as the support it rendered before the Declaration of Independence, and the support it provided after July 4, 1776.

---

[22] A *livre* was a former money of account in France, issued first as a gold coin, then in silver, and discontinued in 1794.

[23] The dummy company was the famous "Rodrigue Hortalez and Company," and its main director was the French playwright and statesman Pierre Augustin Caron de Beaumarchais.

# AID BY SPAIN PRIOR TO THE DECLARATION OF INDEPENDENCE

By at least 23 December 1774, negotiations for supplying the colonists were being made through Joseph Gardoqui & Sons in Bilbao, Spain. Gardoqui, in a letter dated 15 February 1775, responded to an order dated 23 December 1774, from Jeremiah Lee stating that at present he had 300 muskets, 300 bayonets and 600 pistols ready for shipment and would seek to purchase many more to fill the American's order. The gunpowder ordered was recommended to be shipped through Holland.[24] It was perhaps Gardoqui who had provided the arms and gunpowder that the redcoats were seeking at Lexington and Concord on April 19, 1775!

On 28 June 1775, Brigadier General Nathanael Greene wrote to Nicholas Cooke that the colonists should have an ample amount of gunpowder for war with Britain because France was imposing only a small fine on merchants sending gunpowder to the colonists, and that the King of Spain was placing no restrictions of the sale of gunpowder to the colonists.[25]

---

[24] Letter from Joseph Gardoqui & Sons dated 15 February 1775, Naval Documents of the American Revolution, Vol. I, William Bell Clark, Editor, Washington, 1964, p. 401.

[25] Letter from General Nathanael Greene to Nicholas Cooke dated 28 Jun 1775, Id at p. 769.

Only a few days later, on 5 July 1775, Elbridge Gerry submitted another order to Gardoqui on behalf of the Massachusetts Committee of Supplies.[26] On 29 July 1775, 14 tons of gunpowder arrived in Philadelphia from Spain, which was immediately shipped to the rebels besieging Boston.[27]

According to one scholar[28], in August 1775, King George III demanded and Parliament issued a declaration that the American colonies were in a state of rebellion. This was followed in November by a Prohibitory Act instituting a naval blockade of the American coastline.

Professor Cummins reported that in October 1775, two Spanish merchant ships which had sailed from Central America, in violation of the British blockade, called at the port of Charleston, SC[29]. According to his report, they sold gunpowder and supplies

---

[26] Letter from Elbridge Gerry to Joseph Gardoqui & Sons dated 5 Jul 1775, Id at p. 818.

[27] Letter to Philip Stephens, Secretary of the Colonial Admiralty dated at Philadelphia dated 29 Jul 1775

[28] *Spanish Observers and the American Revolution, 1775-1783*, Light Townsend Cummins, LSU Press, Baton Rouge (1985), p. 30, citing a letter from Massarano to Grimaldi, December 15, 1775, no. 150, in the *Sección Estado* of the Spanish Archives in Madrid.

[29] Although he offers no footnotes, in February 2010, Thomas E. Fortin, Executive Producer of New Albion Pictures, mentions this episode as being a segment in his upcoming movie entitled "Forgotten Southern Heroes: South Carolinians, Hispanics, and American Independence!"

to the local rebel commander. As a result, Cummins reported that "Massarano, the British Ambassador in Madrid" filed a formal protest with the Crown. To placate the British, the Marques de Grimaldi, Spain's Minister of State ordered that one of the captains be tried for violating the commercial laws that prohibited trade outside Spain's colonies. A trial was reportedly held in Cádiz in June 1776, which resulted in the captain's acquittal.[30]

Upon researching the records at the British Archives in London, it appears there are several problems with the facts stated in Professor Cummin's thesis:

The "embargo" referenced appears to have been the New England Restraining Act of March 1775, which was amended in April 1775, to include Pennsylvania, New Jersey, Maryland, Virginia and South Carolina.[31]

"British Ambassador Massarano" was in fact Prince Masserano, the Spanish Ambassador to Britain. The British Ambassador to Spain was Thomas Robinson, 2nd Baron Grantham, who served from 1771 until war broke out with Spain in 1779.[32]

A search of the British Newspaper Archive, The United Kingdom National Archives Discovery database, the United States Department of State[33], The National Maritime Museum

---

[30] Unfortunately, this letter has not been located, and Prof. Cummins has declined an invitation to provide a copy of this letter.

[31] UK National Archives, Kew ref: ADM1/240.
[32] Ref: The Peerage, p.272.
[33] *http://history.state.gov*

(Greenwich), and the Franklin Papers[34] all failed to yield any verification of details of the second incident (the violation of the British Blockade) by two Spanish merchant ships at Charleston.

After several days researching this issue at the United Kingdom National Archives in Kew, London, no documents were found that would shed any light on the Charleston incident. Based upon this research, another source was identified as potential source material: The records of the High Court of Admiralty (HCA) held at the United Kingdom National Archives may contain relevant information about the alleged incident. There is however a problem with these records in that they are indexed by ships' names and not dates. Therefore, unless the names of the ships are known, then a search there is not likely to yield any information.

There are no records that could be identified that would record this information at the United Kingdom National Archives. An enquiry was made with the archivist at this repository and he was of the opinion that if such records exist then these would more than likely be deposited in a Spanish repository.

Of interest are the following excerpts from a letter from the Colonial Governor, Lord William Campbell dated 19 Sept. 1775, to Secretary of State of the British Colonial Office in London from onboard *HMS Tamen,* which was anchored in Charleston Harbor. In effect, he had been forced to move onto the *HMS Tamen* and give up residence in the Governor's mansion.[35]

---

[34] *http://frankinpapers.org*

[35] The original of this letter was obtained from the South Carolina Department of Archives and History.

*Some time ago a Spanish (Ship?) from the Havannah (sic) bound to Cádiz arrived off this Bar dismasted and in great distress. As the peoples from the Town would give no assistance, Captain Thornbrow sent at my desire the pilot of the king's ship, who brought her safely in. To prevent any imposition, I recommended proper people to refit her, but after the ship got up to Town, the Committee fixed on others of their own stamp. I would have persuaded the master to have left his powder with Captain Thornbrow till he returns, but the poor man was so afraid of being turned out of the port in the distressed situation he was in that I could not prevail upon him to do it voluntarily. & as I wished to avoid even the appearance of harshness to a Spanish ship at this juncture, Captain Thornborough[36] did not insist on it, especially as the small quantity he had on board, should the rebels seize it, was of no consequence to people who so amply supplied.*

*Some days after another Spanish ship arrived, which was conducted safely into the Harbor in the same manner. This (ship) was inbound from Honduras to Cádiz, & I noted is immensely rich. He (the captain?) was sickly and wanted provisions, but the ship had received no damage; he has however thought proper to quit the protection of the men of war & has carried his ship to Town without the least necessity, & that I cannot be responsible for any consequences that may*

---

[36] Notice two different spellings of the Captain's surname in the original letter.

follow. *I thought it very necessary to acquaint your Lordship with these particulars & inclose (sic) the names of the ships & if your Lordship should think proper to acquaint the ambassador of Spain with the attention His Majesty's Officers in this part of the world show to his Catholic Majesty's subjects in distress, & the tenderness with which they are treated.*"[37]

Three years later, there were still rumblings in Madrid and London from the report of Governor Campbell:

*Madrid 28th December 1778*

*My Lord,*

*I have received the honor of your Lordship's No. 25 and No. 6 and have communicated to M. Grimaldi a particular account of the attentions shewn by Lord William Campbell to the two Spanish Vessels which were driven into the Harbour at Charlestown.*

*He blamed the Spanish Vessels for not putting themselves entirely under the protection of the King's ships, and experienced the greatest satisfaction at the very friendly treatment which the King's officers had offered and given them."*

---

[37] Excerpts from a letter from Lord William Campbell dated September 19, 1775 to Secretary of State of the British Colonial Office in London; from onboard *HMS Tamen* anchored in Charleston Harbor. The original of this letter is in the South Carolina Department of Archives and History, Columbia, South Carolina.

*Lord Viscount Weymouth*[38]

From the above, it is clear that two Spanish ships did enter Charlestown harbor after the British blockade, but from the records on hand it is impossible to conclude that they brought supplies to the rebels.

Perhaps the ship mentioned by Professor Cummins was the Spanish merchant ship *the St. John the Baptist,* which landed at Rebellion Road near Charleston on Saturday October 7, 1775. It was under the command of Don Joseph Lorenzo Zubigary. It had departed Honduras 39 days before. It was said to be the richest ship ever to arrive in Charlestown.[39]

**Continental Congress Committee on Secret Correspondence**:

In 1775 the Continental Congress realized that every discussion of its members was being relayed to King George. Based upon a recommendation from Benjamin Franklin in late 1775, a "Committee on Secret Correspondence" was created to drastically limit the number of eyes viewing important negotiations between the colonists, France, Spain, and others.

On November 29, 1775, Congress established a Committee of Secret Correspondence, with the specific task of seeking foreign

---

[38] Letter from Lord Viscount Weymouth to British Home Secretary, dated 28 December 1778, United Kingdom Archives, Kew, London, England, document SP 94/199 1775.

[39] *South- Carolina and American General Gazette, Vol. XVIII*, October 13, 1775, p. 1

aid. Since Spain and France had a long history of fighting England, they were the first countries contacted.

It was secret because several colonial leaders had let it be known that they intended to remain loyal to the Crown. Information from the proceedings of the Continental Congress was being leaked to the crown. The five committee members chosen were Mr. Harrison; Dr. Franklin, Mr. Johnson, Mr. Dickinson and Mr. Jay. This committee operated many secret agents in England, France and Spain, the most famous of whom was Silas Deane.

The five Secret Committee members were to covertly acquire foreign assistance without sharing the assistance origin from other Congressional members. Through negotiations between Franklin and Prince Gabriel Antonio de Borbón of Spain, muskets, ammunition and salt were made available through Spanish islands in the Caribbean.

By letter dated 9 November 1775, Baron Grantham, British Ambassador to Spain, wrote to Lord Rochford about arms being shipped from Spain to the colonies. He advised that he had an agreement from Ambassador Grimaldi that no warlike goods would be shipped from Spain to the Colonies on English ships. He also noted that unless the situation between Spain and Portugal was resolved soon, England would be forced to reinforce British troops in Buenos Aires.[40]

---

[40] *Naval Documents of the American Revolution*, William James Morgan, ed., Naval History Div., Dept of the Navy, Washington, 1976, Vol. 3, p. 356.

On 12 December 1775, Benjamin Franklin received a letter through the Spanish Ambassador from Gabriel Antonio de Borbón, Prince of Spain. The Prince stated that since Spain and the American Colonists were neighbors that there should be friendship between them.[41] On this same date, Joseph Hewes wrote that his orders from Mr. Smith were to obtain wine, proceed to the island of Saltitudas for salt, and then continue to another Spanish location to pick up gunpowder and muskets.

In February 1776, a letter likely written by John Adams indicated "Measures to Be Pursued in Congress," by foreign aid from France, Spain, Holland, and Denmark. These measures included the Alliance of France and Spain, and the representatives to be sent to each Court[42]; obtaining loans to pay for the upcoming conflict; the commodities needed such as weapons, ammunition, lead and salt, etc.; the treaties of commerce desired; discussions with the foreign courts to prepare for the Declaration for Independence.[43]

---

[41] December 12, 1775, Philadelphia, Gabriel Antonio de Borbón, *Letters of Delegates to Congress, Volume 2*, p. 479.

[42] These representatives were to have the authority normally possessed by ambassadors, but since the colonists were still English, the appointment of an Ambassador at this time would have been inappropriate.

[43] February 9-23, 1776, Philadelphia, Measures to Be Pursued in Congress, *Letters of Delegates to Congress, Volume 3*, p. 219.

An entry in Richard Smith's diary, dated 29 February 1776, included mention of the foreign commercial alliances existing with foreign nations, chiefly with France and Spain.[44] On 2 March 1776, Benjamin Franklin wrote to John Dickinson. Franklin advised that Silas Deane was to travel under cover as a merchant to France for the purpose of secretly meeting certain persons representing the royal courts of France and Spain. Deane was under orders to seek loans, clothing, ammunition, arms, etc. for the purpose of preparing for the upcoming demand for freedom.[45]

France and Spain used Bilbao, Spain as the port from which this contraband was shipped. The agent used by both was the famous family business of Joseph Gardoqui and Sons, utilizing the fictitious Hortalez merchant companies in covert aid to American Colonials. Use of the French Company created a false impression that all of the aid sent through it was coming from France. In truth and fact, Spain was forwarding at least 50%.

In addition, all Spanish ports were open to American ships and for commerce. Supplies, arms, ammunition, money and more were sent to Caribbean island ports in order to avoid direct British contact. France and Spain acted together time wise, even if in a different and covert manner. American Revolution foreign assistance began over a year before the actual Declaration of Independence and continued until the 1783 Treaty

---

[44] February 29, 1776, *Richard Smith's Diary, Volume 3*, p.312.

[45] March 2, 1776, Philadelphia, Minutes of Proceedings, *Letters of Delegates to Congress, Volume 3*, p.321.

of Paris, which included the American Colonies, England, France and Spain.

Mr. Warren, Speaker of the Massachusetts House of Representatives, reported that in the spring of 1776, months before the Declaration of Independence, an American ship carrying 21 1/2 tons of gunpowder provided by Joseph Gardoqui & Sons in Bilbao, Spain was detained by the British near Boston. An identical shipment of gunpowder from the Gardoqui firm already had arrived, together with 5 tons of saltpeter and 300 muskets. Latest news from North Carolina advised that 5 tons of gunpowder had arrived there.[46]

King Carlos III of Spain issued instructions to all Spanish Naval Commanders in the West Indies on 26 February 1776. He gave detailed instructions on where the Spanish ships should sail so as best to monitor the naval movements of the British - presumably to prepare for war. In these instructions he specifically ordered that:

    1) They should hide as much as possible, even from their crews, the purpose of their cruise.
    2) They should exchange intelligence about course, speed, distance, etc. of English ships
    3) They should detain and inspect British merchant ships pretending that they are trying to prevent smuggling. Their goal was to skillfully obtain information about the ships' cargo, destination, movements and the business of the British fleet.
    4) Each time they discovered important information,

---

[46] *Naval Documents of the American Revolution, Id* at Vol. 4, pp. 198-199.

they should communicate it to the Spanish commanders or Governors.

5) Also, all such intelligence should be reported to the French Colonial Commanders, at which time they should endeavor to obtain intelligence from the French.

6) They should share their intelligence with captains of French ships they encounter, and obtain intelligence from the French.

7) Stop all ships returning to Spain and/or headed towards the American Colonies from Spain and use them as a messengers to deliver reports to Spanish governors and the Spanish Ministry.

So, over four months prior to the Declaration of Independence, the King of Spain had instructed all his naval officers that they should spy against the British! These instructions were provided by the Spanish Court to Sartine, the French Minister of Marine, who in turn provided similar instructions to all French ship captains and fleet commanders.[47]

On 6 March 1776, Elbridge Gerry wrote to James Warren, Speaker of the Massachusetts House of Representatives, in which he warned that it was important for the coastal communities to be well armed with adequate gunpowder to defend themselves against the British. He expressed fear that his ship might have been detained by the English. It was returning

---

[47] *Id* at Vol. 4, pp 933-934

from Spain with a cargo of 21 1/2 tons of gunpowder, five tons of saltpeter and 300 stands of arms headed to Boston.[48]

Nicholas Brown, at Providence, R.I., wrote to the Secret Committee of the Continental Congress on 20 Mar 1776, concerning an order made in January 1776 of warlike stores. He advised them that a small sloop had just returned from the Dutch port of Statia (St. Eustatia, Netherlands Antilles), including sail cloth, swivel guns, small arms, gunpowder and cannon balls.[49]

The minutes of the New York Committee of Safety on 22 March 1776, reflected that they were receiving all the gunpowder they needed from Spain, France and Holland.[50]

Reports from British war ship captains to the British Admiralty stated that several American men-of-war were being fitted out with cannon at Ca'diz, Spain and that an American brig mounting several carriage guns was taking on gunpowder and other stores for transport to America.[51]

Based upon British intelligence dated 20 June 1776, regarding Spanish and French naval preparations, a squadron of Spanish ships sailed from Cádiz, Spain, under the command of an admiral, consisting of 5 ships of 70 guns each; two frigates of 26

---

[48] Letter from Elbridge Gerry to James Warren dated March 6, 1776, *Id* at Vol. 4, pp. 198-199.

[49] *Naval Documents of the American Revolution*, *Id* at Vol. 4, p. 419.

[50] *Id* at Vol. 4, p. 453

[51] *Id* at Vol . 4, pp. 1044-1046.

guns each; two sloops of 10 guns each, and one Xebeck[52] of 30 guns. In Barcelona, Spain, it was reported that the Spaniards were preparing for shipment of a number of tents, a great train of artillery, baggage wagons and all sorts of necessities". The British were concerned that Spain and France combined had, or soon would have a larger fleet than Great Britain. [53]

British Royal Navy Captain Henry Bryne, reported from Antigua, to Vice Admiral James Young at the British Admiralty, that his squadron on 10 May 1776, had encountered four large Spanish warships, one of which was carrying a large force of 800-900 troops from Cádiz bound for Puerto Rico. The captain of the latter ship advised Captain Bryne that the other three ships were men-of-war, also headed to Puerto Rico.[54] This Spanish fleet was probably beefing up the Spanish presence in the West Indies in anticipation of war with Britain.

On 31 May 1776, Gabriel de Sartine delivered instructions to all French captains in the American Sea,[55] which were almost identical to the instructions given by HRM Carlos III on 26

---

[52] A small three masted sailing vessel used mostly in the Mediterranean.

[53] British Intelligence Regarding French and Spanish Naval Preparations dated 20 June 1776, *Naval Documents of the American Revolution, Id* at Vol. 6, pp. 427-428.

[54] *Id* at Vol. 5, p. 197.

[55] Gulf of México.

February 1776. Therein, he advised his captains of the routes to be taken by them and by the Spanish ships.[56]

In May 1776, a Spanish merchant ship was seized by the British in Delaware Bay, with $14,000 on board in a box marked "W M," presumably belonging to Willing and Morris[57]. Congress was notified on 1 June 1776.[58]

Captain William Sinclair wrote to Elbridge Gerry on 4 June 1776 to inform him about the March 1776 seizure of the merchant ship *Rockingham*, loaded with gunpowder from Joseph Gardoqui & Sons in Bilbao, Spain.[59]

The committee of Secret Correspondence sent Silas Deane to Paris. He arrived on July 7, 1776.[60]

On 26 June 1776, a large fleet of 15 Spanish gunships was spotted heading towards Santa Dominica, with flags on three

---

[56] *Naval Documents of the American Revolution, Id* at Vol. 6, pp. 393-397.

[57] Willing and Morris were representing the colonists in the purchase of arms and ammunition from Spain and France.

[58] Letter from Maryland Council of Safety to the Maryland Delegates in the Continental Congress dated 1 June 1776, *Naval Documents of the American Revolution, Id* at Vol. 5, p. 341.

[59] Letter from William Sinclair to Elbridge Gerry on 4 June 1776, *Id* at Vol. 5, p. 369.

[60] *Spain and the Independence of the United States: An Intrinsic Gift*, Thomas E. Chavez, Univ. of NM Press, Albuquerque, 2002, p.49.

ships indicating that there were three general officers in this squadron.[61]

In June 1776, a ship load of arms, ammunition and other supplies from Spain arrived in New Orleans from Spain. It sometimes took months for merchant ships to cross from Spain to the colonies. Yet in the month before the Declaration of Independence was signed, large amounts of military supplies had already arrived from Spain.

As evidence that Spain and France had put their secret plan into action before July 4, 1776 is the letter from Charles Carroll, Sr. on August 1, 1776.[62] He wrote that a French ship landed at Chester, Massachusetts with arms and ammunition (from Gardoqui in Spain), with a letter that France intended to assist the colonists in their attempt to break away from the British. In those days it took from three to six months for a ship to sail from northern Spain to the colonies. **This means that the cargo left Bilbao sometime between February and April, 1776!** This delivery was confirmed by Stephen Ceronio, who wrote on 23 October 1776, that agents for the Roderigue Hortalez Company had delivered arms, ammunition, and clothing for the continental

---

[61] Report dated 26 June 1776, from Count D'Argout to Gabriel de Sartine, French Minister of Marine and Governor of Martinique, *Id* at Vol. 5, p. 747.

[62] August 1, 1776, Philadelphia, Charles Carroll, Sr., *Letters of Delegates to Congress, Volume 4*, p.596.

defense.[63] It should be noted that this shipment was paid for with funds donated by France and Spain.

Before June 1776, "supplies had been going on . . . through the ports of Spain, France and Holland, as ship captains from America picked up arms and ammunition in personal trading ventures. Moreover, much important trade of this nature had been going on through the Spanish ports in the West Indies. Using these same ports as bases, American captains had been able to prey upon British merchant vessels during the first months of the war."[64]

Thus, in June 1776, when the American Revolution was just about to begin, we find both Spain and France acting officially, though under the seal of secrecy, as allies of the English colonies against their mother country. Even before this date, however, supplies had been going out on a haphazard basis through the ports of Spain, France, and Holland, as ship captains from America picked up arms and ammunition in personal trading ventures. Moreover, much important trade of this nature had been going on through the Spanish ports in the West Indies for many years.

---

[63] October 23, 1776, Philadelphia, *Committee of Secret Correspondence, Volume 5*, p.367.

[64] *Independence Broadside*, News From the Revolution For the NSSAR Congress, Vol. 8, Issue 1, July 9, 2012, p.2; reprinted from *New Orleans Genesis*, a pub. of the Gen'l. Research Soc. of New Orleans, Vol. 71 (June 1779), pp. 269-270.

Spain had given "Most Favored Nation" trading privileges to American colonists well before July 4, 1776. Using these same ports as bases, American privateer captains had been able to prey upon British merchant vessels during the first months of the war.

**Eastern Portion of New Spain Adjoining the Mississippi River**

On 1 September 1776, another Spanish ship from Bilbao, Spain arrived in New Orleans with military supplies for the Colonists. About the same time, other goods from Spain arrived at the port of Philadelphia. This was less than two months after the Declaration of Independence, ergo, these goods were also shipped well before July 4, 1776. General Charles Henry Lee, second in command to General George Washington, sent Captain George Gibson, with a group of 16 colonists, from Ft. Pitt to New Orleans, to obtain those supplies from Spain.

## SPAIN CONTINUED TO SEND SUPPLIES TO THE AMERICANS UP THE MISSISSIPPI RIVER AND ON THE EAST COAST

## JUNE 1776 TO THE END OF THE WAR

" . . . [I]n May 1776, the (Virginia) Committee of Safety sent George Gibson and William Linn down the Mississippi River to New Orleans, where with the help of Robert Morris' agent, Oliver Pollock, they secured ten thousand pounds of gunpowder from the Spanish. Captain Gibson took 1,000 pounds through the Gulf of México and up the Eastern Seaboard to Philadelphia. The remaining 9,000 pounds was taken up the Mississippi and Ohio Rivers by Lieutenant Linn and Gibson's Lambs. The Ohio River was iced over during a very harsh winter, and the flatboats were unable to move. It took Linn until the spring of 1777 to bring the bulk of the purchases back up the Mississippi and Ohio Rivers to Wheeling in Western Virginia . . . ."[65]

It is interesting to note that an earlier shipment of guns, gunpowder, blankets and medicine arrived in New Orleans from Spain in June 1776. How did the Committee of Safety know that there would be a shipment in New Orleans before the ship arrived?

New Orleans businessman, Oliver Pollock introduced Captain Gibson to Spanish Governor Unzaga, who agreed to supply the colonists.

---

[65] *The Revolution in Virginia, 1775-1783*, by John E. Selby, Univ. of Virginia Press, Charlottesville, 1988, p. 170.

"Virginia interest in the west had grown considerably since Gibson and Linn had traveled to New Orleans to purchase gunpowder for the state. That expedition greatly broadened people's awareness of the area's geography and the possibilities for trade with the Spanish. Merchants, land speculators and the new Governor of Louisiana, Bernardo de Gálvez, were all intrigued with the idea of establishing communications via the Mississippi, but it was Virginia's military commander at Harrods Bay, George Rogers Clark, who came up with the plan for significant Virginia involvement in the West."[66]

In anticipation of Bernardo de Gálvez assuming his post as Governor, on 25 November 1776, Carlos III ordered Gálvez to collect information about the British colonies. Subsequently, he was told by King Carlos that Spain would soon enter the American Revolutionary War, and ordered him to render secret help to the colonists. In early 1777, Governor Unzaga introduced Pollock to General Gálvez. By July 1777, Spain sent another 2,000 barrels of gunpowder, lead and clothing up the Mississippi to assist the colonists in their revolutionary cause. Carlos III made secret loans to the colonists of 1,000,000 *Livres*. Additional arms, ammunition and provisions were sent by the Spaniards to George Rogers Clark's Ohio River posts and to George Washington's continental army via Fort Pitt.

---

[66] *Id* at p. 189.

**Typical Mississippi River Boat in late 1700's. At places on the river these boats were pulled upstream by horses and mules, sometimes with the assistance of crewmen. Upstream travel on the river was slow and arduous.**

In 1777, Benjamin Franklin, American representative in France, arranged for the secret transport from Spain to the colonies of 215 bronze cannons; 4,000 tents; 13,000 grenades; 30,000 each muskets, bayonets, and uniforms; over 50,000 musket balls and 300,000 pounds of gunpowder. A subsequent letter of thanks from Franklin to the Count of Aranda for 12,000 muskets sent to Boston from Spain was found.[67]

---

[67] *The Vital Contribution of Spain in the Winning of the American Revolution*, Robert H. Thonhoff, self published, p. 2

On 10 February 1777, the Massachusetts Board of War shipped to Joseph Gardoqui & Sons, 2,210 Quintals[68] of cod fish on the brig *Benjamin*, with an order for 3,000 blankets, 1,000 firearms, 20 tons of iron, 30 tons of cordage, 200 yards of Raven duck (for tents), 100 yards of Russian duck, and two tons of steel.[69]

On 16 March 1777, from Victoria, Spain, Arthur Lee advised Benjamin Franklin and Silas Deane that 3,000 barrels of gunpowder and loads of clothing arrived in New Orleans from the house of Gardoqui in Bilbao, Spain. Lee also advised that Gardoqui intended to load three ships in Bilbao.[70]

Arthur Lee obtained an agreement with Joseph Gardoqui to dispatch a ship from Bilbao, Spain to Massachusetts with a cargo of salt, sail and tent cloth, cordage, blankets, an assortment of drugs and medications to fight the three prevailing camp diseases, and other war stores that he could procure quickly. The proceeds of that shipment were to be used to purchase war supplies. Further, Lee requested of Gardoqui, that he provide

---

[68] A quintal equals 112 pounds of fish. So, the 2,210 quintals equals 247, 520 pounds of fish.

[69] Letter from the Massachusetts Board of War to Joseph Gardoqui & Sons, Bilboa, Spain dated February 10, 1777. *Naval Documents of the American Revolution, Id* at Vol. 7, p. 1156.

[70] Letter from Arthur Lee to Benjamin Franklin and Silas Deane dated March 16, 1777. *Naval Documents of the American Revolution, Id* at Vol. 8, p. 680.

additional supplies to all American ship captains who call at the port of Bilbao.[71]

The schooner *Glover* departed Marblehead, Mass. on 25 April 1777, with 1,256 quintals of fish consigned to Joseph Gardoqui and Sons in Bilbao, Spain, valued at 2,292 Pounds English currency, to fund the purchase and shipment of war supplies.[72]

On 27 April 1777, Joseph Gardoqui informed the colonists that his firm would accept several commodities to establish an account from which the costs of arms, ammunition and other war supplies could be paid. Those commodities included fish, rice, tobacco, pitch, tar, turpentine, whale oil, whale bone, masts, yards and spars.[73]

Joseph Gardoqui & Sons shipped via the *Success* to Arthur Lee in the colonies the following supplies: "757 harricks of salt, 16 anchors weighing 238 hundred, 3 cables from 16 to 18 1/2 inches, 3 hawsers, 234 coyles of cordage, 31 cases containing 2,247 pair of strong shoes, 2,532 ready- made shirts, 243 1/4 dozen stockings, 1,500 good hats, 18 large kettles, 92 bales containing 2,186 good large blankets, 28 pieces of shirting, and 2

---

[71] Letter from Arthur Lee to the Committee of Secret Correspondence. *Naval Documents of the American Revolution, Id* at Vol. 8, pp. 691-692.

[72] Shipping Articles For Schooner *Glover* from the Massachusetts War Board, dated 3 May 1777. *Naval Documents of the American Revolution, Id* at Vol. 8, p. 906.

[73] Letter from Joseph Gardoqui & Sons to Samuel Phillips Savage of the Massachusetts Board of War dated 27 April 1777. *Naval Documents of the American Revolution, Id* at Vol. 8, pp. 797-798.

small cases and a barrel with Jesuits Bark, rhubarb, ipcacuan, tart, emetic, mercury sublimate, purgers salts and opium."[74]

On 21 July 1777, Captain Gustavus Conyngham wrote to Benjamin Baily, Prize Master, advising that he had appointed Captain James Smith as captain of the recently captured English Brig *Northampton*. Captain Smith was ordered to Bilbao, Spain where he was to present himself to Messers Gardoqui, and present their order for goods. In the event of recapture, Smith was provided with a fake set of orders, which he was to turn over after destroying his true orders and the letter from Conyngham to Gardoqui.[75]

In a letter from Lord Weymouth to Lord Grantham, the above subterfuge by Captain Conyngham was discovered when the British recaptured the Brig *Northampton,* together with both sets of orders and the letter to the Gardoquie firm. The latter letter informed the Gardoquie's of the plan for American privateers to bring their prizes into the ports of Spain.[76]

The Joseph Gardoqui firm was more than just an agent. It made purchases of arms, ammunition and other military supplies for the colonists. When the schooner *Glover* from Boston, Massachusetts was damaged by a British war ship, Gardoqui

---

[74] Letter from Joseph Gardoqui to Arthur Lee dated 10 May 1777. *Naval Documents of the American Revolution, Id* at vol. 8, pp. 837-838.

[75] *Naval Documents of the American Revolution, Id* at Vol. 9, p. 517.

[76] *Naval Documents of the American Revolution, Id* at Vol. 5, p. 544.

arranged assistance to refloat it after it ran ashore. Gardoqui then made arrangements for the necessary repairs.[77]

By September 1777, Spain had already furnished the American insurgents with 1,870,000 *livres*. Before long, it became apparent to the court of Madrid that the funds which had been given equally by the two nations were being credited, by the Americans, solely to the Court of France. To this day, some French historians dispute Spain's equal contributions made through the dummy corporation.

In October 1777, Virginia Governor Patrick Henry wrote two letters to General Gálvez, and another in January 1778. In each of those letters he requested more supplies. Henry also suggested in those letters that the two Floridas that Spain lost to England in 1763, should revert back to Spain. In each letter Henry expressed his appreciation to Gálvez and Spain for their assistance.

In March 1778, U.S. Captain James Willing left Ft. Pitt with an expedition of 30 men. They raided and plundered British forts and property along the Ohio and Mississippi Rivers. They captured boats, barges, an armed British ship, and slaves.

When Willing arrived in New Orleans with his flotilla of boats of various sizes and function, the expedition had grown to 150 men. Gálvez welcomed Willing and his men. He provided them with quarters and gave them free reign of the city. They auctioned off their British plunder in New Orleans. With the

---

[77] *Letter from Joseph Gardoqui & Sons to Samuel Phillips Savage dated 31 August 1777, Naval Documents of the American Revolution, Id* at Vol. 9, p. 621.

proceeds, they purchased military supplies for the Continental army from Gálvez for their return trip.

George Rogers Clark, headquartered at Ft. Nelson, current day Louisville, Kentucky received a considerable amount of his supplies which he used in his victories over the British at Kaskaskia, Cahokia and Vincennes in 1778-1779, up the Mississippi River from Gálvez. Again, Oliver Pollock was instrumental in the transactions.[78]

On 18 November 1777, the Massachusetts Board of War submitted an order for military supplies to Joseph Gardoqui & Sons: "bar iron as ballast, 2,000 blankets, 100 pieces of Revens Duck or Russia flatts, 100 pieces of Russia or Holland duck, 100 pieces of blue cloth and a few pieces of red cloth, 100 pieces of one yard wide coarse linen, 2,000 pair of large stout shoes, and 2,000 pair of stockings."[79]

On 20 December 1777, the following military supplies were invoiced by Joseph Gardoqui & Sons to Elbridge Gerry. The goods had been shipped:
    via the schooner *Tabby (sailed March 24, 1777)* -"119 pieces of Russian Duck (for tents), 42 pieces of tent cloth, 252 pounds of sewing twine, and 400 sail needles";
    via the *Alexander* (sailed April 25, 1777) - "185 shirts, 8 anchors, together with 342 hundred weight of cables and

---

[78] *Spain And The Independence Of The United States: An Intrinsic Gift, Id* at pp. 97-98.

[79] Order from Massachusetts Board of War to Joseph Gardoqui & Sons dated 18 November 1777, , *Naval Documents of the American Revolution, Id* at Vol. 10, p. 530.

cordage";

by the *Charlotte* (sailed April 25, 1777) -100 shirts, 30 pieces of tent cloth, 24 pieces of Russia duck (for sails), 8 anchors@199 hundred weight, cables, and cordage";

via the *Lydia* -"27 pieces of blue cloth, 331 shirts, 12 blankets, 8 anchors @ 102 hundred weight, cables and 234 coils of cordage";

by the *Success (sailed May 8, 1777)* - 757 farricks of salt, 16 anchors @ 238 hundred weight, cables, 3 hawsers, 234 coils of cordage, 2,247 pair of shoes, 2,532 shirts, 243 1/2 dozen stockings, 1,500 hats, 18 large kettles, 2,186 large blankets, 28 shirts, 2 small cases & a barrel with Jesuits bark, Rhubarb, ipecacuanha, tartar emertic, mercury sublimate, purging salts and opium";

and by the schooner *Marblehead (sailed May 14, 1777)* -salt, and an unknown quantity of duck and tent cloth.[80]

During the period 1776-1779, Spain further provided a credit of about 8 million *reales*, which provided military and medical supplies of all kinds, and food to the colonists. Nevertheless, Spain was still maintaining in 1777, the cloak of secrecy over its operations, a secrecy believed to be vital to the security of its American dominion. In the fall of 1777, Washington, his army short of clothing and war supplies, was facing the winter that might well decide the fate of his country. Desperate agents of the colonies were becoming more and more indiscreet,

---

[80] Invoice from Joseph Gardoqui & Sons to Elbrige Gerry dated 20 December 1777, *Naval Documents of the American Revolution, Id at* Vol. 10, pp. 1130-1131.

announcing openly the sources of aid to America. By giving the strong impression that Spain and France were actually their open allies, they hoped to weaken England's will to continue the war.

Gálvez knew that a formal declaration of war was soon to come. Under the guise of recruiting an army for the defense of New Orleans, he prepared for formal war. Up until 21 June 1779, all of Spain's support for the colonists was secret. Much of the support was funneled through the French government, which took credit for all these gifts and loans. On 21 June 1779, Spain formally declared war upon Great Britain.

**General Bernardo de Gálvez**

## SPAIN THROUGHOUT THE AMERICAN REVOLUTIONARY WAR CONTINUED TO ENLARGE ITS FLEET AND MILITARY IN THE CARIBBEAN

### AND

## SPAIN FEIGNED AN ATTACK ON GREAT BRITAIN WHICH KEPT A LARGE PART OF ITS FLEET AND ARMY AT HOME

So as to be able to quickly form a task force to assist the Americans, Spain was constantly sending warships and troops to the Caribbean, primarily to Havana and Puerto Rico. Many of these ships and troops were later placed under the command of General Bernardo de Gálvez.

Lieutenant Thomas Lloyd, R.N.[81], in the journal of H. M. sloop *Atalanta* wrote on 15 February 1777, that when he was in the Havana, Cuba harbor to deliver a letter to the governor, he saw a Spanish 74 gun ship and about 12 additional Spanish ships of war, four of which were two-decked.[82]

On 6 April 1777 Beaumarchais wrote to Count de Vergennes, suggesting that the French and Spanish fleets maneuver around Great Britain in hopes that the English would by necessity elect to keep much of their army and navy at home, rather than

---

[81] Royal Navy

[82] Journal of H. M Sloop *Atalanta*. *Naval Documents of the American Revolution*, William James Morgan, Ed., Naval History Div., Dept. of the Navy, Washington, 1976, Vol. 7, p. 1214.

sending them to North America.[83] Throughout the conflict both France and Spain made periodic visits to the home waters of Great Britain. These patrols resulted in a sizeable number of warships and thousands of troops being kept at home to guard against a Franco-Spanish attack.

On April 7, 1777, Benjamin Franklin, wrote a letter to Conde[84] D' Aranda requesting that the Spanish declare war on England. Pursuant to a Resolution of Congress dated 30 December 1776, Franklin promised that if Spain would join in the war between the colonies and England, the United States would assist in providing the town and port of Pensacola to Spain. Franklin noted two provisions: that Spain would grant to the United States free access to the port of Pensacola and free navigation of the Mississippi River.[85]

Both the residents and English military at Port Royal, Jamaica, were in fear of an immediate attack by the Spaniards. On 27 May 1777, Admiral Gayton dispatched a small vessel to assess the Spanish maritime strength in Havana, which was reported to be the following Men of War: the *Monorca,* 70 guns; the *St. Damar*, 64 guns; the *Septentrion*, with 64 guns; the *St. Joseph*, with 70 guns; the *America* with 64 guns and the *Poderose*, with 70 guns. In addition there were five frigates in the Havana Harbor: *Venus*, 26 guns; *Xabeque*, 30 guns; *St. Rosa*, 20 guns;

---

[83] Letter from Beauarchias to Vergennes dated 6 April 1777, *Id* at Vol. 8, p. 749.

[84] French for "Count".

[85] Letter from Benjamin Franklin to Conde D' Aranda dated 7 April 1777. *Id* at Vol. 8, pp. 749-750.

*St. Clara*, 26 guns; and the *Liebra*, with 28 guns. The report also included two bombs, four fire ships, 40 transport ships, and 30 battalions of 100 men each.[86]

British Vice Admiral Clark Gayton in a letter dated 5 August 1777, reported to Philip Stevens of the British Admiralty that several large Spanish warships had been sighted east of Cuba. On July 5, 1777, the *Southhampton* sighted two Spanish 74-gun ships full of troops from Spain, bound for Havana. The following day he fell in with another 74-gun Spanish ship also bound for Havana[87].

Although Spain and England were not at war, British privateers often attacked Spanish merchant ships. One such incident was reported in a letter dated September 15, 1777, from Governor Bernardo de Gálvez to his uncle, Jose' de Gálvez. The governor stated that the Spanish brigantine *Principe de Asturias* on August 28, 1777 sailed from New Orleans to Havana, where she was to take on mail for Vera Cruz. On September 1st, she was stopped on the Mississippi River by a British privateer sloop, which fired shots of metal and stone into her.

The governor decided to reinforce the mail ship with the *San Joachin*, with 25 grenadiers in addition to the normal crew. They were ordered to get underway as soon as possible and to capture the English privateer and bring it to New Orleans. Before reinforcements arrived, the privateer must have received

---

[86] Extract of a Letter from Mr. Collinsworth, a midshipman on board Admiral Gayton's ship, dated Port Royal Harbour, May 27, 1777. *Id* at Vol. 8, p. 1036.

[87] *Id at Vol. 9, p. 716*

word that the *San Joachin* was on the way. They released the mail ship and slipped into the Gulf.[88]

Spain and France threatened an invasion of England. This was the longest military action by Spain during the American Revolutionary War. Spain and France attempted to assemble an armada only to have substantial numbers of the ships' crews succumb to disease. This kept many English regiments and ships of the line in England preparing to defend against the threatened invasion, which ships and troops otherwise could have been sent to the colonies. The raids of Captain John Paul Jones kept the threat of invasion alive - which kept hundreds of ships and thousands of troops in Great Britain.

---

[88] *Id* at Vol. 9, pp. 929-930.

# THE AMERICAN REVOLUTIONARY WAR WAS PART OF A GLOBAL WAR

Most historians limit their discussion of the American Revolutionary War to the land area encompassed by the original 13 colonies. Spain's contribution along the coast of the Gulf of México and up the Mississippi River, as far as St. Louis was significant, as it prevented England from opening a second front on either the Gulf or along the Mississippi. Also, the Mississippi and Ohio Rivers remained as a lifeline to Washington's troops through New Orleans.[89]

To have a full and complete understanding of the direct interaction of the French and Spanish allies, one must examine the events occurring in what is now referred to as the Midwest, the Louisiana Territory and the Caribbean. To comprehend the full impact of the actions of our allies, one must understand that it was a global conflict.

## GIBRALTAR AND MINORCA

Between 16 June 1779 and 7 February 1783, France and Spain laid siege on Gibraltar, occupying a large number of ships of the English navy, thereby keeping those ships away from the war in the American colonies. At one point, the Franco-Spanish army attacking Gibraltar totaled 33,000. During the attack by Spain on Gibraltar beginning on 21 July 1781, Spain used 50 ships of the line and a large number of frigates, plus it had troops embarked on 46 troop transports.

---

[89] "Spain's Involvement in the American Revolutionary War", Edward F. Butler, Sr., The *SAR Magazine*, Summer 2009, Vol. 104, No. 1, pp. 20-25.

Because of the strong fortifications and the tunnels that catacombed Gibraltar, the British were able to hold out because they were resupplied from sea three times.

The invasion of Minorca in 1781 was a success, as Minorca surrendered the following year. Minorca was restored to Spain after the war.

**GREAT BRITAIN, SPAIN, MAJORCA & MINORCA**

**Captain John Paul Jones**

Commander John Paul Jones aboard the USS *Ranger,* a sloop, with his crew of 140 men on April 10, 1778, set sail from the French naval port at Brest, France. He headed toward the Irish Sea to begin raids on British gunships. This was the first mission where any American ship was to prey on English shipping in home waters during the Revolutionary War.

That year the USS *Ranger* raided the port at Whitehaven, England, where, about 400 British merchant ships were anchored. Jones was hoping to reach the port at midnight, when the ebb tide would leave the ships at their most vulnerable.

Because Whitehaven was a shallow port, Jones and his 30 volunteers had to row to the port, which was protected by two forts. As strange as it might appear, they attacked in two row boats. Jones' boat attacked the southern fort, disabling its cannon. Jones then set fire to the southern fort which spread quickly, so as to engulf the entire town.

After the raid on Whitehaven, Jones raided several coastal towns. He continued to the Irish Sea to Carrickfergus, where his *Ranger* crew captured the HMS *Drake* after delivering fatal wounds to the British ship's captain and lieutenant.

Jones was resupplied by Joseph Gardoqui and Sons in Bilbao, Spain in between raids on England and English shipping. Jones asked Benjamin Franklin to seek a new ship for him from France. He was awarded an old French East Indian frigate, which was renamed the USS *Bonhomme Richard,* named for Benjamin Franklin.

**Captain John Paul Jones**

In September 1779, Jones next set sail with a squadron of French and American ships to the western edge of Ireland. There he captured twelve British merchant vessels. The squadron dispersed at the Firth of Forth, and Jones set his sights on a heading south with three vessels. On September 23, 1779, the Americans encountered a convoy of British ships off Flamborough Head. There, he fought one of the fiercest battles in naval history.

At the approach of the American ships, the British merchantmen made for the coast while two of the Royal Navy escorts remained to face Jones. Initially, Jones fought the *Serapis* at long range with his eighteen-pound cannon. After one of the guns exploded, Jones engaged the *Serapis* at close range. As the ships touched sides, Jones lashed his crippled ship to the British frigate. After a battle that raged through the night, British commander Richard Pearson asked Jones if he'd had enough. Jones reportedly replied, "I have not yet begun to fight!"

The USS *Bonhomme Richard* was struck by cannon fire; it began taking on water and caught fire. Only a few hours later, the captain of the *Serapis* surrendered. Jones reluctantly abandoned ship and transferred his crew to the captured *Serapis*.

John Paul Jones's raids along the English coast were the only time that British home territory was attacked during the American Revolutionary war. It brought the war home to British Continental Navy raiders and privateers.[90] His raids succeeded where conventional land warfare could not. Their highly publicized actions helped turn the tide of popular British opinion away from the war, forcing the government to sue for peace.

**CENTRAL AMERICA AND THE CARIBBEAN**

The English navy was involved in smuggling operations along the South American Atlantic coast. They were confronted by the Spanish navy. Sea battles between the British and Spanish navies were frequent in Central America and the Caribbean.

---

[90] One of the important Spanish privateers was Captain Jorge Farragut. He was the father of Admiral David Farragut, the first American Admiral.

**Central America**

England had important outposts and ports in East Florida, West Florida, Bermuda, the Bahamas, Jamaica, and Honduras. Spain controlled West Florida, the Louisiana Territory (everything west of the Mississippi River), New Spain (which included what is now Texas, Arizona, New México, California, Colorado, Utah, Nevada and México), as well as most of Central America, and the West Indies (Cuba, Hispaniola and Puerto Rico). France controlled what is now Haiti, Martinique, and Guadalupe.

When Spain entered the War in 1779, England initiated an attack on Spanish Nicaragua. The British attacked San Fernando de Omoa in October 1779, and were soundly defeated by the Spanish. The following year, the British attacked Fort San Juan, Nicaragua. Although the British won the battle, it was a shallow victory, as the bulk of their garrison fell to yellow fever and other tropical diseases. The remaining British troops were forced to relinquish their conquest and return to Jamaica.[91]

**FLASHPOINTS AROUND THE WORLD**

During the course of the American Revolutionary War, battles between England, France and Spain also occurred in Buenos Aires, South Africa and India. English ships were on alert all around the world. To the extent that English gunships and English troops were involved, those were gunships and troops that could not attack America.

To give an idea of the importance of these world conflicts, a look at the number of gunships captured by each side is informative:

**LOSS OF SPANISH SHIPS:**

>Action of 8 January 1780: The armed merchantman *Guipuzcoano* was captured by the Royal Navy.

>Action of 8 January 1780: The 16-gun private corvette *San Fermín* was captured by the Royal Navy.

>Battle of Cape St. Vincent, 16 January 1780: The 70-gun *Diligente* was captured by the Royal Navy.

>Battle of Cape St. Vincent, 16 January 1780: The 80-gun *Fénix* was captured by the Royal Navy.

>Battle of Cape St. Vincent, 16 January 1780: The 68-gun *Monarca* was captured by the Royal Navy.

---

[91] *The Kimble Papers, Vol.1*, 10 August 1780, Stephen Kimble, New York Historical Society, Vol.. 17, New York City, 1932.

Battle of Cape St. Vincent, 16 January 1780: The 70-gun *Princesa* was captured by the Royal Navy.

Battle of Cape St. Vincent, 16 January 1780: The 70-gun *San Miguel* was captured by the Royal Navy.

Siege of Gibraltar, 1782: The new 74-gun *San Miguel* (named for the ship captured in 1780) was captured by the Royal Navy.

**BRITISH SHIPS CAPTURED BY SPAIN:**

On 9 August 1780 the Spanish Fleet from Cádiz captured 55 British ships, including the following gunships, which were incorporated into the Spanish fleet with upgrades:

The 28-gun East India Company's Indiaman *Gatton*

The 28-gun East India Company's Indiaman *Godfrey*

The 30-gun East India Company's Indiaman *Hillsborough*

The 28-gun East India Company's Indiaman *Mountstuart*

The 28-gun East India Company's Indiaman *Royal George*

The 16-gun sloop **HMS Saint Fermin** was captured on 3 April 1781 by the Spanish Navy's *San Antonio* and *San Luis*. The schooner **HMS West Florida** was captured by Captain William Pickles, on 21 July 1779. It's name was changed to the *Gálveztown,* and placed into service by Gálvez on Lake Pontchartrain, Louisiana.

The 18-gun sloop **HMS Port Royal***,* was captured by Gálvez at the Siege of Pensacola on 8 May 1781.

# DON BERNARDO DE GÁLVEZ Y MADRID

Bernardo de Gálvez was from a very prominent family in Spain.

His uncle, Jose' de Gálvez was a successful lawyer, who won many lawsuits against the royal government. These legal successes brought him to the attention of Carlos III. In 1765 the king appointed him Inspector General of New Spain. Later he was named President of the Council of the Indies, placing him in charge of Spain's colonial empire in America.

DON BERNARDO DE GÁLVEZ
CONDE DE GÁLVEZ
VIRREY de Nueva España

Jose' took good care of his three brothers. Jose' named his brother Matias (Bernardós father) as Governor of the Kingdom of Guatemala, which at that time included all of present day Central America. Gálvez' brother Antonio was a high ranking military officer who later became a Field Marshall. His third brother Miguel was Spanish Minister to Prussia, and later was Minister to Russia. Miguel's adopted daughter, Mar'ia Rosa, who was probably the illegitimate child of Carlos III, was the mistress of Manuel Godoy, Spanish Prime Minister under King Carlos IV.

Matias' son was Bernardo de Gálvez, who was named Governor General of New Orleans on 19 September 1776, but did not assume office until late 1776. Before leaving Spain, Carlos III had advised Bernardo that soon Spain would enter the hostilities between the Americans and Great Britain. Upon his arrival in New Orleans he immediately set out to form a strong militia.

For his militia he recruited male residents of New Orleans, recently arrived immigrants from the Canary Islands, residents of the German Coast; and Acadians (Cajuns), who had recently been involuntarily uprooted from their homes in Acadia, Canada and moved to Louisiana by the English. To that mix, he added native Americans and free men of color. Soon after the arrival of Bernardo de Gálvez in New Orleans in late 1776, a steady flow of Spanish army reinforcements began arriving from Spain. Carlos' plan was to reinforce Cuba, Puerto Rico and other bases in the "American Sea".[92]

---

[92] Gulf of México

In his many battles on the Mississippi River and along the Gulf Coast, Gálvez led troops from Spain, Majorca, México, Venezuela, Cuba, Puerto Rico, Hispaniola, México, Ireland, France, as well as Acadians, Germans, Canary Islanders, Indians, Mestizos, and both free and enslaved Blacks. He even had about 30 Americans from the South Carolina Navy under his command, plus a few Texans and a contingent of the First Continental Marines, a part of the South Carolina Navy.[93]

At the siege of Pensacola he commanded part of the French Fleet. After the battle, he provided money and supplies to reprovision these French ships, which later participated in the battle of Yorktown. Major General Geronimo Girón, one of Gálvez' top officers was a direct descendant of Montezuma. Francisco Miranda, his aide-de-camp was involved in Venezuelan independence.[94]

"[I]n May 1776 the [Virginia] Committee of Safety sent George Gibson and William Linn down the Mississippi River to New Orleans, where with the help of Robert Morris' agent, Oliver Pollock, they secured over nine thousand pounds of gunpowder from Gálvez. It took Lynn until the Spring of 1777 to bring the bulk of the purchases back up the Mississippi and Ohio Rivers to

---

[93] *The Vital Contribution Of Spain In the Winning of the American Revolution*, by Robert H. Thonhoff, self published 2000, p. 5.

[94] *El Fuerte del Cibolo*, Robert H. Thonhoff (Privately published in Karnes City, Texas) 2002, at p. 75.

Wheeling in western Virginia . . . ."[95] The supplies from Spain were enough to save Fort Pitt and Willing from defeat.[96]

On November 26, 1776, Governor Bernardo de Gálvez received orders from his uncle, Josef de Gálvez, the Minister of the West Indies, to start shipping gunpowder to the colonists. By year's end he had shipped $70,000[97] worth of gunpowder. In that directive, he was also instructed to send secret commissioners to the English colonies. These commissioners were to collect information.[98]

A Royal Order dated December 24, 1776, instructed all Spanish officials, including the Governors of Havana and Louisiana, "to quickly supply the 'Americanos' with what gunpowder and rifles or muskets, and 'fusiles' where available." The governors were instructed to ship these war materials on free merchant ships.[99] This latter instruction was because neither Spain nor France, as neutrals, could openly give aid to rebels in another country.

---

[95] *The Revolutionary War in Virginia, 1775-1783*, John E. Selby, U. of VA. Press, Charlottesville, 1988, p. 170

[96] *Spain and the Independence of the United States: An Intrinsic Gift, Ibid*.

[97] $1,969,100 in 2013 dollars.

[98] *Spain's Louisiana Patriots in its 1779-1783 War with England During the American Revolution, Part Six, Spanish Borderlands Studies*, Granville W. and N.C. Hough, p. 2.

[99] *Spain and the Independence of the United States: An Intrinsic Gift*, Thomas E. Chavez, Univ. of NM Press, Albuquerque, 2002, p.49.

Pollock was only able to secure goods from the Spanish in New Orleans.

England's plan was to encircle the Americans. Their army would attack from Canada down the Ohio and Mississippi Rivers. At the same time, their naval forces would attack New Orleans from the Gulf with its military then in West Florida. This would prevent the colonists from being supplied up the Mississippi. Gálvez warned Leyba, his Deputy in St. Louis to prepare for an attack.

It was through Gálvez' leadership that the British were defeated at Fort San Carlos, and that the Spanish garrison there defeated the British and destroyed their stores in Michigan, thereby ending any thought of a campaign down the Mississippi. It was also Gálvez who defeated the English in Baton Rouge, Manchac,[100] Natchez, Mobile, Pensacola and the Bahamas. Clearly, he took the war to the British and won.

By 1784, his official title was Bernardo de Gálvez y Madrid, Viscount of Galveston and Count of Gálvez. Following the end

---

[100] Manchac (also known as Akers) is an unincorporated community in Tangipahoa Parish, Louisiana. Fort Bute or Manchac Post, named after the then British Prime Minister John Stuart, 3rd Earl of Bute, was established in 1763 at the junction of Iberville River (Bayou Manchac) with the Mississippi River, and remained an important British military and trading post in West Florida until captured by Spanish forces under Bernardo de Gálvez of Louisiana on September 7, 1779, during what became known as Battle of Fort Bute of the American Revolutionary War. Manchac was raided in February 1778 by American forces under the command of James Willing. See Arthur H. DeRosier, Jr.: *William Dunbar: scientific pioneer of the old Southwest*, University Press of Kentucky, Lexington, Ky., 2007, pp. 39-44.

of the war, in 1785 Gálvez was named Captain General of Havana. His father died later that year, at which time Gálvez was named Viceroy of New Spain. He immediately moved to México City with his wife Felicite, and three minor children, Adelaide, Matilde, and Michael.

Gálvez arrived in the midst of a famine and yellow fever epidemic. He contributed much of his personal fortune to feed the hungry and tend to the sick. As a result he was loved by the people. Among his accomplishments were the re-building of the opulent Chapultepec Castle and the completion of the Cathedral of México in México City – the largest church in the Western Hemisphere.[101]

Unfortunately, Bernardo died in the epidemic on November 30, 1786, just 12 days before another child, Guadalupe was born on December 12, 1786. He is entombed in the walls of La Iglesia de San Fernando in México City. His heart was placed in an urn that was interred in the Cathedral of México, which he completed while serving as Viceroy.[102] Both he and his father are entombed within the altar wall of the San Fernando Church.

When Gálvez arrived in New Orleans in late 1776, his rank was as a Colonel. After capturing Manchac, Baton Rouge, and

---

[101] *El Fuerte del Cibolo, id at pp. 75-76.*

[102] *The Vital Contribution of Spain in the Winning of the American Revolution: An Essay on a Forgotten Chapter in the History of the American Revolution* (Privately published in Karnes City, Texas, 200), p. 13.

Natchez in 1779, he was promoted to Brigadier General. He was promoted to Field Marshal following his victory at Mobile that year. His success at Pensacola was significant. Following that conquest, King Carlos made him Count of Gálvez and Viscount of Gálveztown.

He was also made Governor and Captain-General of Louisiana, with a salary of 10,000 *pesos* per year for the duration of the war.

Further, he was authorized by the king to place a crest on his coat of arms with the words "*Yo Solo*", meaning that he alone was

**Arms of Bernardo de Gálvez**

responsible for the victory at Pensacola. To England, the loss of Pensacola meant loss of control of the Gulf of México and the loss of hope of controlling the Mississippi River.

# Gulf Coast Campaign
## Spain's Dominance of the Gulf and Mississippi River

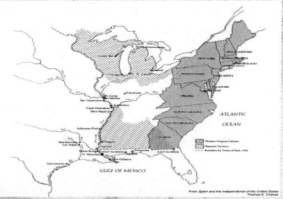

**War declared on Britain by the King of Spain, 12 April 1779**

- Battle of Fort Bute, Manchac, Louisiana 22 Aug to 7 Sept 1779
- Battle of Baton Rouge, Louisiana 9 Sept 1779
- Surrender of Fort Panmure, Natchez 9 Sept 1779
- Battle of Lake Pontchartrain, HMS West Florida vs. USS Morris 10 Sept 1779
- Battle of Fort Charlotte, Mobile, Alabama 20 Feb to 9 March 1780
- Battle of Fort San Carlos, St. Louis, Missouri 26 May 1780
- Battle of Fort Saint Joseph, Niles, Michigan 12 Feb 1781
- Battle of Pensacola, Florida 3 March to 9 May 1782

The HMS West Florida was captured by the USS Morris in the naval battle of Lake Pontchartrain on 10 Sept 1779. The West Florida was taken by Galvez and christened the Galveztown.

The final day of the siege of Pensacola, there was a stall when the joint Spanish and French fleets refused to cross the sand bar due to fear of floundering. General Galvez stood on the deck of the Galveztown and proclaimed "YO SOLO VOY" (I alone will go) and proceeded across the sand bar to attack. The fleet followed and the battle was won. The King of Spain bestowed the title of "Yo Solo" to Bernardo de Galvez and added the caption of "Yo Solo" over an image of the Galveztown to his coat of arms.

## Gulf Coast Campaign

The original of the nine foot panel on the previous page, along with four others were designed and constructed by a committee of the "Texas Connection with the American Revolution Association," which included the author. These panels were part of a display about Bernardo de Gálvez at Texas A & M University, San Antonio, Texas in March 2013. They were also on exhibition at the Menger Hotel in San Antonio, Texas during the Texas Heritage Societies annual meeting October 23-27, 2013.

# OLIVER POLLOCK

Oliver Pollock was an individual to whom all Americans owe a debt of gratitude. He was appointed as the agent of both the Continental Congress and of Virginia. Based in New Orleans, as a merchant, it was his duty to arrange for the purchase, storage, financing and transporting of military weapons and supplies for the Americans. Most of the supplies he arranged for were shipped from Spain to New Orleans, and from New Orleans up the Mississippi.

Much of it went directly to General George Rogers Clark at Fort Nelson (Louisville), but substantial amounts supplied American Forces at Point Pleasant (WV), Wheeling (WV) and Ft. Pitt. From Ft. Pitt the continental army was supplied. Pollock also was charged with purchasing or chartering ships to deliver supplies from Spain to ports on the eastern seaboard of the United States.

**Oliver Pollock**

To accomplish his duties it was often necessary for him to place his personal guaranty on substantial advances. The Continental Congress and Virginia respectively were honor bound to reimburse him. The system was fairly simple: Clark and Pollock would issue Bills of Credit on Virginia or the Continental Congress, with the face amount being paid by Pollock. Simply put, Spain supplied the goods on the personal guarantee of Pollock or Clark that if Virginia or congress failed to pay the Bill of Credit, they would pay it.

Lamentably, this reimbursement was not forthcoming. Pollock at the end of the war ended up in debtor's prison.

Pollock and Clark were left with huge unsecured debts. By using their personal credit the transaction was completed much quicker and therefore the supplies reached their destination sooner. Reimbursements were not made timely, and the fall of Philadelphia caused a failure of reimbursement. By the time that Spain declared war in 1779, Pollock had been forced to mortgage his personal holdings to keep the flow of goods in the stream to the Americans.[103]

The following quotation reflects how important was Pollock's contribution to defeat of the British in the Northwest Territories:

> *Colonel Clark also faced difficult and persistent supply problems. He could expect little help from Virginia, and the Kentucky settlements could not spare much from their insufficient stores. Some foodstuffs could be*

---

[103] James, "Oliver Pollock: Financier," 73-74.

> *obtained in the Illinois country when money was available to make purchases, and a trickle of welcome goods came from the friendly Spanish authorities on the far bank of the Mississippi River.* **But Oliver Pollock, the New Orleans fiscal agent for both Virginia and the Continental Congress did more than anybody to help. Indefatigable in his efforts, Pollock overcame innumerable obstacles to keep Clark supplied with the goods he had to have.**
>
> *Pollock was critically handicapped by the failure of the state and Continental governments to honor the bills drawn on them by Clark and others operating in the west, and he was forced to pledge his own property and credit to maintain the flow of supplies.* **His subsequent bankruptcy was a tribute to the zeal with which he supported the American cause. Clark could not have maintained his position in Illinois as long as he did had it not been for Pollock's efforts.**[104]
> *[emphasis added]*

Oliver Pollock is best known for being the first to use the "$" sign. He originally abbreviated Pesos as "ps." His handwriting was horrible. He wrote the "s" on to the "p", and it looked like a dollar sign.

Oliver Pollock, the New Orleans fiscal agent for both Virginia and the Continental Congress did more than anybody else to help. Indefatigable in his efforts, Pollack overcame innumerable

---

[104] *George Roger Clark and the War in the West*, by Lowell W. Harrison, Univ. Press of Kentucky, 1976, pp. 36-37.

obstacles to keep General Clark supplied with the goods he had to have. Pollock's success was due to Spain's willingness to provide the supplies, and a direct result in the efforts of General Bernardo de Gálvez.

## GÁLVEZ CAPTURES MANCHAC:

### 7 September 1779

Gálvez' spies had been watching the movement of British troops, especially at Pensacola. Reports showed that the British were deploying additional troops, far beyond those needed to defend the fort. Gálvez believed they were preparing for an assault on New Orleans. Thus, he was presented with a decision: should he wait for the British to attack, or should he fire the first shot?

He spent his time wisely in creating and training a strong militia. Spain declared war on Great Britain on 21 June 1779, making Spain and the Americans allies. Gálvez had known since his 1776 briefing by King Carlos that war was coming. He was ready!

On 27 August 1779, Gálvez led his multicultural army 90 miles up the Mississippi to Ft. Bute at Manchac (in current Louisiana). He started with a force of 667 men, which included 170 veteran Spanish soldiers; 330 Spanish recruits newly arrived from México and the Canary Islands, and an assortment of Cubans, Dominicans, Puerto Ricans, militiamen, free Blacks and Mulattoes, and 7 American volunteers, including Oliver Pollock. Part of the force traveled in a flotilla of four boats, under the command of Juan A'lvarez, while the main body went by land.

The great majority of Gálvez' army consisted of Spanish troops and the Louisiana Spanish Militia. **These Spanish troops were the first foreign troops to fight for American independence on American soil.**

Along the way Gálvez enlisted an additional 600 men from the German and Acadian coasts and 160 Indians. When he finally arrived to confront the British, his force consisted of 1,427 men of every color, class and nation. They endured many hardships in the two week long journey. They had to pass through a wilderness including alligator infested swamps, impassable roads and dense wooded areas. They had to fight alligators, snakes and other animals. All of these hurdles impeded their progress. They had no tents to protect them from the elements and very few supplies. About one-third were forced to drop out along the way due to sickness or fatigue.

When they reached Manchac, the British had not yet heard that Spain had declared war against them. This gave Gálvez a decisive advantage of "surprise". Victory for Gálvez came quickly.

They attacked and seized Manchac on 7 September 1779, taking 20 prisoners. Nearby was the town of Gálveztown, which had recently been settled by the Canary Islanders.[105]

---

[105] Many Canary Islanders settled in and around San Antonio.

## GÁLVEZ CAPTURES FT. NEW RICHMOND AT BATON ROUGE AND FT. PANMURE AT NATCHEZ:

### 21 September 1779

Unknown to Gálvez at the time, Carlos III had issued a proclamation on 29 August 1779, stating that the main objective of the Spanish troops in American was to drive the British out of the Gulf of México and the Mississippi River.

The British fort at Baton Rouge, Fort New Richmond, was a substantial one. To avoid sizeable losses of his invading force, Gálvez drew up a plan to deceive the English. He divided his force into two elements. One group was instructed to enter the woods on the far side of the fort, and to make as much noise as possible. It was his intent to fool the English into thinking that his main body was in the woods. That group sustained very little damage as they were protected by the dense woods. The second element, under concealment of a fence surrounding an orchard, secretly dug trenches near the fort.

On September 20, 1779, his army attacked the fort. After only a few short hours the British surrendered. As a condition of their surrender Gálvez also insisted that Fort Panmure in Natchez (now Mississippi) also be surrendered. Thus, Fort Panmure was surrendered without a shot being fired. Gálvez took 375 prisoners from Baton Rouge and an additional 80 from Natchez. Gálvez' force consisted of the Louisiana Regiment (500), American Dragoons (20), a white militia company (60), a Black militia Company (80), Indians (160), and patriot traders (7).

In less than a month, the English army had been removed from the lower Mississippi by a small hybrid army. During the next few years, with the aid of the militia companies of the colony, Gálvez went on to wage successful battles against the other British held forts of Mobile and Pensacola, thus returning the Florida Territory to the control of Spain.

By clearing the Mississippi, this allowed Captain William Pickles to bring an American schooner onto Lake Pontchartrain. Captain Pickles boarded and seized the English privateer, *West Florida*, which had dominated the lake for two years. The Canary Islanders took other prize ships at Gálveztown.

## GÁLVEZ ATTACKS FT. CHARLOTTE AT MOBILE:

## 11 January1780 to 9 March 1780

Because King Carlos III in 1776, had instructed Bernardo de Gálvez to begin preparing for war, Gálvez had created a large militia in New Orleans composed of men from many different countries.

Within only two months after Spain entered the American Revolutionary War in June 1779, Bernardo de Gálvez, immediately began to make preparations for war. In September 1779, he gained complete control over the lower Mississippi River by capturing Fort Bute, Baton Rouge and Natchez. His next goal was to remove the British from Mobile and Pensacola, the only British presence in the province of West Florida. The British acquired Ft. Charlotte from the French as part of the Treaty of 1763, which ended the French and Indian War.

In early January, 1780, he made a request for additional troops before departing New Orleans for an attack on Fort Charlotte. That fort guarded the entrance into Mobile Bay. As the closest British fortress to New Orleans, it posed a threat to Gálvez' troops in New Orleans.

On January 11, 1780, his fleet of twelve ships carrying 754 men set sail from New Orleans. A week later they reached the mouth of the Mississippi. Two days later, on January 20, they rendezvoused with the American ship *West Florida*, under the command of Captain William Pickles. It had a crew of 58.

On February 6, a storm scattered the fleet, but within three days, the Spanish fleet arrived outside Mobile Bay. Gálvez had inadequate intelligence on the entrance to Mobile Bay. This resulted in several ships running aground on sand bars. One of his ships, the *Volante*, was severely damaged. Gálvez, made lemonade out of the lemons dealt him, and salvaged the guns from the *Volante* wreck. He set them up as an artillery battery at Mobile Point to protect the bay entrance.

On February 20, 1780, an additional 1,412 Spanish troops arrived from Havana, giving Gálvez an attacking force of about 2,400. The troops were landed near Ft. Charlotte on February 25, 1780, on the shores of the Dog River, about 10 miles (16 km) from Fort Charlotte. A deserter told the Spanish that the fort was garrisoned by 300 men.

A two-week siege followed. On March 1, Gálvez asked Captain Elias Durnford to surrender, which he politely rejected. The following day, Gálvez began setting up gun batteries around the fort. Durnford had requested that General John Campbell at Pensacola send him reinforcements. On March 5 and 6, a large number of soldiers of the Pensacola garrison left on a march toward Mobile. They were delayed by difficult river crossings, and were unable to assist the Fort Charlotte garrison.

While the Spanish engaged in siege operations to move their guns nearer the fort, Gálvez and Durnford engaged in a courteous written dialogue. Simultaneously, the Spanish continued to dig trenches and began to bombard the fort. On March 13, the walls of Fort Charlotte were breached, and Durnford capitulated the next day, surrendering his garrison. The British were greatly outnumbered, but fought tenaciously until Spanish bombardment breeched the fortress walls. As British Commander Captain Elias Durnford was outnumbered, he was forced to surrender on 9 March 1780. The capture of Ft. Charlotte opened the way for an attack on Pensacola.

At the opposite end of Mobile Bay, Gálvez established a small military garrison called "The Village". The garrison was manned by the New Orleans Negro Military Company (40) and a company from the España Regiment (40). The garrison was defended by 8 military cannon of various sizes, operated by naval gun crews (60). This small group successfully defended a British attack on 7 January 1781. Nearly every British officer was killed or severely wounded in that attack.

For his victory, Gálvez was promoted to Field Marshall and given command of all Spanish operations in America. Before departing Mobile, he assigned a detachment of 500 militia to garrison the fort. The garrison at Mobile successfully fended off a counterattack by the British in January 1781. Between the victory at Mobile and the victory at Pensacola, many Spanish soldiers, while out foraging and hunting for food, were killed by Indians allied with the British.

# THE SPANISH ARMADA HEADING TO PENSACOLA WAS DESTROYED IN A HURRICANE

## 16 October to 18 October 1780

Pensacola was originally settled by the Spanish in 1539.[106] Tristan De Luna founded a Spanish colony there in 1559, which lasted for only two years. The settlers were devastated by a hurricane. The first permanent settlement by the Spaniards was not until 1698. The French took Pensacola in 1719, but then traded it for New Orleans. In the 1763 treaty settling the French and Indian War, Britain was given Cuba and Spain was awarded the Floridas. Immediately, Spain traded the Floridas for Cuba.

During the American Revolutionary War, in 1779 the British constructed Fort George. Gálvez knew that Pensacola was strongly defended by British troops with large and powerful cannon. Rather than attack while the British were disorganized following their defeat at Mobile, he instead wrote to Havana requesting large-scale naval support, and additional troops from Spain. In April 1780, he learned that England had reinforced Pensacola with additional troops, and several warships.

Without the requested reinforcements, he left a garrison in Mobile, and departed for Havana to raise the troops and equipment needed for an attack on Pensacola. He had learned that there were many "foot draggers" in the administration in Havana, and felt that he needed to appear personally to argue his case.

---

[106] Sixty eight years before the English established their settlement at Jamestowne, Virginia.

**Spanish Ships Fight Storm**

Gálvez went to Havana to plan for an assault on Pensacola and to supervise the operation. By 16 October 1779, he was ready. On that day he sailed from Havana with 7 gunships, 5 frigates, 3 smaller warships and 49 transport ships. His force totaled 164 officers and 3,829 men.

Little did Gálvez know when his armada cleared Havana harbor, that they would encounter a hurricane. His plan to capture Pensacola from the English was dashed for the time being. About half his warships and troop transports were sent to the bottom of the Gulf of México. The British press claimed that 2,000 men had been lost. The remainder of his fleet with their crews was cast upon the shores of the Gulf from the Yucatan of

México to the shores of Alabama. The survivors retreated to Havana.[107]

For fear that the British might seek to retake Mobile before he could take Pensacola; Gálvez dispatched two gunships and 500 soldiers to reinforce Mobile. Because of this reinforcement, the Spanish were able to defeat a British counter attack in January1781.

It was not until 28 February 1781 that his second invasion force was prepared to set sail from Havana. This smaller force consisted of one man of war, three frigates, one packet and several smaller transports, with a force of only 1,315 soldiers. He had previously sent word to New Orleans and Mobile respectively to have troops from those posts to join in the attack.[108]

---

[107] *Spain And The Independence of the United States, Id.* at p. 182.

[108] *Id* at p. 189.

# SPANISH SIEGE OF FT. GEORGE AT PENSACOLA TOOK TWO MONTHS:

## *THE MOST DECISIVE BATTLE OF THE AMERICAN REVOLUTIONARY WAR[109]*

### 13 February - 9 Mar, 1781

"Dammit Calvo! Order your fleet into the Bay!" Gálvez shouted at no one in particular. Captain José Calvo de Irazabal was in command of the Spanish fleet. Calvo had the entire Spanish fleet jammed up at the entrance to Pensacola Bay. There was a narrow entrance between Santa Rosa Island and Perdido Key - both of which had British cannon bombarding the fleet. Calvós' ship, the 64-cannon *San Ramón* had grounded in its attempt to transit the straits. By flag

**Pensacola Bay**

message he ordered his fleet to hold fast, citing the danger that British guns on both Santa Rosa Island and Perdido Key seemed

---

[109] For an in depth account of the Battle of Pensacola, see *The Longest Siege of the American Revolution: Pensacola*, by Wesley S. Odom, self published, 2009.

to have range to the bay entrance.[110] "Imbecile!" said Gálvez when he received this message.

Gálvez transferred his flag to the *Gálveztown*[111], and as Governor, he was also commander of the Spanish forces from Louisiana. He sailed the *Galvestown* through the channel, past the incredulous Calvo watching from the quarterdeck, and into Pensacola Bay. He was followed by the three other Louisiana warships. Calvo, with a red face dripping with sweat reluctantly ordered the remainder of the fleet to follow. The following day he sent a message to Gálvez that he had completed his mission of escorting Gálvez' invasion forces to Pensacola, with which he sailed the San Ramon back to Havana.[112]

**Background**

After Spain declared war on England on June 21, 1779, General John Campbell beefed up his English military forces to defend Pensacola. Pensacola was vitally important to England strategically due to its Caribbean possessions. In addition to the 16th Infantry Regiment, a batallion from the 60th Infantry Regiment, and a company from the 16th Regiment of Royal Artillery, his forces also included the Third Regiment of Waldeck, the Maryland Loyalist Battalion, and some Pennsylvania Loyalists, plus about 500 Native Americans. The

---

[110] Dupuy, R. Ernest; Hammerman, Gay; Hayes, Grace P (1977). *The American Revolution: A Global War*. New York: David McKay. ISBN 0-679-50648-9., p. 151

[111] The *Gálveztown* was the British brigantine his forces captured on Lake Ponctharetrain.

[112] Dupuy, *Ibid*.

garrison was housed in Fort George, which was an earthen works upon which was placed a wooden palisade. To the north was the Prince Of Wales Redoubt, called "The Sombrero". Still further north and east was the Queen's Redoubt, known as "The Crescent".

Artillery batteries were placed on both Santa Rosa Island and Perdido Key to defend the entrance to Pensacola Bay. Two additional forts provided the British with additional protection of Pensacola Bay. Red Cliff Fort, about 7 miles southwest of Fort George, fired about 140 cannon shot at the Spanish armada.

Only nominal damage was incurred, as the British guns could not be lowered to fire at the closest ships. The magazine of Fort Half Moon was destroyed by a Spanish cannon shot, which resulted in the Spanish taking 1,100 British soldiers, the *HMS Port Royal*, a ship of the line, a frigate, two small warships and several English sloops.

The Spanish invasion force sailed from Havana on 13 February 1781. The fleet reached the entrance to Pensacola Bay on 9 March. Irish troops and light artillery were landed on Santa Rosa Island. Their mission was to locate and destroy the British troops on the island and to dispatch the cannon defending the entrance to the Bay. Auroro ÓNeil, Gálvez' Irish commander ordered the Spanish artillery to fire upon all British ships in the bay within range.

On 28 February 1781, a second (and smaller) Spanish flotilla, with 1,315 soldiers, sailed from Havana, Cuba to assist General Bernardo de Gálvez in his attack on Pensacola. Gálvez had previously ordered troops stationed in New Orleans and Mobile to join in the attack on Pensacola. Mobile sent 500 men, and 1,400 arrived from New Orleans.

The two month siege of Pensacola began on 9 March 1781. His total force consisted of about 3,500 men.

Gálvez had no intelligence on the depth of the channel. Prudence dictated that some of the cargo be offloaded from ships in the fleet to make them ride higher in the water. It was on 19 March that Gálvez sailed into Pensacola Bay.

By 24 March Santa Rosa Island had been cleared of British soldiers, all of whom had either been killed or taken prisoner. On that day Irish forces reached the mainland. They were immediately attacked by about 400 Choctaw Indians allied with the British.

On 12 April 1781, Gálvez was wounded in the arm by gunfire. After his wound was treated, his arm was placed into a sling.[113]

Some 1,600 reinforcements from Havana arrived on 19 April.

---

[113] Martín-Merás, Luisa (2007). *"The Capture of Pensacola through Maps, 1781" in Legacy: Spain and the United States in the Age of Independence, 1763-1848.* Washington, DC: Smithsonian Institution. ISBN 978-84-95146-36-6, p. 82.

About the same time, four French frigates joined in the battle, together with 725 French soldiers. By 23 April Gálvez commanded a force of 7,800 men.

On 19 April 1781, the same day a large Spanish and French fleet from Havana was sighted heading towards the bay. The Spanish fleet, including four French warships together with 725 French soldiers, was manned by a crew of 1,700. It included transports carrying about 1,600 Spanish soldiers, which raised the total Spanish force commanded by Gálvez to about 8,000 men.[114]

**Gálvez Monument at Pensacola Battlefield**

---

[114] Martín-Merás, Luisa, id at p. 85.

This number is highly significant, as Washington's Continental Line consisted on only about 6,000, being about the same number of French soldiers and sailors at Yorktown.

**Author at Pensocola Gálvez Monument**

The end of April was the beginning of the end for the British. On 30 April 1781, the Spanish batteries finally were in place to open fire.

The siege on Pensacola's fortifications was now in full swing. Because of another hurricane on 5 and 6 May, five of the Spanish ships were forced to depart to avoid damage to the wooden hulls. If left at anchor, the wooden ships would have crashed on the shore.

The army was on its own to continue the siege. Hurricane downpours flooded the trenches which dampened the spirits of the soldiers. Those spirits were raised when the troops were granted a ration of brandy from Gálvez.[115]

Spanish troops set up a make-shift camp. Hundreds of engineers and workers transported supplies and armaments to the battlefield. The men dug trenches, bunkers, and redoubts and constructed a covered road to shield the troops from the constant fire of British cannons.[116]

On 8 May 1781, Spanish artillery struck the British powder magazine in the Fort Crescent redoubt. A series of explosions destroyed the fortification, killing 57 British soldiers and wounded scores more. More importantly, parts of the fortress were destroyed.

Fort Crescent was immediately occupied by Spanish forces. Artillery was without delay positioned in the redoubt to bombard the remaining British positions. Two days later on 3 May, Campbell surrendered to Gálvez. British prisoners taken included: the Maryland Loyalist Regiment; the Pennsylvania Loyalists; British 60th Foot (Royal Americans); British 16th Foot, and the German Waldeck Regiment. British prisoners

---

[115] Mitchell, Barbara (Autumn 2010). "America's Spanish Savior: Bernardo de Gálvez Marches to Rescue the Colonies". *MHQ (Military History Quarterly)*. pps. 98–104.

[116] Gálvez, Bernardo (1781). *Diario de las operaciones de la expedicion contra la Plaza de Panzacola concluida por las Armas de S. M. Católica, baxo las órdenes del mariscal de campo*. México, pp. 20, 26.

totaled 1,113, and an additional 300 were allowed to return to Georgia, with their promise not to rejoin the British army.

The British had sustained 200 casualties. The Spanish lost 74 men, with 198 wounded.[117] The terms of the surrender granted all of West Florida to Spain. All of the British arms, ammunition, cannon and military supplies were forfeited to Spain as well as a British sloop, the 18-gun *HMS Port Royal*. Spain captured 153 artillery pieces.

The prisoners were transported to Havana. Later they were exchanged in New York for Spanish prisoners, who had endured the horrors of the English prison ships in New York harbor.[118]

For the next four weeks, and after the terms of the surrender had been agreed upon, Gálvez supervised the reconstruction of the fort. He moved a former British battery closer to the bay and enlarged the batteries on Santa Rosa Island and Perdido Key to defend against a future invasion. Almost a month after the surrender, Gálvez sailed out of Pensacola for Havana along with the Spanish fleet. ÓNeill remained, having been appointed by Gálvez as Governor of West Florida.

On 30 May, Gálvez and his men were welcomed as heroes when they arrived in Havana. King Carlos promoted Gálvez to lieutenant general, added to Gálvez' titles "Count of Gálvez, and Viscount of Gálveztown.[119] Gálvez also was named

---

[117] Caughey, John W., id at 209-211.

[118] It has been estimated that over 10,000 Americans died on the infamous British prison ships in New York Harbor.

[119] Martín-Merás, Luisa, *id* at p. 85.

governor of both West Florida and Louisiana.

The impact of the British surrender of Pensacola was the final blow in eliminating the British from the west and from the gulf coast. They were no longer in a position to consider an attack on the Americans from the west or from the south. By his victory at Pensacola, he insured that the Americans would not have to fight a second front.

Following General Cornwallis' surrender at Yorktown on 19 October 1781, but before the Treaty of Paris was signed between the colonists and England in 1783, Gálvez continued in his attacks against the English. He personally supervised the attack on the Bahamas and its surrender on 6 May 1782. His army consisted on 274 regulars and 338 militiamen. They captured 12 privateer ships and 65 English merchant vessels.

An American historian called the siege of Pensacola "a decisive factor in the outcome of the Revolution and one of the most brilliantly executed battles of the war. He said that General Gálvez' campaign broke the British' will to fight."[120]

---

[120] Dr. Granville Hough at the Galvez Gala on 12 October 2003 in the city of Long Beach, California.

**BERNARDO DE GÁLVEZ**

Don Bernardo de Gálvez, Spanish Governor of Louisiana, 1776-1783, in a brilliant campaign, with the aid of regular troops, militia, volunteers, and a few Americans, captured Baton Rouge from the British on September 21, 1779. Terms included the surrender of Fort Panmure in Natchez, which was accepted by the British troops on October 9, 1779. The signing of the Treaty of San Lorenzo on October 27, 1795 ended Spanish control of Natchez.

The place of *Don Bernardo de Gálvez* in American history rests not only on his military conquests but on the man himself—what we might call his style.

There was something quintessentially American about him. The emergence of such a man from Spain's rigid empire stirs thoughts about such personal elements as chance, destiny and luck.

Unquestionably, Bernardo de Gálvez was the right man in the right place at the right time for the United States of America.

Fort Matanzas
National Park
U.S. Department of the Interior

### The Battle of Yorktown

The Battle of Yorktown was the last major engagement on American soil during the American Revolution.

Its victory was due to the timely arrival of Admiral de Grasse's fleet to blockade the Harbor preventing the weaker British fleet from evacuating Lord Cornwallis and his troops.

De Grasse had sailed from Cuba, having been outfitted and funded by Spanish Citizens.

Routes of Washington and Rochambeau in 1781

### Malaga Cathedral

The Citizens of Malaga voted to have monies set aside to construct the second tower at the Malaga Cathedral sent to help the American Colonies instead. 200,000 reales were donated. The second tower of the cathedral was never finished.

### Admiral de Grasse's Expedition

Admiral de Grasse's expedition was funded by the efforts of 28 Havana, Cuba residents who together provided 4.5 million reales to ensure victory at Yorktown, 16 August 1781.

Each ship represents 100,000 Reales

## GÁLVEZ TAKES THE BAHAMAS

### 6 May 1782

Although Cornwallis had surrendered on October 19, 1781, at Yorktown, negotiations on a peace treaty languished on for another two years. In the interim, military actions continued in the Northwest Territories and on the high seas. For many years Gálvez had vowed to attack Nassau, the capital of The Bahamas, which served as a major British privateering base.

**An 1803 map showing New Providence and Nassau**

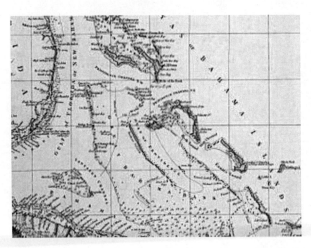

A Spanish force under the command of Juan Manuel de Cagigal, Spanish Governor of Havana, sailed from Havana on 18 April 1782. His armada consisted of 64 troop transports with 2,500 troops embarked, 7 ships of the line, and 7 frigates. He had also managed to secure additional warships and troop transport from American privateers led by Alexander Gillon.

On May 6, 1782 Governor Cagigal's ships came into view of Nassau. He convinced the British commander, Vice Admiral John Maxwell, to surrender without opening a formal siege of the town. Maxwell offered twelve articles of surrender, a list which was mildly revised by Cagigal before he accepted the surrender. Spanish forces then occupied the town, taking the 600-strong British garrison as prisoners and capturing several ships, including a frigate.

For the duration of the American Revolutionary War, the Bahamas was removed as a threat from both the British Navy and British privateers. It also served as a new port where American and allied ships could obtain repairs, provisions and supplies. More importantly, it denied the British of a port from which to operate.

The following year, the British traded its interest in the Floridas, for the return of the Bahamas. This action returned St. Augustine and its strong fortress into the hands of the Spanish. The American colonists no longer had to fear a British attack from the south, west, or southeast Atlantic.

## GÁLVEZ DEFEATS THE BRITISH IN THE
## UPPER MISSISSIPPI VALLEY:

Gálvez' forces also secured the upper Mississippi and Ohio Rivers. His Spanish forces defeated the British at Fort San Carlos (St. Louis, Missouri), and San Jose (St. Joseph, Michigan). Spanish forces also assisted General George Rogers Clark at Vincennes (Indiana), Kaskaskia and Cahokia (Illinois).

Following his victory at Pensacola, Gálvez gave the French flotilla that participated in the battle of Pensacola, some 500,000 pesos. The French used this money to reprovision and repair their ships. Those ships were part of the French fleet which blockaded Yorktown, which led to the surrender of the British on 19 October 1781. In 1782 Gálvez forced the British out of the Bahamas.

Thomas Fleming said the following about Gálvez:

> *His place in American history rests not only on his military conquests but on the man himself - what today's pundits would call his style. There was something quintessentially American about him. The emergence of such a man from Spain's rigid empire stirs thoughts about such historic imponderables as chance, destiny, and luck.*
> *Unquestionably, Bernardo Gálvez was the right man in*

*the right place at the right time - for the United States of America.*"[121]

## Mississippi River Valley Map[122]

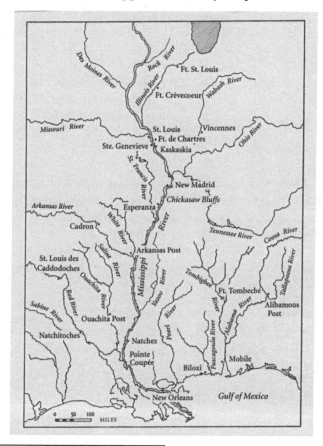

---

[121] Address given by Dr. Granville Hough at the Gálvez Gala on 12 October 2003, in Long Beach, CA.

[122] *Colonial Arkansas, 1686-1804: A Social And Cultural History*, Morris S. Arnold, Univ. of Ark Press, Fayetteville, 1991.

# SPAIN'S ASSISTANCE IN THE MIDWEST: GENERAL GEORGE ROGERS CLARK[123]

As a result of the treaty ending the French and Indian Wars in 1763, Great Britain made it illegal for colonists to travel west beyond the Allegheny Mountains.

The Treaty of Stanwix, was entered into at Ft. Stanwix in New York between the English and the Iroquois, because thousands of settlers were entering the Ohio River Valley.[124] George Rogers Clark was among the first white men to travel to Kentucky[125]. He traveled on the Ohio River.

In 1774 Clark was organizing an expedition of 90 men to explore the Ohio River Valley, when war broke out with the Indian tribes living in the area. The colonists had not been a party to the treaty between Great Britain and the Cherokee, which ceded their Kentucky hunting grounds to the British. This war was named "Lord Dunmore's War." Clark was appointed a Captain in the Militia.[126]

---

[123] For an excellent review of the extensive activities of General Clark during the American Revolutionary War, see *George Rogers Clark and the War in the West*, by Lowell H. Harrison, Univ. Press of Kentucky, Louisville, 1976.

[124] *Conquest of the Country Northwest of the River Ohio,* by William Hayden English, 1896.

[125] Thanks to Mrs. Lanny R. "Ann " Patten for research assistance on her ancestor, George Rogers Clark.

[126] *Clark of the Ohio: A Life of George Rogers Clark*, Frederick Palmer, Kessinger Publishing Co., 2004.

In 1777, as attacks led by British Indian allies increased in Kentucky, Governor Patrick Henry commissioned Clark as a lieutenant colonel in the Virginia Militia, and authorized him to recruit troops for an expedition to capture the British forts in Illinois and Indiana.

"Virginia's interest in the West had grown considerably since Gibson and Linn had traveled to New Orleans to purchase gunpowder for the state. That expedition greatly broadened peoples' awareness of the area's geography and the possibilities of trade with the Spanish. Merchants, land speculators, and the new governor of Louisiana, Bernardo de Gálvez, were all intrigued with the idea of establishing communication via the Mississippi, but it was the state's military commander at Harrods Bay, George Rogers Clark, who came up with the plan for Virginia's involvement in the West."[127]

**George Rogers Clark**
November 19, 1752 – February 13, 1818
(aged 65)

---

[127] *The Revolutionary War in Virginia, 1775-1783*, John E. Selby, U. of VA. Press, Charlottesville, 1988, p. 189.

In 1778 and 79, Virginia's George Rogers Clark campaigned in the Mississippi Valley against the British outposts. Eventually, running low on supplies, Clark came to St. Louis to ask the Spanish Lieutenant Governor, Don Fernando de Leyba, for help. Clark was aware that Spain had been providing arms, ammunition, food and other supplies through New Orleans, and had been transporting it upriver to Ft. Pitt since 1776.

Upon their first meeting, each man was surprised by the other. When Clark met Leyba, he expected a stuffy bureaucrat, and remarked that he had "never before [been] in Compy (sic) of any Spanish gent." Clark continued by saying that Leyba was not reserved and had entertained him well.

Following his victory at Vincennes, Clark was promoted to Brigadier General by Governor Thomas Jefferson. At the same time he was made Commanding General for all troops in Kentucky County and Illinois County, Virginia. The latter, along with Indiana and Ohio, having been called Illinois County, Virginia by Gov. Patrick Henry.[128]

Major General George Rogers Clark has been recognized as the "Conqueror of the Old Northwest", serving as the highest ranking American military officer on the northwest frontier during the American Revolutionary War. He conducted battles in Illinois, Indiana, Ohio, and Kentucky. Historians credit Clark with doubling the size of the United States by conquering the Northwest.

For his part, Leyba had expected a wild, unlettered frontiersman, but instead took to the open and friendly Clark immediately. Leyba described putting on a party which lasted two days:

---

[128] *Ibid.*

**President Generals Butler and Sympson at Sycamore Shoals.**

"Dances were given for him both nights and a supper to the ladies and the dancers, and lodging in my house with as much formality as was possible for me."

Leyba urged the St. Louis merchants and traders to advance supplies to Clark on credit. Many went broke in doing so. Tensions increased as some of Clark's men, encamped at Cahokia and Kaskaskia, deserted and caused trouble in St. Louis and Ste. Genevieve.

In 1779 Spain, after years of covert help to the American cause, entered the war against England as an ally of France. [Spain never signed a formal treaty with the Americans]. Spanish Royal Governor Gálvez sent reinforcements to St. Louis, then attacked and reduced British posts on the lower Mississippi.

At the end of the war, General Clark credited Spain for his victories in the Midwest because it was Spain that provided him with arms, ammunition and vital supplies. Many historians have agreed:

> *The authorities at St. Louis aided George Rogers Clark in the conquest of the territories northwest of the Ohio River, and rallied to defeat a combined Great Britain and Indian attack in St. Louis in 1780. This was a significant victory of the American Revolution, for it consolidated the defense of the frontier against British expeditions and Indian raids, at the same time it preserved the Mississippi - Ohio route for supplies and the American Army.*[129]

Much of the early aid to the colonists went through the West Indies Dutch and French ports, where it was reloaded into American vessels. Most of the subsequent aid from Spain was transported directly to New Orleans, from where it was shipped up the Mississippi and Ohio Rivers.

---

[129] *Missouri, A Guide to the Show Me State*, part of the American Guide Series, Missouri State Highway Dept, Duell, Sloan and Pearce, NYC, 1941, pp. 42-43.

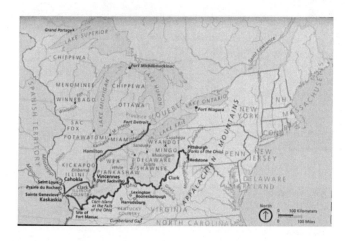

**Map of Battles and Forts in the Northwest Territories**

General George Rogers Clark, the General in charge of the Western Frontier, was the recipient of much of the Spanish assistance, while some of it went to what is now Wheeling, West Virginia, and Ft. Pitt.

The metal and gunpowder industries of México secretly furnished weapons to the Americans. Much of the guns and ammunition and other military supplies sent by Spain to the colonists came from central México to Veracruz, Mexico where it was shipped to Havana, and then New Orleans.[130]

---

[130] *Spain's Patriots of Northwestern New Spain from South of the US Border in its 1779-1783 War with England During the American Revolution, Part 8, Spanish Borderland Studies*, by Granville W. and N.C. Hough, pp.1-2.

In the early stages of the war, General George Rogers Clark stated "If [Kaskaskia] was in our possession . . . it would bring the connection of the two great rivers into our hands, which would enable us to get supply of goods from the Spanish . . . ."[131] He later was appointed by Virginia to lead the Virginia Militia in Kentucky County. Subsequently, Clark was named by the Continental Congress to lead American forces in the Midwest.

---

[131] *Illustrated Guide to Sites of the American Revolution*, Diane ___, Bereman Design and Books, Ltd, NY, 2004.

# FORT KASKASKIA, ILLINOIS

## 24 June to 4 July 1778

Kaskaskia, Illinois was established in 1703 by French Jesuits as a mission. The site had been an Indian village. The Indian congregation built a stone church in 1714. In 1741, King Louis XV sent a bell to the church. Most of the Indians farmed, growing wheat and corn, which they sold in New Orleans.

The nearby fort was constructed by the French in 1733, only to be destroyed by the British in 1763 toward the end of the French and Indian War. Following the treaty at the end of the war, many of the French inhabitants moved across the river into country ceded to Spain and settled at Ft. San Carlos at present day St. Louis, or a bit south at St. Genevieve, an outlying Spanish settlement.

Kaskaskia was the Illinois state capital until 1820, when it was moved to Vandalia. At its peak, it had a population of about 7,000. It is located on the east bank of the Mississippi River south of present day St. Louis, Missouri. During its early period, it was a major French colonial town, which was established for trading with the Indians.

On 24 June 1778, General Clark, together with 175 men left Corn Island and headed toward Kaskaskia. Corn Island is located in the middle of the Ohio River, near present day downtown Louisville, KY. He had been placed in charge of the militia. His plan to attack the British forts had been approved, and he had been promoted to Lieutenant Colonel. Although they were upstream from the "Falls", they portaged their boats about a mile further upstream to obtain a good point to enter the river to shoot the rapids.

Since Clark knew that the English monitored river traffic where the two rivers merged, he ordered that the oars be padded to reduce noise on the river. Rather than travel to the confluence of the Ohio and Mississippi, and travel up the Mississippi River, they disembarked near the mouth of the Tennessee River in the vicinity of the abandoned Fort Massac. The following morning, 29 June, 1778, the marauders began their arduous march of 120 miles overland to Kaskaskia during the heat of summer.

Clark had ordered that his men travel light. They were instructed to take with them only their long rifle, powder horn, bullets, hunting knife, tomahawk and hunting pouch, plus any other items they considered essential. They were expected to live off the land. They marched in single file to reduce the chance of discovery by Indian scouts.

Neither Virginia nor the Continental Congress was able to supply Clark. They had no available funds or supplies. He was totally reliant upon the support he received from Spain, and his ability to recruit from among the French settlers in the area.[132]

As they got within a two day march to Kaskaskia, no hunting was allowed, for fear the British or their Indian allies would discover their presence by hearing gunfire. Food supplies dwindled and the men lived on berries. By the evening of 4 July 1778, the attacking force had reached a farmhouse on the eastern bank of the Kaskaskia River, less than a mile from the fort.

---

[132] Jack M. Sosin, *The Revolutionary Frontier, 1763-1783* (Albuquerque: University of New Mexico Press, 1967), 127.

About half the men went with Clark to attack the fort, while the other half went to the town, which was occupied by about 500 whites and an equal number of Negroes.

The occupants had been warned three days earlier about a possible attack, but as the days passed, fears of an attack subsided. The occupants of the fort were totally unprepared for an attack. Clark's forces just walked into the fort and took it over within minutes. British Governor Rocheblave and his wife were captured in the fort, along with much recent correspondence from British military headquarters in Detroit. This latest intelligence aided Clark tremendously. Many of the French living in the town had no love for the English, and they signed their allegiance to the Americans and were allowed to become part of the Kentucky militia.

Following the capture of Fort Kaskaskia, Clark was delighted with the warm welcome he received from the Spanish residents across the river at Fort San Carlos. It was at this time that he first began correspondence with Captain Fernando de Leyba, Commander of the Spanish forces at Fort San Carlos. Clark set aside many of the restrictive rules and regulations established by the British. Both the French and Indian inhabitants were appreciative, and many of both groups formally aligned themselves with Clark.

It was at this point in 1778, well before Spain officially declared war against England, that Leyba offered to assist Clark by providing arms, ammunition and supplies. Leyba even offered to supply part of his military detachment to Clark in the event of an attack on Fort Kaskaskia.[133]

---

[133] Letter from Clark to Patrick Henry, Governor of Virginia dated 16 September 1778. *Patrick Henry, Vol. III*, p. 194.

# FORT VINCENNES, INDIANA

## 7 February to 8 March 1779

Fort Sackville at Vincennes, in present day Indiana, had been taken from the British by George Rogers Clark in 1778. Lieutenant Governor Henry Hamilton, the British commander, with a force of 275 officers and men, left Detroit in mid October 1778 for an attack on Vincennes. His force traveled the 600 miles through the snowy wilderness in 71 days, arriving in Vincennes on 17 December 1778. Many of the American garrison were French. Most of them had turned in their weapons and departed. Only a few Americans remained to defend the fort.

In early January 1779, the English attacked and retook Fort Sackville. With only four loyal men upon which to depend, the commander surrendered without a shot having been fired. Before the surrender, the commander penned a note to Clark, advising him of the surrender.

On 7 February 1779, Clark, with 170 armed men, departed Kaskaskia on the Mississippi. His army consisted of Kentucky Militia and French volunteers. Their journey to Fort Sackville was about 200 miles. Deep snow and icy flood waters covered their route. Their supplies were carried by pack horses and a large riverboat, the "Willing" upon which were mounted a nine-pounder cannon, two four pounders, and four swivel guns. The ship also carried ammunition and food, and a crew of about 45 men.

Captain John Rogers, a cousin of the general, was made Captain of the *Willing*. His instructions were to proceed via the Kaskaskia, Mississippi and the Ohio Rivers to the Wabash River, where he was to move upstream to a point just south of Vincennes. If the British garrison sought to escape, his crew was to stop them. Otherwise he was to be ready to offer support to Clark's land forces. The *Willing* departed on 5 February 1779.

After 16 days of tiring travel the land contingent reached Fort Sackville on 21 February 1779. Game was readily available while on this march, so none of the frozen soldiers were hungry until they were two days from Fort Sackville. From that point onward, there could be no hunting, for fear of being discovered. A company of volunteers from Cahokia arrived on 4 February 1779, who also were hungry. Like an answered prayer, Clark's men captured an Indian canoe, filled with food - buffalo meat and corn - allowing each member of the party to have a small portion of food.

**U.S. Commemorative Stamp issued in 1929 to honor Clark.**

The first part of the attack required that the troops be transported across the frozen Wabash River. By this time only two canoes were available for this chore. The horses had to be left behind.

Clark had anticipated that the garrison at Fort Sackville was 600 men strong. Fortunately, at the time there were only 40 British soldiers and an additional 40 French volunteers in the fort. Their supplies were low and they were exhausted. Hamilton had no reason to expect an attack by Clark in the middle of winter, some 180 miles away, through snow and ice.

It should be noted that France formally recognized the United States on February 6, 1778, with the signing of the treaty. Britain declared war on France on March 17, 1778. Inside Ft. Sackville and in cabins around the fort there were many Frenchmen who had been allied with the British. When Clark's men arrived, many of the French joined him and provided his troops with provisions. Many of the Frenchmen who had not gone over to Clark refused to fire on their French friends who had joined Clark. This adversely affected British morale.

Some local Frenchmen dug up a hidden cache of gunpowder and gave it to Clark. Here it should be noted that although France has formally become an ally of the colonists, many Frenchmen fought with the British and their Indian allies. So, it can be said that Frenchmen fought on both sides of the conflict. There is no evidence that any Spaniard fought for the English.

Clark was a great strategist. To leave the impression that his force was much greater than his 170 men, he had them display a large number of flags that would have been indicative of 500 troops or more. His woodsmen were expert riflemen. As a result they could fire so rapidly, it appeared to the British that he had twice the number of riflemen actually on hand.

On 24 February 1779, Clark sent a message demanding surrender of the fort. Hamilton was warned against destroying arms, ammunition, supplies and correspondence; and that if he disobeyed, he would be treated like the murderer he was. Colonel Hamilton declined to surrender.

War with the Indians had been bloody. Indians took scalps and sold them to the English. Colonel Hamilton was known among the local Indians as the "hair buyer." Clark believed in fighting fire with fire. When an Indian raiding party attempted to return to the fort, Clark's men captured or killed all but five of them. On 25 February 1779, Clark had those five Indians brutally killed by tomahawk within sight of the fort. With that act, Clark secured the surrender of the British garrison under the command of Lieutenant Governor Henry Hamilton. Nothing had been destroyed! This brutal act also served as a message to the Indian allies of the British, that the British could not protect them.

When the American flag was again raised over Fort Sackville, it marked the high point of the career of General George Rogers Clark. But, the best was yet to come. After the victory Clark learned that several boats were coming down the Wabash River with food, trade goods and supplies for the British garrison.

The *Willing* finally arrived in Vincennes on 27 February. Clark ordered Captain Helm to take the *Willing* and several volunteers upstream and capture these supplies. The British boats were captured in the first few days of March 1779, without a shot being fired.

The British supplies and 40 prisoners captured upstream reached Ft. Sackville on 5 March. The loot consisted of much needed uniforms, wine and food. What was not needed immediately was auctioned off. The proceeds totaled almost 10,000 English Pounds, and the money was divided among Clark's men. The French prisoners were paroled upon their respective promises to

**SAR President General Ed Butler and wife, Robin, participated in a wreath laying ceremony at the George Rogers Clark Memorial in Vincennes, Indiana in March, 2010.**

never take up arms against the Americans again. On 8 March, 26 British officers and men were shipped back to Virginia to be imprisoned.

The above photo was taken at the George Rogers Clark National Memorial Park in Vincennes, Indiana. Shown are President General Judge Ed Butler, First Lady Robin Butler and members of the Indiana SAR Color Guard and the state regent of the Indiana DAR. The author led a wreath laying ceremony in Clark's honor in March, 2010.

As a result of his success, Clark was promoted to Colonel. The Virginia legislature voted to present Clark with a handsome sword, and set aside 150,000 acres of land on the north shore of the Ohio River near the Falls at Louisville to be apportioned among all those men who had participated in the campaign.[134]

---

[134] Indiana Historical Bureau. "Plat of Clark's Grant".

# FORT CAHOKIA, ILLLINOIS

The Cahokia, Illinois area was originally a Mississippi Indian tribal home. Burial Mounds have been discovered placing the tribe in the area in the early 17th century. A French priest, Father Pinet, established a mission in late 1696. It was his goal to convert the Cahokian and Tamaroa Indians to Christianity. Father Pinet and his Indian congregation built a log church. It was dedicated to the Holy Family. Cahokia was located across the Mississippi River from Fort San Carlos (present day St. Louis, Missouri).

Over the next century, Cahokia became one of the largest French colonial towns in the Illinois Country. Harmony existed between its Indians and the large number of French Canadian settlers. The primary economy was built around fur trapping and agriculture. The main crops were wheat and corn, much of which was transported down the Mississippi to New Orleans for sale. Most of the land between Kaskaskia and Cahokia was under cultivation. The 50 mile stretch of land adjacent to the Mississippi was rich with deposits of topsoil after each flood.

By the time of the 1763 treaty ending the French and Indian War, the town had grown to about 3,000. As the French were forced to give up the land east of the Mississippi to the English, Cahokia suffered. Most of the inhabitants moved to Spanish territory west of the Mississippi for one of two reasons:
1) they wanted to live in a Catholic country, and
2) they feared the British.

In 1778, during the American Revolutionary War, George Rogers Clark set up a court in Cahokia. In earlier years Cahokia was an independent city state. Cahokia officially became part of the United States on July 5, 1778. Soon after that the 105

Cahokia "heads of household" pledged loyalty to the Continental Congress of the United States.

Later, Cahokia was named the county seat of St. Clair County. The Cahokia Courthouse acted as a United States territorial courthouse and a major political center for the next 24 years. When St. Clair County was enlarged in 1801, Henry Harrison named the Cahokia Courthouse the legal and governmental center of a sizeable area extending to the Canadian border. By 1814, other counties and territories had been organized, and St. Clair County was defined as its current size. The county seat was moved to Belleville, Illinois.

East of St. Louis, 300 Indians went with pro-British Frenchman, Jean Marie Ducharme (who was a former St. Louisan) to attack Cahokia. Ducharme's attack on Cahokia was defeated. George Roger Clark's Virginians along with artillery scared off the Indian attackers.

Clark remained in Cahokia for five weeks. During that time he negotiated peace treaties with at least 10 Indian tribes. He followed up by placing American agents in each tribe to monitor their respective activities and to insure that they did not breach the treaty.

Most historians agree that the most important achievement of Clark's 1778 campaign was not the occupation of the Illinois country, but his success in neutralizing a large part of the Illinois Indian military power on which the British had relied.

## FORT JEFFERSON, KENTUCKY

## 1780

With all the battles on or near the Mississippi, Virginia Governor Thomas Jefferson was of the view that the United States should have a fort on the Mississippi, to protect our interests against the British. He felt this was necessary to insure the speedy flow of commerce and communication up the Mississippi. George Rogers Clark agreed with Governor Jefferson.

They concluded that the best spot for a new fort would be on the Mississippi, just south of the confluence of the Ohio River - about one mile south of Wickliffe, Kentucky, in the southwestern corner of the state in an area that was subject to frequent flooding. Clark suggested a garrison of 200 men. He added that the construction of a new fort, would result in approximately 100 families migrating to the fort. Their crops would help feed the troops.

Fort Jefferson and the nearby Borough of Campbell was completed in 1780 on a bluff overlooking the Mississippi, and occupied in 1781. Each of the settlers was granted 400 acres of land near the fort upon their agreement to make part of their crops available to the fort. The Chickasaw Indians were very upset that a fort was built on their property without permission. Jefferson had assumed that Clark would purchase the land from the Indians, but Clark just took it.

After construction was complete, Clark returned to Ft. Jefferson. An attack on 25 July 1780 by the Chickasaw was the beginning of a two week siege. In mid August, the main army of the

Chickasaw nation, under the command of a white British officer - Scotsman James Colbert, attacked. While the fort was under siege, warriors burned crops and killed livestock. Many of the soldiers and the pioneers died from malnutrition, food poisoning and malaria. The fort was abandoned later that year.

Because of all its battles with the British and their Indian allies, the Commonwealth of Virginia was almost bankrupt. Many of the Fort Jefferson settlers lost their grants because their land had not been surveyed. After the 1780 Battle of Fort Jefferson the settlers began to leave Fort Jefferson and returned east or traveled west to seek their fortune under the Spanish flag.

Only about 100 stayed with Captain James Piggott and Captain Joseph Hunter. Joseph Hunter led a group of settlers across the Mississippi to Spanish Louisiana (Arkansas and Missouri), while in the Fall of 1781, James Piggott led the first large group of American settlers - 17 families - into the Illinois Country. They settled in what is now known as East St. Louis, Illinois.[135]

---

[135] "Piggot History", *Metro East Journal* (East St. Louis, Illinois), April 28, 1969.

# FORT SAN CARLOS, MISSOURI (Saint Louis)[136]

## 26 MAY 1780

**"Those British bastards! We will repay them for this attack!** These were the angry words of Captain Don Fernando de Leyba, Lieutenant Governor of the Spanish Province of Northern Louisiana, and Commandant of Fort San Carlos (present day St. Louis). On 26 May 1780, between 1,300 and 2,000 British-led Indian warriors attacked Fort San Carlos, named for Carlos III, King of Spain. Included in the attack were 300 English soldiers. Before discussing the battle, let's look at the history of the fort.

History of Fort San Carlos:

The first settlement in this area was in the 1660s when French fur traders established a small settlement. Later French priests moved into the area to convert the local Indians. In 1763, when the French lost the French and Indian War, the area west of the Mississippi River, fell to the Spaniards; while the lands to the west of the Allegheny Mountains and the lands north of the Ohio River went to the British. The main English fortress was at Detroit. By 1779, the English had devised a plan to encircle the rebelling colonists. That plan involved invading and securing the Mississippi River down to the Gulf of México, and the British planned to capture of New Orleans from the Gulf.

---

[136] With research assistance by Gerald Burkland, member of the Michigan SAR Society.

On the eve of the American Revolutionary War, the lands along the Mississippi River were sparsely settled, with English outposts in present day Memphis, Tennessee; Natchez, Mississippi; Baton Rouge and Manchac, Louisiana; Kaskaskia and Cahokia, Illinois; Detroit and Fort St. Joseph, Michigan; together with many smaller settlements. The Spanish occupied New Orleans, Louisiana; Arkansas Post, Arkansas; and Fort San Carlos and St. Genevieve, Missouri. The Americans, in violation of the treaty[137] which settled the French and Indian War, occupied Fort Nelson, Kentucky. Clearly, the English intended to capture Fort San Carlos, St. Genevieve, Arkansas Post and New Orleans.

In 1777 there were only 1,448 people in the Illinois country, which included Ft. San Carlos.[138] That year Gálvez asked for help to defend the frontier. He was promised 700 volunteers from the Canary Islands for the Louisiana Infantry Regiment. These Canary Islanders were transported, starting in 1778, and many saw action in the Louisiana territory.[139]

In June 1778, Fernando de Leyba was appointed Lieutenant Governor and the administrative assistant to General Bernardo de Gálvez [for Fort St. Louis] by the Governor General at New

---

[137] The treaty forbad settlement by English colonists west of the Allegheny Mountains. This land was reserved for the Indians, which enhanced the fur trade with Mother England.

[138] *Spain's Louisiana Patriots in its 1779-1783 War with England During the American Revolution, Part Six, Spanish Borderlands Studies*, Granville W. and N.C. Hough, p. 2.

[139] *Id* at p. 4.

Orleans to superintend the affairs of the entire territory extending from the Arkansas River to the Canadian line."[140] He was also at that time appointed as the commandant of Ft. San Carlos, named in honor of Carlos III, and St. Genevieve, a small Spanish settlement about 30 miles south. Ft. San Carlos was located at the current St. Louis, just south of the confluence of the Missouri and Mississippi Rivers.

Virginia's George Rogers Clark had been fighting the British and their Indian allies during 1778-1779. Even before Spain officially declared war on England on June 21, 1779, Clark had been receiving arms, ammunition and supplies from General Bernardo de Gálvez in New Orleans. This aid was obtained through Don Fernando de Leyba, Commandant of Fort San Carlos.

When Leyba took over, the village was a trading post without any fortifications or defensive emplacements. He brought with him secret instructions from Gálvez about the impending war between Spain and England. Leyba witnessed the massive amounts of aid coming up river bound for the Americans.

Britain had persuaded many Indian tribes to ally with them against the Americans. With Britain's new strategy to sweep down the Mississippi to New Orleans, Spanish settlements along the western side of the river were soon to be targeted. Britain planned to make this massive sweep primarily with the assistance of their Indian allies. This would allow them to

---

[140] *Missouri: A Guide to the Show Me State, American Guide Series*, NY, 1941, p. 42

surround the colonists and strangle their supply route up the Mississippi and Ohio Rivers.

In St. Louis, Don Fernando de Leyba, learning that his country was at war, urged the construction of a series of four stone towers and entrenchments to protect the town. Many St. Louisans thought such preparation foolish, and did not want to invest money in it. They were convinced that St. Louis would never be attacked, and that life would go on indefinitely the way

**Model of gun tower at Fort San Carlos in 1780 battle.**

it always had. But Leyba pushed for money and laborers. At the top of a hill at the corner of today's Walnut and Broadway, the first of the towers, called Fort San Carlos, was completed by April 1780, and a trench was dug around the town.

Leyba knew an attack might come soon. His health was failing, his wife had already died here in the wilderness, and all he wanted was to take his two young daughters back to Barcelona. Instead, tensions mounted in St. Louis, which was wide open to attack and protected by only 16 Spanish soldiers and the able-bodied men of the town who comprised the militia.

His duties were to develop and maintain friendly relations with the nearby Indians; to build good relationships with the nearby trappers and settlers, most of whom were French; to develop agriculture; and to recruit and train a militia. He was provided with a small detachment of Spanish army troops.

Earlier King George III had entered into a treaty with the Indians under which the colonists were forbidden to settle west of the Allegheny Mountains. Land west to the Mississippi River was reserved for the Indians. There were very few British troops in the Northwest Territory, with the largest concentration in present day Detroit. These troops were under the command of Colonel Henry Hamilton, who Leyba considered unscrupulous.

Leyba was impressed by Clark's brilliant victory at Vincennes in Feb, 1779. They became fast friends following Clark's victory at Kaskaskia in early July 1778. Clark had visited Fort San Carlos, and Leyba had also visited Clark at Fort Nelson.

During Clark's first visit, Leyba had ordered a two day celebration, including an artillery salute, a formal dinner with 30 guests, and dances on two nights, followed by late suppers each night at Leyba's home.

A popular novel[141] indicates that Clark became enamored with Theresa de Leyba, the Commandant's sister, but there is no evidence of that romance. Leyba also asked the local merchants and traders to advance supplies on credit. Clark was never reimbursed for the debts he created for military supplies received from Fort San Carlos or New Orleans, and became destitute after the war.

When war with England was declared by Spain, Gálvez sent reinforcements to Fort San Carlos. In March 1780, Clark warned Leyba that the British were planning to attack Spanish settlements in the Mississippi River Valley. Leyba immediately began digging entrenchments, fortifications and the first tower was completed by April 1780. Leyba spent much of his personal fortune to pay for the construction of the fortifications at Fort San Carlos.

On May 26, 1780, between 1,300 and 2,000[142] British-led Sioux, Sac, Fox and Winnebago warriors, British soldiers and French Canadian soldiers suddenly fell upon the unsuspecting community of 900 people. The attack was led by Captain Emanuel Hesse, an English officer from Detroit. The Indians killed several settlers and slaves who were tending their fields on the outskirts of town. The firing alerted St. Louis's militia, who

---

[141] *Long Knife: The story of a great American hero, George Rogers Clark*, by James Alexander Thom, Ballentine Books, NY, 1979.

[142] Some reports indicate there were between 2,000 and 3,000 British led attackers.

ran to the barely-completed entrenchments. The attackers were hit with a withering fire from militia musketry of the 300 defenders. Fear of the deafening cannon caused many of Great Britain's Indian allies to run from the battlefield. The battle lasted for two hours, with 21 villagers killed and 71 captured.

Under the command of Captain Leyba, the residents had been preparing for months against such an attack. The fortifications extended over a mile. The residents had constructed a stone tower with three four-pounders and two six-pounder cannons.

The defenders were greatly outnumbered. The Spanish militia numbered just under 170 men. With the 34 Spanish regulars and the 60 or so militia from Ste. Genevieve, the defenders were only about 265 strong. During the battle they were joined by other residents of the fort.

The Indian allies of the British on this raid were 200 Santee Sioux under the leadership of Chief Wabasha; a war party of Chippewa, commanded by Chief Matchekewis; a large contingent of Winnebagoes and Menominees; 250 Sauk and Fox warriors, and war parties from a half dozen other tribes.

At the time, there were about 900 people living in the fortress and the adjoining village. In addition to killing and capturing many of the residents of Ft. San Carlos, Hesse's forces also captured a party of 46 whites upriver. No accurate reports of enemy casualties exist. The British reported four Indians killed and four wounded. This was probably an understatement, especially since their operation was a failure.

In addition to Ducharme, Joseph Calve, was another St. Louis Frenchmen who betrayed his native land in favor of the British. He is the one credited with convincing the Sauk/Fox tribe to send warriors for the attack on St. Louis. The Sauk Fox nation redeemed itself on 12 Feb. 1781, when it joined the St. Louis counterattack on the British supply depot at the fort at St. Joseph (Michigan).

About 60 militiamen from Ste. Genevieve (now Missouri) participated in this battle.[143] This was a significant victory of the American Revolution, for it consolidated the defense of the frontier against British expeditions and Indian raids. At the same time it preserved the Mississippi – Ohio River route for supplies to the American Army.[144]

The attack on Fort San Carlos was planned by the British in conjunction with a simultaneous attack on Cahokia (present day Illinois), which was led by pro-English Frenchman, Jean Marie Ducharme, who formerly lived at Fort San Carlos. Ducharme was defeated at Cahokia by General George Rogers Clark's Virginians, who had marched from Fort Nelson (present day Louisville).

Expecting an attack by the British, Leyba had constructed a fortress with a stone tower upon which he had placed two six pounder cannon. He had planned well, as the attacking Indians scattered after the first round of grapeshot was fired. The English soldiers remained out of range. They retreated with their

---

[143] *Spain's Louisiana Patriots in its 1779-1783 War with England During the American Revolution, Part Six, Spanish Borderlands Studies*, Granville W. and N.C. Hough, p. 6.

[144] *Missouri: A Guide to the Show Me State, American Guide Series*, NY, 1941, p. 42-43.

Indian allies. The defeat of the English at Fort San Carlos thwarted their plan to conquer the Mississippi River valley.

George Rogers Clark and his Americans drove off a simultaneous British attack against Cahokia on the east side of the river. Several good citizens were buried in the churchyard that week. The successful, if costly, defense of St. Louis prevented the British from obtaining control of the Mississippi River Valley. The St. Louis battle was fought by the predominantly French citizens, who were members of the Spanish Militia, under a Spanish governor and a small number of Spanish troops, African-American slaves, and a smattering of American settlers.

No further attempts were made by the English to take St. Louis from the Spanish. Sadly, the real hero of the battle, Lieutenant Governor Leyba, died of illness one month afterward. He had provided defenses for a defenseless town and saved the Mississippi River Valley from British control, but never saw Barcelona again.

"Meanwhile, in a series of brilliant campaigns, Bernardo de Gálvez took Mobile from the British in 1780, and Pensacola in 1781. By 1781, British power in the western theater had been nullified by the efforts of George Rogers Clark and the Spanish under Gálvez."[145]

Clark was a frequent guest in Leyba's home. The two men became good friends. Over the years Leyba honored him with

---

[145] *The Battle of Fort San Carlos, from The Lewis and Clark Journey of Discovery*, National Park Service web site at http://www.nps.gov/archive/jeff/lewisclark2/circa1804/StLouis/blockinfo/Block100FortSanCarlosBattle1780.htm

gala banquets, dinners and dances, and the two men frequently corresponded. It was through Leyba that Clark received the military supplies sent up river by Gálvez. Both Leyba and Clark wanted to keep both the Mississippi and Ohio Rivers free of the British and their Indian allies. Leyba's replacement, Don Francisco Cruzat arrived in late 1780.[146]

The battle of Ft. San Carlos was the only battle of the American Revolutionary War fought west of the Mississippi River.[147]

---

[146] *Ibid.*

[147] *The Battle of Fort San Carlos*, May 26, 1780, Commemoration Committee publication.

# SPANISH ATTACK BRITISH
# FORT ST. JOSEPH, MICHIGAN

## 2 JANUARY to 12 FEBRUARY 1781

Fort St. Joseph (near present day Niles, Michigan) was constructed by the French government to defend against the Iroquois Indians in the 1680s. It was on the banks of the St. Joseph River, which emptied into Lake Michigan. It later became the French commercial center for the southern Great Lakes. It became the center for fur trade at the southern end of Lake Michigan.

In 1763, by the terms of the treaty, the fort came under the control of the English. During the American Revolutionary War, the fort was used by the English to supply the Miami, Potawatomie and other American Indians who the British had incited to make war on the Americans.

During the summer of 1779, the English commandant of nearby Fort Michilimackinac learned that George Rogers Clark, with a force of about 700 men, planned to attack Detroit. He assumed that Clark would pass nearby Fort St. Joseph. He sent his second in command with a force of about 75 militia and some 200 Indians to intercept Clark. Clark's plan was to attack Fort St. Joseph, but his plans were thwarted by lack of supplies. In 1780, Fort St. Joseph included 8 houses and 7 shanties; a population of 45 Frenchmen; and a small detachment of English soldiers.

A French officer, Augustin de La Balme, sent a group of 16 Cahokians, commanded by Jean Baptiste Hamelin, on a successful raid of Fort St. Joseph in late 1780. This British storage depot contained enough corn to feed the British army for the duration of their planned attack down the Mississippi River valley all the way to New Orleans. The British commander caught up with them on December 6, 1780, and regained all of the captured supplies. Only three survivors escaped through the woods.

Later that month, Frenchmen and Indians met with Lieutenant Governor Cruzat, and demanded that he outfit an expeditionary force to retaliate. Cruzat feared a second attack on Fort San Carlos the following spring. He felt that if he could plan a successful raid, Spanish strength in the area would be displayed and such an attack on Fort San Carlos might be avoided. He knew that if he could recapture the stockpiled corn, the English army could not make a successful attack down the Mississippi River.

Captain Leyba had planned his revenge, but did not live to see it. The San Carlos Spanish expeditionary force under the command of Captain Eugene Pourré left Fort San Carlos on January 2, 1781. They took three weeks to travel the 600 miles in the dead of winter. They were joined by 20 townsmen from Cahokia; by an additional 12 Spanish soldiers, and by a large party of 60 Pottawatomie, Sauk and Fox Indians.

Each man was on foot and carried his own provisions and equipment. This motley army canoed up the Illinois River as far as Lake Peoria. They walked the remaining snow covered 300 miles; much of which was frozen swamps, in the dead of winter.

On February 12, 1781, 60 Spanish militia and an unknown number of Spanish soldiers, (including the reinforcement sent by Gálvez to reinforce the garrison at Ft. San Carlos when Spain declared war) joined by warriors of the Sauk/Fox Indian Nation (who had been allied with the British in the attack on Fort San Carlos), attacked and captured the British fort and supply depot at what is now Niles, Michigan.

The fort was lightly defended, and victory was immediate. For the second time in History, the Spanish flag was raised over what is now Michigan.[148] Don Eugenio Pourré proclaimed that all the land below Lake Michigan and the Illinois River henceforth belonged to "His Most Catholic Majesty the King of Spain."

What they could not carry with them was distributed among local friendly tribes, and the rest was burned, along with the fort. For all intents and purposes, The "Spanish Raid" was the end of Fort St. Joseph - and the end of the British second front. Don Pouré's troops left the following day, returning home on March 6, 1781, proudly displaying the captured English flag. One can only imagine the cold, fatigue, hunger and other privations suffered by this heroic band. Yet, not a single man was lost.

In a letter from Lieutenant Gov. Cruzat to Gov. Gálvez, he stated that his reason for the attack on Fort St. Joseph was not so much for revenge as it was to both appear strong to his Indian allies, and to negatively influence English allies. Leyba's Reward: Upon learning of Leyba's successful defense of Fort San Carlos, King Carlos promoted Captain Fernando de Leyba to the rank of Lieutenant Colonel. Unfortunately, the commission arrived after his death.

---

[148] In 1766 English Major Robert Rogers, a native of New Hampshire, was tried by Courts Martial for treason as a result of his surrendering Fort Michilimackinac to the Spanish in 1762.

The Spanish successful defense of the upper Mississippi River valley at Fort San Carlos and their successful attack on Fort St. Joseph denied the British the use of the Mississippi River, and prevented the British from strangling the struggling Americans. By keeping the river open Gálvez was allowed to continue supplying General George Rogers Clark at Fort Nelson, and the Ohio River was kept open to supply George Washington's army at Fort Pitt. Although the number of Spanish soldiers involved was small, the results of these British defeats at the hands of the Spanish, was significant; and the ultimate victory of the Americans over England was assured.[149]

---

[149] *Old Fort St. Joseph, or Michigan Under Four Flags*, by McCoy, Daniel, pp. 5-8, Delivered before the Michigan Pioneer and Historical Society at its Thirty–Second Annual Meeting, June 7, 1906; Wynkoop Hallenbeck Crawford Co., State Printers, Lansing, 1907; see also "The St. Joseph Mission" by Pare, George in *Mississippi Valley Historical Review, Vol. 17*, pp. 46-54.

# FORT NELSON, KENTUCKY[150]

## 27 May 1778 to 12 February 1781

Kentucky County, Virginia was officially created in early December, 1776. The rationale was argued by General George Rogers Clark that "the Kentucky settlements were essential for the protection of the Virginia frontier." George Rogers Clark was named as the Commander of the Kentucky County, Virginia Militia. He had hoped to recruit about 500 volunteers from Virginia, but he and his other officers were able to recruit only about 150, most of whom were from Fauquier and Frederick Counties.

Gunpowder that arrived in New Orleans from Spain in September, 1776 had been shipped to Ft. Pitt, present day Pittsburgh, Pennsylvania. Clark transported the gunpowder and distributed it to several Kentucky stations.

By 1777, the English were able to induce the Indians to attack the American settlers in the area. This came from a direct order of King George. Clark decided the only way to protect the Kentucky settlers and ultimately protect Virginia, was to sweep the British from the upper Mississippi Valley.

Ft. Nelson was originally established on Corn Island in the center of the Ohio River, just offshore from downtown Louisville, Kentucky. Later, because of frequent flooding of

---

[150] *George Rogers Clark and the War in the West*, Lowell H. Harrison, Univ. Press of Kentucky, Louisville, 1976.

Corn Island, Clark repositioned the fort to the high banks of what is now Louisville.[151] It was at Ft. Nelson where Clark planned his attacks on Cahokia, Illinois; Kaskaskia, Illinois; and Vincennes, Indiana. Clark opined that if he could defeat the British at these three key forts, he could neutralize their Indian allies.

At the same time as the attack on Fort San Carlos, a contingent of the English forces under the command of Captain Henry Bird, was sent down the Mississippi to block George Rogers Clark from coming to the rescue of Fort San Carlos. Their attack centered on Fort Nelson at the Falls of the Ohio.

Bird's Indian allies didn't want to attack Ft. Nelson, because it was well defended. Instead, at Licking Creek the Indians persuaded Bird to go into the interior of Kentucky, where the Indians would obtain more loot. This English contingent captured Ruddle's Fort and Martin Station.[152] Nevertheless, because of the British defeat at Fort San Carlos, and the capture and destruction of Ft. St. Joseph, they dropped their plans to attack down the Mississippi.

---

[151] The new headquarters of the National Society Sons of the American Revolution is located on Main Street in Louisville, within the footprint of Ft. Nelson.

[152] *Spain's Louisiana Patriots in its 1779-1783 War with England During the American Revolution, Part Six*, Spanish Borderlands Studies, Granville W. and N.C. Hough, p. 190; See also "When Detroit Invaded Kentucky", by Milo M. Quaife, *Filson Club History Quarterly, Vol. 1*, No. 2, (January1927, pp. 53-67).

Clark's command was so small that to give the appearance that it was larger, he began referring to his command as the "Headquarters Western American Army, Falls of the Ohio, Illinois, Detachment."

# ARKANSAS POST

## 22 November 1780

The settlement at Arkansas Post was established on the banks of the Arkansas River in 1674 by French explorers Marquette and Joliet. It was located near the confluence of the Arkansas and Mississippi Rivers and only a 10 day march to the point where the Mississippi empties into the Gulf of México. It was abandoned by the French in the early 1700's. On February 10, 1763, a treaty was signed ending the Seven Years War,[153] in which Spain was ceded the former French lands west of the Mississippi. When Spanish forces took over, the post was renamed as Ft. Carlos III, in honor of the Spanish king. This fort should not be confused with Ft. San Carlos at St. Louis.

Arkansas Post was a good mid-way stopping point for travelers between New Orleans and St. Louis. Upstream expeditions were informed about the positions of English troops and their Indian allies. This information kept Spanish supply lines open during the war. In 1776 the dilapidated fort was manned by about 50 whites and only 16 Spanish soldiers. The Commandant relied heavily upon Indian allies to raid the nearby English fort on the eastern bank of the Mississippi.[154]

---

[153] Also called the French and Indian War.

[154] *The Arkansas Post Story* by Roger E. Coleman, Southwest Cultural Resources Center, Professional Papers No. 12, Eastern National, 1987, p. 59.

Upon learning that Spain has entered the war, on November 22, 1780, Spanish Commandant Villiers crossed the Mississippi from Arkansas Post with a detachment of Spanish soldiers and captured the English Fort Concordia, (across the Mississippi River from Arkansas Post) and formally took possession of it.[155] The capture of this English outpost helped force the English from the Mississippi basin. The final battle of the American Revolutionary War was fought at Ft. Carlos in April, 1783.

---

[155] *Id* at p. 60

# SPANISH SOLDIERS WERE AT THE READY AT CALIFORNIA PRESIDIOS

## 1779-1783

All along the California coast Spanish Presidios were manned by Spanish soldiers. They were prepared for an attack by Captain James Cook. Captain Cook was well known for his Pacific Ocean explorations starting in 1761. The Spanish did not know where he was, but they knew that he was in the Pacific Ocean. Although Cook was murdered in Hawaii in 1779, word of his death did not reach California for many months. Spanish soldiers were on duty at the following California presidios:

San Diego de Alcala

Royal Presidio at Monterey

Our Lady of San Francisco de Asis

Santa Barbara Presidio

San Gabriel

San Juan Capistrano

San Buenaventura

San Luis Obispo

San Antonio

Santa Clara

In the words of Sir Winston Churchill: "They also serve, who only sit and wait." The map below shows Alta California in 1784. At that time there were nine missions, four presidios and two pueblos, all of which were built in 15 years.

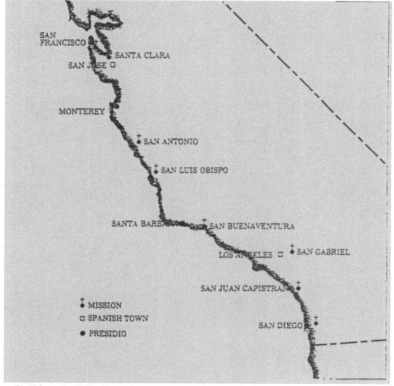

**California Missions, towns and Presidios.**
**Courtesy of Dr. Mildred L. Murry, CASDAR**

As will be demonstrated in the chapter on the *Donativo*, the Spanish soldiers in California gave well more than requested of them by King Carlos III. Because of their respective "*donativos*", the descendants of these "patriots" are eligible to join the SAR and DAR.

# SPANISH FLEET CAPTURES 55 SHIPS OF THE ENGLISH FLEET 9 AUGUST 1780

On 9 August 1780, the main Spanish fleet, led by Admiral Luis de Córdova y Córdova, which had just departed from Cádiz, Spain captured 55 British ships which were part of a convoy of sixty-three vessels which had just departed Portsmouth, England. Admiral Córdova commanded the 120-gun ship of the line *Santísima Trinidad*, flagship of the Spanish fleet. Historical records indicate this was one of the most complete naval victories in history![156]

This was the largest single capture of an opponent's fleet during the American Revolutionary War, and one of the largest naval captures in history. Needless to say, this caused a severe blow to British commerce. The British financial losses were estimated at £ 1,500,000.[157] In addition to the loss of the 55 ships, 3,144 men, including the 90th Regiment of Foot[158] and goods worth

---

[156] *The Encyclopedia of London*, p. 483

[157] Parkinson, N.C. *The Trade Winds: A Study of British Overseas Trade, the French Wars, 1793-1815*, Routledge: Reprint Edition. ISBN (78-0-415-38191-8, p.38.

[158] Volo, M. James. *Blue Water Patriots: The American Revolution Afloat*, Rowman & Littlefield Publishers, Inc. (2008) ISBN 978-0-7425-6120-5, at p. 77.

£1.5 million, the convoy's capture helped derail a secret British diplomatic effort to make a separate peace with Spain.[159]

Although most of the ships captured were merchants ships, the Spanish fleet also captured several British gunships, including the 30-gun *HMS Hillsborough*, and the *HMS Ramillies*. All 55 of the captured ships were placed in the Spanish Navy.

The captured British ships were brought into Cádiz, an unusual spectacle since the capture of such a great enemy convoy by any navy was an uncommon event; Córdova's fleet produced this feat upon two occasions. All the ships including the five East Indiaman frigates were brought into the Spanish navy.[160] This was a major intelligence failure, for the British Admiralty did not learn of the sailing of this Spanish fleet until 4 August.[161]

The following message was from one of the captains of the ships captured:

---

[159] Syrett, David. *The Royal Navy in European Waters during the American Revolutionary War*. University of South Carolina Press. ISBN 978-1-57003-238-7, at pp. 136-137.

[160] Guthrie, William & Ferguson, James. *A New Geographical, Historical, and Commercial Grammar And Present Of The World*. J & J House Booksellers, London (1806), at p. 360.

[161] Syrett, David. *The Royal Navy in European Waters during the American Revolutionary War, Id* at p. 136

> *We received fourteen shot from one of the seventy-four's and six wounded, our bowspirit (sic) shot and shivered up as far as the gammoning, when we struck to the Ferme, a 74 (Spanish). We were all, except the ladies and their husbands, the captains, first and second officers, and about six other gentlemen, ordered on board the Ferme: but on going on board, had it in our option to return; which we all did; and we met with the greatest civility, humanity, and generosity on board [...] The great kindness of the Spaniards makes our situation scarcely felt, as everything is done by them to alleviate our misfortune; and we have never yet felt that we were prisoners.*

—Officer of East Indiaman *HMS Hillsborough*, Cádiz.

As might be expected, this Spanish victory, caused a financial crisis among the marine insurance underwriters throughout Europe.[163] This caused the cost of maritime insurance to sky rocket. It also caused a lack of public confidence in the Royal Navy. The five British East Indiaman were brought into Spanish service, giving them an entire new squadron of frigates as follows:

---

[162] *The Scots Magazine, MDCCLXXXIII, Vol. XLV*, Edinburgh, Printed by Murray and Cochran, October 1780, p. 547.

[163] Volo, M. James. *Blue Water Patriots: The American Revolution Afloat, Id at p. 78.*

30-gun *HMS Hillsborough* became the 34-gun *Santa Balbina*

28-gun *HMS Mountstuart* became the 34-gun *Santa Bibiana*

28-gun *HMS Royal George* became the 40-gun *Real Jorge*

28-gun *HMS Godfrey became the* 34-gun *Santa Paula*

28-gun *HMS Gatton* became the 30-gun *Colón*.[164]

---

[164] Jose' Montero y Arostegui. *Historia y descripcion de la Cuidad y Departamento naval del Ferrol*, p. 688; and Rodgiguez Gonzales y Agustin Ramon. *Victorias por mar de los Espanoles*. Biblioteca de Historia, Madrid (2006), at p. 232.

# THE TEXAS CONNECTION[165]:

## 1779-1782

In 1779 a hurricane hit New Orleans and surrounding areas. It not only killed large herds of cattle being used by Gálvez' army for beef, the hurricane also flooded the wheat fields and destroyed the crop of hay which was intended to feed the cattle. Gálvez, from his days as an officer in what is now Texas, knew there were large herds of Texas long horn cattle in the San Antonio area. He sent an emissary, Francisco Garcia, with a letter to Governor Domingo Cabello, requesting a cattle drive from the San Antonio area to Louisiana.

It is well known that an army travels on its stomach. A well fed army is a good army. During the period 1779-1782, somewhere between 9,000 and 15,000 head of cattle were provided to Gálvez' army by ranchers living along the San Antonio River between San Antonio and Goliad. In addition, this area sent several hundred head of horses and many bulls to perpetuate the herds, as well as thousands of pounds of hay and other grains to feed these animals.

These herds of cattle, bulls, and horses were driven from San Antonio, Texas, area to Louisiana by Spanish soldiers,

---

[165] For an excellent and very comprehensive discussion of Texans' role in the American Revolutionary War, see *The Texas Connection With the American Revolution,* by Robert H. Thonhoff, Eakin Press, Burnet, TX, 1981.

militiamen, Indians, and vaqueros[166] from, San Antonio de Bexar (a fort no longer standing, in what is now Karnes County). Some of these men stayed in Louisiana, and fought with Gálvez' army.

Hundreds, if not thousands of Tejanos, as they were then called, responded to the call for donations issued by Charles III, providing thousands of silver dollars in aid to the war effort.[167]

## THE PRESIDIO, MISSIONS, PUEBLAS AND RANCHEROS OF SOUTH TEXAS:

The area of our primary concern was called Nueva Espana (New Spain). It was divided into five provinces: La Provincia de Nuevo México (New México), which included Santa Fe, the capital of which was El Paso; La Provincia de Nueva Vizcaya (New Biscay, the capitol of which was Chihuahua, and which included the Big Bend area of present day Texas); La Provincia de Nueva Estremadura (Coahuila - which included Laredo, and north west along the Rio Grande to the Big Bend); and La Provincia de Nuevo Santander (New Santander, now called Tamaulipas, Mexico); and lastly, La Provincia de Texas ó Las Nuevas Filipinas (The Province of Texas or The New Philippines), which extended from the Nueces River on the south and west to the Red River on the north and east; and from the Gulf Coast on the south to the "Arctic snows" on the north.

---

[166] Spanish for "Cowboys."

[167] Robert H. Thonhoff, *The Vital Contribution of Texas in the Winning of the American Revolution*, (Self Published, Karnes City, Texas, 2006), p. 6.

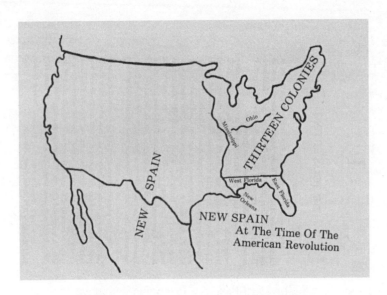

**Map Courtesy of Robert H. Thonhoff**

Although described as a large chunk of present day United States and Canada, the hostile Indians limited the land actually occupied by the Spanish to present day Texas and Louisiana. The attention of this section will be directed to the Province of Texas.

Spain followed a very rigid order of settlement in New Spain. In each settlement there were four pillars: the presidio, the missions, the pueblos, and the rancheros. San Antonio de Bexar became the provincial capitol in 1773. At that time it contained five active missions, a villa and a presidio.

1. **The presidio**, like a fort, is where the soldiers were garrisoned. On a typical day at the presidio of San Antonio, which normally had a roster of between 81-106 men; about 25% of the men were on duty at the presidio; 25% were guarding the horse herd; while another 25% were out looking for Indians. Of

the remainder, about 20 were stationed at El Fuente del Cibolo, to guard the ranchers; while between 4-7 were assigned guard duty for the mail and payroll.

2. **The missions**, each of which included a small settlement of Indians and those who worked the rancheros owned and operated by the mission. San Antonio had five missions, all of which were built along the banks of the San Antonio River. They are listed in the order of their respective location along the river:

a)     **The Alamo**. Construction began in 1724. It was nearest to the presidio and near the governor's mansion.

b)     **Mission Conceptión** was originally built in East Texas in 1716. It was moved to San Antonio in 1731. It boasts Moorish archways and intricately carved stone.

c)     **Mission San José** was founded in 1720, and is famous for its stone rose window. There was a wheat mill on the mission grounds. It is the only mission that has been fully restored, and is still operated as a Franciscan parish church.

d)     **Mission San Juan**. It also was founded in East Texas. This 1716 church was also moved to San Antonio in 1731. It is known for its distinctive bell towers and a laminated, carved altar. Pataguilla, was a ranch run by the Indians of this mission.

e)     **Mission Espada** is the oldest of the five. Founded in 1690 in East Texas, it was the third of these missions to be moved to San Antonio in 1731. This mission owned and operated Las Cabras Ranch, which was later owned by Manuel Barrera. The foundation walls, a granary, a two story convent, workshops and Indian apartments are still standing. There is now a small museum featuring ranching traditions.

3. **The pueblos,** or villas are where the remaining settlers and Indians lived. All men, including Indians, over 16 years of age, were part of the militia. They provided their own horses, saddles, weapons and ammunition. They were called up as the need arose, primarily to fend off attacks by raiding Indians. The main town was San Antonio. Other place names in the area were:

**Las Islitas** was a settlement of Canary Islanders who lived near "Sheep Crossing", on the present road to Elmendorf; **Paso de Maldonado** was probably named for the Maldonado family. It was located near present Graytown; **Los Chayopines**, near present day Floresville, was a ranch owned by Francisco de Ábrego; **El Fuerte de Santa Cruz del Cíbolo.** Don Andrés Hernández built the headquarters for his ranch, San Bartolo, nearby; **Ojos de Santa Cruz** "Holy Cross Springs", now Sutherland Springs; **La Bahía** (Goliad), which had two missions: **Espíritu Santo** and **Rosario.** These two missions had the largest herds of cattle and largest pastures of all the ranches; and **Nogales** ("walnuts"), which later became Walnut Springs; now, Seguin.

4. **The ranchos**, where longhorn cattle were raised included over 65 Ranchos on the San Antonio River, and its branches on Leon Creek, Salado Creek, Cibolo Creek, Marcelina Creek, and Ecleto Creek. Also, the longhorns and other livestock were driven from ranchos on the Medina River, Atascosa River, and Aransas River.

# The Texas Connection

## Cattle Drives

Approximately *10,000* head of cattle were herded by San Antonio Vaqueros from the San Antonio area to Goliad (La Bahia), on to Nacogdoches, then to Natchitoches, and finally to Opelousas. From there they were ferried up the Mississippi River to the Ohio River and into Pennsylvania, or down the Mississippi River to New Orleans and used in support of the Army.

## Ranchos

The 10,000 head of cattle provided to Bernardo de Galvez came from the missions and ranches situated in El Rincon, the area between the Cibolo and San Antonio Rivers. ***Texas A&M-San Antonio*** is located on one of these ranches.

Because of hostile Indians in southeast Texas, the cattle were driven to New Orleans by way of Nacogdoches. Antonio Gil Ybarbo, Lieutenant Governor of the Texas Province, owned a ranch called Elat Lobanillo, at Lobanillo, near Nacogdoches. He was also the militia leader. When the cattle drive went through Nacogdoches, Ybarbo also supplied cattle to Gálvez. From there the herds went through Nachitoches and Opelousas to New Orleans. A list of the ranches providing cattle to General Gálvez is contained in Appendix G.

**TEXAS WAS PRIME CATTLE COUNTRY:**

In the Texas census of 1783, there were 1,248 men, women and children living in the presidio and adjacent San Antonio de Bexar area. Another 554 lived in the missions. The total population of Texas in 1783 was 2,819. This census labeled each resident by name, age group, sex, and heritage. The heritage categories included Spaniard, Frenchmen, Mestizo, Mulatto, Lobo (Indian and mulatto cross), Coyote (Indian and Mestizo cross), Indian and slave.[168]

The San Antonio population included immigrants from the Canary Islands, who began arriving in 1731. Six of the 23 towns in New Spain between the Nueces River and Laredo were on the San Antonio River.

The prime cattle raising areas of Texas in those days were in a rough diamond -shaped area with San Antonio in the north; Brownsville in the south; Laredo on the west; and Old Indianola

---

[168] Texas Census of 1783.

in the east. The nucleus of the best land was between San Antonio and Goliad, along the San Antonio, Cibolo and Guadalupe Rivers.

The ranchers who sold beef to Gálvez and the drovers were all patriots. Additionally, all the men who were members of the Spanish army and the local militia during the time in question, qualify as patriots within the definition of the Sons of the American Revolution. In addition to their service in the army and/or the militia, each Tejano male over 18 most likely made a financial contribution to the war, as requested by Carlos III in August, 1781.

Each Spanish male over 18 was expected to donate 2 pesos, while Indians and those of mixed blood were asked to donate 1 peso. Collections continued until 1784, when news of the peace treaty finally arrived. Few contributor lists survive, but there are census records.

The king's declaration of war included a request for public prayer directed to all priests and church officials. The priests complied, praying both in Spanish and in the local Indian dialects on a regular basis. Thus, each of the mission priests and the church hierarchy in New Spain were also patriots.

# SPAIN AND FRANCE PREPARE TO ATTACK THE BRITISH AT JAMAICA

## 24 October 1781 to 20 January 1783

The island of Jamaica was the largest thorn in the side of the Spanish and the French in the Caribbean. It not only served as the largest British port in the Caribbean for His Majesty's navy, it was also a hornet's nest of British privateers, who for many years had feasted on the gold and silver from the Spanish Main.

Just five days after the victory over Cornwallis at Yorktown on October 19, 1781, Francisco de Saavedra, a special emissary of the Spanish King, left for México, where he remained for two months, making financial arrangements for an invasion of Jamaica. Through his efforts, three shipments totaling 9,500,000 *pesos* were to be delivered to Havana for the Americans within the following six months.

Since the attack was to be a joint Spanish and French operation, it was necessary to establish the chain of command. That was determined in Versailles, France on 3 November 1781. Gálvez was to be the supreme commander of the Spanish-French armada and the commander of all troops placed ashore.

From the outset Gálvez was besieged with logistical problems. His father, General Matías de Gálvez needed more troops in Honduras, so it was necessary for him to deploy a regiment to Cartagena. He intended to delay the attack on the Bahamas, but the officer in charge of that attack had disobeyed an order and seized the Bahamas. This deprived Gálvez of the ships and troops involved there.

On 12 December 1781, several English ships came upon the French convoy transporting 10,000 French troops. The ensuing battle left the French fleet widely dispersed. While the French fleet was still disorganized, a great storm came upon them on Christmas day. France then rearranged its priorities, leaving Jamaica a priority after its military needs in Europe and India.

It was agreed that all ships involved in the attack and all the French and Spanish soldiers to be involved would marshal at Cape Francais (present day Haiti) to coordinate the attack. The main body of 79 Spanish ships and over 5,000 soldiers did not depart Havana until 5 March 1782.

De Grasse' fleet, with his troop convoy, encountered the British fleet under Admiral George Romney on 12 April 1782. They met in battle near the Iles des Saintes on the island of Guadalupe. Both fleets were severely damaged. Rodney captured five French ships of the line, including DeGrasse's flagship, with him aboard.

Because of this loss, it was necessary to delay the attack on the two British forts in Jamaica, until after the summer storm season. Rather than to keep the 20,000 troops assembled and the 29 ships of the line on hold for six months, they were all reassigned to other duties.

An emissary was sent to France to encourage a shifting of its priorities to put the invasion of Jamaica back on the front burner. The diplomatic wheels spun slowly. Before any decision could be reached, the peace treaty was concluded in 1783.

Clearly, the British had become aware of the planned attack on Jamaica. Britain did not want to lose Jamaica. This was a factor in it signing the peace treaty. The armistice between the Europeans and Americans was signed on 20 January 1783, at which time the invasion of Jamaica became a moot issue. The war was over!

The treaty was signed by England, Spain, France, and the United States. It terminated the war and recognized the boundaries of the United States as the Great Lakes to the North and the Mississippi River to the west. Spain was awarded Florida.

George Washington's troops gathered at Newburg, NY, where they remained until the last British ship, with the last British soldier, left New York harbor.

## CURRENT DESCENDANTS OF SPANISH PATRIOTS ARE ELIGIBLE FOR MEMBERSHIP IN PATRIOTIC LINEAGE SOCIETIES

An exhaustive list of known soldiers garrisoned in Texas; the priests and citizens of the pueblos; the ranchers who sold the cattle and vaqueros who drove the cattle to Louisiana; the mission Indians, including those who served as scouts and interpreters, and other patriots of the American Revolution are contained in *Spain's Texas Patriots in its 1779-1783 War with England During the American Revolution* by Granville W. and N.C. Hough, which also contains the names of many of their wives.

Additional names of many other patriots are also found in *The Texas Connection With The American Revolution*, by Robert H. Thonhoff, Eakin Press, Burnett, TX, 1981, including the names and positions of the "Cavalry Company of the Royal Presidio of La Bahia del Espiritu Santo."

Also, muster rolls, *Donitivo* lists and family histories can be found in *Tejano Patriots of the American Revolution; 1776-1783*, by Jesse O. Villarreal, Sr., edited and annotated by Judge Robert H. Thonhoff, self pub. (2011). Mr. Villarreal has a second book coming out in late 2014, in which he will list the muster rolls of the presidios in the Province of Texas, 1776-1783.

It should be noted that at the present time the National Society, Daughters of the American Revolution (DAR) accepts descendants of King Carlos III; General Bernardo de Gálvez and members of his army in Louisiana, which are referred to as "Louisiana Patriots." Those who served as early as 1776 are accepted by the DAR based on Spain's covert support of the colonists. They also accept the descendants of those Tejano ranchers who provided cattle to General Gálvez' army.

To date however, it is not believed that the DAR has accepted as patriots, those members of the Spanish army and/or militia who served during the period after Spain's declaration of war; those non-military colonists who answered King Carlos' call for contributions; or those who served as drovers on the cattle drive to Louisiana. Perhaps no one has applied for membership in the DAR using one of these men as their proposed patriot. Mr. Hough's comprehensive studies of the Spanish involvement in Texas, California, Arizona and New México have been donated to the libraries of both the DAR and the SAR.

It is certain that many of these early Spanish patriots' descendants still reside in Texas. Hopefully, many of them will take the time to apply for membership in the Sons of the American Revolution[169] and the Daughters of the American Revolution. It will be up to the membership chairman of each chapter to encourage this group of descendants to apply for membership.

---

[169] Any man interested in joining the Sons of the American Revolution can obtain information from the SAR web site at www.SAR.org.

# DESCENDANTS OF SPANISH ROYALTY ARE ELIGIBLE FOR MEMBERSHIP IN PATRIOTIC ORGANIZATIONS:

The descendants of Carlos III, King of Spain, during the American Revolution, are eligible for membership in patriotic lineage organizations. His Royal Highness, Juan Carlos I, who until June, 2014, was King of Spain, was inducted into the Sons of the American Revolution (SAR) in 2000.

Current King Felipe VI de Borbón is also a member of the SAR. His cousin, His Highness, Don Francisco Enrique de Borbón y Escasny, Duke of Seville, was inducted into the SAR in May 2001, and was the Charter President of the Spain SAR Society, chartered in May, 2010.

Additionally, descendants of those serving as Spanish Prime Minister or Ambassador, Admirals, Colonels and ship captains, qualify as qualifying "patriots".  Additionally, those who were involved in the purchase of the arms, ammunition and supplies, such as the members of the Joseph Gardoqui and Sons company, Robert Morris, and any Spaniard involved in the warehousing, loading, and transporting the goods, including the seamen who brought the goods to North America also qualify.

## THE *DONATIVO*

As Spain's war with England bore on, the assets of the Spanish treasury declined severely. King Carlos III issued a proclamation on 17 August 1780, to all Spanish citizens in Spain and abroad. He asked that they donate two pesos and that all Indians, Mestizos, Negros and those of mixed blood donate one peso to help pay for the war.

Based upon surviving records, in one year, in Texas alone, the residents donated 1,659 pesos.[170] Others may have made a donation, for which no evidence still exists. Attached as Appendix H is a copy of the list of those making the requested donation from the Bahia Presidio in Texas.[171]

Then, as now, a request from the monarch was equivalent to an order. Although many of the records relating to the collection of the "*donativo*" have been lost or destroyed, enough of those records exist. They reflect that every person at every mission, Spanish town and presidio contributed. It is of interest to note that of the 67 soldiers from the Bahia Presidio in Texas, who made a contribution, only one gave the minimum requested of two *peso*s. The breakdown of donations from the one Presidio was as follows:

| Amount Contributed | Number of Soldiers Contributing that amount |
|---|---|

---

[170] Letter of appreciation for individual and military contributions by Texas citizens, Bexar Archives, 9 March 1784, CAH.

[171] Texas Archives, Center For American History, U. T. Austin.

| | |
|---|---|
| 2 *pesos* | 1 |
| 4 *pesos* | 1 |
| 6 *pesos* | 3 |
| 7 *pesos* | 1 |
| 8 *pesos* | 26 |
| 9 *pesos* | 9 |
| 10 *pesos* | 20 |
| 19 *pesos* | 1 |
| 25 *pesos* | 1 |
| 29 *pesos* | 1 |

Thus, from this one Presidio in Texas, the average donation was 13.43 pesos - a very sizeable amount in 1780. Clearly, Spanish soldiers and citizens were all supportive of the American Revolutionary War.

To reflect the universality of responses, also attached is Appendix I, a list of those from California, who contributed. The contribution from the California missions alone amounted to $2,683 Spanish Silver Dollars.

Proof of a direct lineal ancestor donating constitutes the requisite "patriotic service" required for membership in the Daughters of the American Revolution, Sons of the American Revolution and the Children of the American Revolution.

# CHRONOLOGICAL SUMMARY OF SPAIN'S ASSISTANCE TO THE AMERICANS:

## 1776 to 1783[172]

Between Spain's Declaration of War against the British in 1779, and the end of the war in 1783, there were at a minimum some 17,000 Spanish soldiers and sailors who served on what is now American soil or the adjoining waters within cannon shot distance. This brave group of warriors killed thousands of British and their allies; captured tens of thousands of British prisoners and their personal arms, including their French and Indian allies; captured hundreds of British ships; thousands of artillery pieces, and tens of thousand pounds of gunpowder.

Additionally, Spain provided to the Americans much needed cannon, cannon balls, muskets, musket balls, gunpowder, medical supplies, tents, uniforms, blankets, shoes, copper, tin, naval stores, plus millions of dollars in cash. They captured English forts in Illinois, Indiana, Ohio, Michigan, Mississippi, Louisiana, Alabama, Florida and the Bahamas. Even the French paid homage to Spain for its efforts during the war:

> "The public treasury was assisted by individuals, ladies even offering their diamonds. Five hours after the arrival of the frigate *Aigutte*, sent by De Grasse, the sum of 1,200,000 Livres was delivered on board.

---

[172] Except where noted, each act of assistance has already been documented.

> "Finally, help would be given to the Americans, and thanks to it, the decisive battle of the war could take place, as well as the defeat of Cornwallis' army.
>
> "This immediate financial aid from sources in Cuba should be considered as coming directly from the Creole inhabitants of Havana. The Creole ladies forming a patriotic type association, and the Creole merchants . . . were involved in the transaction. Cuban merchants hoped that American independence would bring them future economic prosperity, a liberalization of commerce enabling them to maintain exchange relations with the United States. Here we have only a good example of how important and significant the contributions made by Spain were for the final outcome of the American Revolution." [173]

The Spanish military and naval activities at Gibraltar, Menorca, Majorca, India, Great Britain, Central America, and at Buenos Aires, kept hundreds of British ships and tens of thousands of troops away from American Shores.

General Bernardo de Gálvez and his troops were successful in their attempt to remove England from the Gulf of México and the Mississippi and Ohio Rivers. Their actions prevented the British from creating a second front with the Americans, and removed the British soldiers involved from the war with the rebels. Spain's military attacks in the Gulf of México and elsewhere, actually caused England to divert ships and men which could have been used against the Americans. It left the Mississippi and the Ohio Rivers open as a vital life line to the Americans. Spain also provided both directly (through Gálvez

---

[173] *Admiral de Grass*, by Charles Lee Lewis, p. 138

and the dummy corporation) and indirectly (through the French) loans, gifts and much needed supplies.

Spain's entry into the war came at a time that was highly critical for the Americans, who were trying to fight the strongest nation in Europe almost barehanded. In 1778, the center of gravity of the war had been transferred from the North to the South and there the fortunes of war were not exactly favoring the rebels. That year the English took Savannah and Charleston, as well as other towns, causing severe setbacks for the American forces which had lost some 5,000 men.

It was then that the British hastened to implement their plans for the capture of New Orleans. There is little doubt that their success would have given them permanent command of the Mississippi Basin, from Canada to the Gulf. This would have been tragic for the Americans. With the British already controlling all the east coast, Canada, Florida, and the Bahamas, their possession of the Mississippi River valley would have strangled the rebellion to death.

Spain's declaration of war on England forced the British to fight on several fronts at the same time, having to oppose the combined Franco-Spanish fleet of 90 vessels which was laying siege to Gibraltar, and which had continuously threatened to invade England itself. In this way, they tied up a sizeable percentage of the British fleet from the Indian Ocean to the Caribbean, making it impossible for England to affect a blockade on the American Coast. Occupying the British fleet in far flung areas also facilitated the operation of an ever-growing fleet of American and foreign privateers.

The following is a blow-by-blow list in chronological order of the assistance the colonists received directly from Spain:

1774-1783 American colonists were provided arms, ammunition, and supplies from Spanish merchants.

1775 - 1783 American Privateers were given "most favored nation" status and sanctuary at Spanish ports, including Havana, New Orleans, Bilbao, La Coruña, Cádiz, Algeciras, and Santa Cruz de Tenerife. Captain John Paul Jones used La Coruña as his headquarters for 18 months.[174]

1 January 1776 New Spanish muskets from Joseph Gardoqui and Sons of Bilbao, Spain began arriving in Massachusetts, and were distributed to some Massachusetts Continental Regiments.

1 Jun 1776 A Spanish ship loaded with military supplies arrived in New Orleans.

Before July 4, 1776 Spain and France entered into a secret agreement with the colonists to support them in their rebellion against England.[175]

1776-1779 During the three years before Spain declared war on England, it provided credit to the colonists

---

[174] *The Vital Contribution of Spain In the Winning of The American Revolution*, Robert H. Thonhoff, self published, 2000, p. 5.

[175] The promise of secret support from both Spain and France surely gave confidence to the colonists prior to the signing of the Declaration of Independence.

totaling 8 million Reales, for weapons, food, military and medical supplies.

August 1776    General Charles Henry Lee, second in command to General George Washington, sent Captain George Gibson, with a group of 16 colonists, from Ft. Pitt to New Orleans, to obtain weapons, gunpowder and supplies from Spain that had arrived in June, 1776.

September 1776    Spain sent 9,000 pounds of gunpowder to the Americans, which had arrived in New Orleans on 1 September 1776, up the Mississippi River. An additional 1,000 pounds was sent by ship to Philadelphia.

September 1776    General Bernardo de Gálvez arrived in New Orleans to assume his post as Governor. Having been told by King Carlos III that war was imminent, he immediately began to recruit an army, under the guise that it was for the defense of New Orleans.

25 November 1776    Carlos III ordered Gálvez to secretly collect intelligence about the British. Later, Gálvez was ordered to render secret help to the colonies.

24 December 1776    An order was issued by Minister of the Indies, Jose Gálvez, to the Governor Unzaga of Louisiana, instructing him to support the Americans.

Before July 1777    Spain sent another 2,000 barrels of gunpowder, lead and clothing up the Mississippi to assist the Americans. Carlos III made secret loans of 1,000,000 Livres to the rebels.

1777           American Representative[176] in France, Benjamin Franklin, arranged for the secret transport from Spain to the colonies of 215 bronze cannon; 4,000 tents; 13,000 grenades; 30,000 muskets, bayonets and uniforms; 50,000 musket balls; and 300,000 pounds of gunpowder.

September 1777           By this time, Spain had already furnished 1,870,000 *livres* to the Americans. Much of this was contributed through a dummy corporation,[177] for which France mistakenly received total credit.

October 1777           Patrick Henry wrote two letters to General Gálvez, thanking Spain for it's help and requesting more supplies. Henry suggested that the two Floridas which Spain lost to England, should revert back to Spain.

1778-1779           American General George Rogers Clark obtained a considerable amount of his supplies from General Gálvez in New Orleans. These supplies were used in his victories over the British at Kaskaskia, Cahokia and Vincennes.

---

[176] Since the colonies had not obtained their independence from England yet, France could not accept an Ambassador. Yet, Franklin, the "Representative" was afforded all the courtesies normally extended to other Ambassadors.

[177] The famous "Rodrigue Hortalez and Company" served as the conduit for Spanish assistance. Its main director was the French playwright and statesman, Pierre Augustin Caron de Beaumarchais.

January 1778        Patrick Henry wrote another letter to General Gálvez, thanking Spain for its help and requesting more supplies.

February 1778        The "Treaty of Alliance" between France and The United States was executed. Because of the "Borbon Compact" Spain was obligated to assist France against the English.

March 1778        U.S. Captain James Willing left Ft. Pitt with an expedition of 30 men, bound for New Orleans to obtain supplies for the war. They plundered the British settlements along the Ohio and Mississippi Rivers. General Gálvez welcomed them to New Orleans and assisted them in auctioning off of their British plunder. Gálvez sold them military arms and ammunition for their return trip to Ft. Pitt.

1779-1782        Spanish ranchers along the San Antonio River between San Antonio and La Bahia, now Goliad, Texas, sent between 9,000 and 15,000 head of cattle, several hundred horses, mules, bulls and feed to General Bernardo de Gálvez in New Orleans. The cattle were used to feed his troops and to provision George Washington's Continental Army at Valley Forge.

1779        All males, including Indians, over 18 in New Spain were required to become a member of the Militia in their respective areas.

7 Feb 1779        General George Rogers Clark, with supplies provided by Leyba and Gálvez, departed Kaskaskia (current day Illinois) on the Mississippi River with a small army of about 170 men, including Kentucky militia and French

volunteers. This force traveled over 200 miles of land covered by snow and ice, crossing icy flood water until they reached Fort Sackville at Vincennes (Indiana) on 23 February 1779.

25 Feb 1779     The British surrendered Fort Sackville at Vincennes, marking the beginning of the end of British domination in America's Northwest Territory. After winning a short skirmish with Indians allied with the English within view of the fort, Clark secured the surrender of the British garrison under Lieutenant-Governor Henry Hamilton at 10 a.m. on February 25. Upon their arrival in Vincennes, some of the French settlers, allied with the English immediately were converted to supporters of the American Revolution. When the fort was surrendered there were only 40 British soldiers, and about the same number of French, who had changed sides.

April 1779     A secret treaty was entered into between the French Ambassador in Madrid, and Count Floridablanca, Spanish Secretary of State, which drew Spain closer into the conflict between the American Colonies and England.

21 June 1779     Spain declared war on England. Carlos III, King of Spain, ordered Spanish subjects around the world to fight the English wherever they were to be found. General Bernardo Gálvez in New Orleans was ready for battle. French officials were ordered by the French Crown to cooperate with their Spanish neighbors in every way possible. Even de Grasse himself had orders to be of service to the Spaniards in naval operations against the British.

27 August-7 September 1779     General Bernardo de Gálvez led the Spanish Army at New Orleans up the Mississippi River 90

miles to attack Ft. Bute, in Manchac, Louisiana. Ft. Bute was surrendered by the English on 7 September 1779.

29 August 1779    Carlos III, King of Spain, issued a proclamation that the main objective of the Spanish troops in America was to drive the British out of the Gulf of México and the Mississippi River.

20 September 1779    General Gálvez' army captured Baton Rouge, and negotiated the surrender of the British fort at Natchez. By clearing the Mississippi River of British forces, Gálvez allowed Captain William Pickles to bring an American Schooner onto Lake Pontchartrain. Pickles seized the British privateer, *West Florida*, which had dominated the lake for two years. This ship was renamed the "*Galvestown*".

8 November 1779    Thomas Jefferson wrote to General Gálvez, expressing his thanks for Spain's assistance during the revolutionary cause.

1780    Carlos III issued a Royal Order requesting a one-time voluntary donation ("*Donativo*") of two pesos per Spaniard and one peso per Indian in each provincial site in Spain's New World Empire, to defray the expense of the war with England. This request for a "donativo" was viewed as a crown order, followed by a high level of participation.

15 – 20 Jan 1780    John Adams visited Bilbao, Spain and met with Diego Gardoqui of Joseph Gardoqui and Sons. In one of the two letters sent by him from his Inn in Bilbao, John Adams wrote the following: "We have had the pleasure of finding Mr. Gardoqui and sons friends willing to collaborate with us in all aspects". Through the Bilbao merchant "*Joseph*

*Gardoqui e hixos*", Spain sent 120,000 *Reales* to the United States in pieces of eight cash and payment amounting to 50,000 *Reales* on other orders. These coins were used to support the US public debt and gave rise to its own currency, the dollar. Through Gardoqui and Sons, Spain also provided 215 bronze cannon, 30,000 muskets, 30,000 bayonets, 51,314 musket bullets, 300,000 pounds of gunpowder, 12,868 grenades, 30,000 uniforms and 4,000 tents, with a total value of 946,906 *Reales* to the United States.

28 Jan.- 9 Mar. 1780    Gálvez led the attack on Mobile. The Spanish siege lasted from 10 February to 9 March 1779, when the British surrendered. Gálvez was promoted to Field Marshal and was given command of all Spanish operations in America.

April 1780    The Spanish fleet sailed from Cádiz, Spain to America to reinforce the army of General Bernardo Gálvez.

26 May 1780    Spanish troops, Spanish Militia and Indian allies defeated the British and their Indian allies at Fort San Carlos in present day St. Louis, MO.

24 June 1780    Carlos III, by royal order to the Governor of Havana, appointed Francisco de Saavedra as a Special Emissary to represent the Crown, giving him authority to make decisions regarding transfer of funds from the Royal Treasury in Havana.

9 August 1780    On this date there was a naval engagement of the American Revolutionary War in which the main Spanish fleet led by Admiral Luis De Córdova y Córdova, together with a squadron of French ships, captured most of a

heavy British convoy of sixty-three vessels, causing a severe blow to the commerce of Great Britain.[178] The British convoy led by Sir John Moutray, captain of *HMS Ramillies* and three frigates sailed from Portsmouth in late July, and were intercepted on 9 August by the Spanish fleet. During the action the Spaniards managed to capture 55 of the 63 vessels - including five wars ships - making it one of the most complete naval captures ever made.[179] This loss was still bitterly remembered in Great Britain thirty years later at the height of the Napoleonic Wars. The British financial losses were estimated at £ 1,500,000.[180] Can you imagine the current value in 2014 English Pounds?

The five captured British warships were added to the Spanish Navy giving them a new squadron of frigates. The 30-gun *HMS Hillsborough* was added to the Spanish navy as the 34-gun *Santa Balbina*; the 28-gun *HMS Mountstuart* was commissioned as the 34-gun *Santa Bibiana*; the 28-gun *HMS Royal George* became the 40-gun *Real Jorge*; the 28-gun *HMS Gatton* was recommissioned the 30-gun *Colón*; and the *HMS Godfrey* with

---

*153 Universal History Americanized, or an Historical View of the World from the Earliest Records to the Nineteenth Century, with a Particular Reference to the State of Society, Literature, Religion, and Form of Government of the United States of America,* Vol. VI (1819).

[179] *The Encyclopedia of London*, p.483

[180] Syrett, David. *The Royal Navy in European Waters during the American Revolutionary War.* University of South Carolina Press. ISBN 978-1-57003-238-7, pp. 136-137.

its 28-guns transitioned into the 34-gun *Santa Paula*.[181] This action severely limited the naval resources of England and interrupted the logistical resupply of the English army in North America. At the same time it reinforced both the Spanish merchant and war fleets.

16 October 1780　　　　Gálvez led a Spanish fleet of 15 warships and 59 transport ships from Havana to attack Pensacola. Embarked were 164 officers and 3,829 men.

18 October 1780　　　　A hurricane hit the Spanish armada. Many were lost. The survivors retreated to Havana. For fear that the British might seek to retake Mobile before he could take Pensacola; Gálvez dispatched two gunships and 500 soldiers to reinforce Mobile.

November 1780　　　　The Spanish Treasury in Havana paid 152,190 *livres* to France in payment for hospitalization of Spanish soldiers in Cape Francois. Spain loaned the French government an additional 151,300 *pesos*. Spain also paid 60,000 *pesos* to French officials at Cape Francois for the benefit of French troops stationed in Spanish Santa Domingo.

16 February 1781　　　Spanish soldiers, Spanish militia and Indian allies traveled 600 miles from Fort San Carlos in present

---

[181] *Listado de presas británicas capturadas por la escuadra de Luis de Córdoba en 1780 Revista de Historia Naval del Ministerio de Defensa - An incomplete list of the British ships captured by Admiral Luis de Córdova in 1780* (Spanish).

day St. Louis, Missouri, to attack the British fort and supply depot at Ft. St. Joseph, in present day Niles, Michigan. It was from this supply depot that the British planned to feed its army and Indian allies during its planned spring 1781 drive to clear all Spanish from the Mississippi River Valley. With control of the Mississippi they could thwart Spanish supplies to General George Rogers Clark at Ft. Nelson, present day Louisville, Kentucky, and to General Washington's troops in the east through Ft. Pitt. These Spanish soldiers and militia defeated the British, burned the fort and destroyed the food they could not take with them.

28 February 1781    A second (and smaller) Spanish flotilla, with 1,315 soldiers, sailed from Havana, Cuba to assist General Bernardo Gálvez in his attack on Pensacola.

9 March 1781    The two month Spanish siege on Pensacola began. Gálvez had previously ordered Spanish troops stationed in New Orleans and Mobile to join in the attack on Pensacola. Mobile sent 500 men, and 1,400 arrived from New Orleans.

19 April 1781    1,600 reinforcements from Havana arrived at Pensacola.

8 May 1781    The British surrendered at Pensacola. This removed the British threat from both the Gulf of México and the Mississippi River. Gálvez was assisted by four French frigates. He gave them 500,000 *pesos* to reprovision and repair their ships.

June 1781    The Spanish Treasury in Havana paid 23,568 *livres* to France for its aid to Spanish soldiers. Spain loaned 68,656 *pesos* to the French fleet, and loaned an additional 200,000 *pesos* to French officials at Cape Francois. For a list of substantial payments made by the Spanish Treasury in Havana to France, see Appendix K.

July 17 – 19, 1781    French Admiral de Grasse met with Francisco de Saavedra, Special Emissary of the King of Spain at Cape Francois concerning delaying the attack on Jamaica until after the French fleet was sent to Yorktown. De Grasse was concerned about leaving French colonies in the Caribbean unprotected should he take the entire French fleet to Yorktown. Saavedra convinced de Grasse not to divide the French fleet, promising to protect French colonies with the Spanish warships in Havana. Thus, it was only because of the assistance of Spain's Caribbean fleet that de Grasse was enabled to take his entire fleet to Yorktown.

July - August 1781    The French had no specie with which to pay their soldiers and no money to pay for the French fleet to become involved in the siege of Yorktown.

July 29, 1781    When de Grasse wrote to Rochambeau by letter dated July 29, 1781, he advised that Rochambeau could count on de Grasse delivering 1,200,000 *livres* that he had been requested to bring, de Grasse did not yet have those funds.

July 31, 1781    De Grasse's request for loans from wealthy French merchants at Cape Francois fell on deaf ears.

August 1, 1781    The following day de Grasse requested financial help from Spain through Saavedra. Saavedra immediately agreed to make those funds available to de Grasse.

August 3, 1781    Saavedra sailed from Cape Francois on August 3$^{rd}$, bound for Havana to obtain the funds for de Grasse.

August 15, 1781    Saavedra reached Havana on August 15$^{th,}$ only to find the Spanish treasury empty. Jose' Ignaci de Urizza, *Intendant* of Havana and Juan Manuel de Cagigal, Governor of Cuba, received instructions from Saavedra to deliver 1,000,000 p*esos* to French officials. It took them six hours to secure necessary loans from Spanish military officers and merchants, who were promised repayment shortly when the ships ladened with silver coins from the Mexican mint arrived within a few weeks. From Saint-Dominique, French Admiral de Grasse sent a frigate to Havana, Cuba to secure the silver coins from Spain. Not only did Spanish officials provide the needed specie, many women of Havana offered their diamonds for the cause. Merchants and four Spanish Army Regiments loaned a total of 4,520,000 *reales,* from which the Exchequer delivered 4,000,000 *reales*, which at the time equaled 500,000 *pesos*. The merchants charged 2% interest, but the Spanish Army Regiments made interest free loans. Lists of the Spanish military making loans is shown in Appendix L.

August 16 - 17, 1781    General Bernardo de Gálvez arrived in Havana on August 16$^{th}$, and gave his approval of the loan from Havana merchants and the military there. He ordered the transfer of the gold and silver to meet with de Grass' fleet. On the night of August 16, the four French ships that had participated in the Siege on Pensacola, (after they had been repaired and provisioned by Gálvez), transported the silver provided by Havana Spanish merchants to the French frigate, the *Aygrette.*

August 17, 1781    The *Aygrette* rendezvoused with de Grasse off the coast of Cuba the next day. It departed Cuban waters ladened with gold and silver which was to be used for the payment of salaries to the French troops in Virginia, who were threatening to desert because they had not been paid in months. The money was also to pay for food and supplies to feed and clothe the French troops. The French ships then proceeded to join the French blockade of Yorktown, which led to the British surrender.   Some of this silver was loaned by France to American Officials for governmental expenses.

August 1781    General George Washington drank a toast to the kings of France and Spain at the home of Robert Morris, in Philadelphia.

August 1781    The Spanish treasury at Havana paid France 100,000 *pesos* for French troops stationed in Spanish Santa Domingo and loaned 100,000 *pesos* to French officials at Cape Francois.

August – September 1781    French officials loaned money (received from Spain in Havana) to the 13 colonies with which to pay one month's salary to the Continental Army. The French Army also used money from Spain to purchase supplies in Virginia.[182]

---

[182] It should be noted that to a lesser degree, the colonists received aid and assistance from Holland (now the Netherlands) and Sweden. Each allowed American ships the use of their ports. The current king of Sweden has been offered membership in the Sons of the American Revolution.

September 1781      The Spanish treasury at Havana loaned 1,000,000 *pesos* to France to be used in Martinique.

19 October 1781      General Cornwallis surrendered at Yorktown.[183] Although the English army in Virginia surrendered, there were still British troops in New York, Detroit, St. Augustine, and Kingston. Until a treaty was executed, England and the United States remained at war.

6 May 1782      General Gálvez' forces attacked the Bahamas, which surrendered without a shot being fired.

4 February 1783      King George III declared a formal cessation of hostilities in the American Revolutionary War.

3 September 1783      With the signing of the Paris Peace Treaty[184], peace was declared between England, the United States, Spain and France.[159]

---

[183] Although the hostilities between the American and British forces were halted by the surrender, the Revolutionary War was not over. Indians aligned with the British continued to fight in Ohio and Indiana. France and Spain continued their hostilities against the British.

[184] Both the Daughters of the American Revolution and the Sons of the American Revolution recognize service between the period 19 October 1781 and 3 September 1783 as "qualified" patriotic service.

1784          The U.S. Congress formally cited General Bernardo Gálvez and Spain for their aid during the American Revolutionary War.

1785          Upon his father's death, General Bernardo Gálvez was named Viceroy of New Spain.

30 November 1785     General Bernardo de Gálvez died in México City, México.

It was the American historian, Helen Auger who said that

> "Spain shod and dressed the American soldiers, and armed their units with the Spanish musket, at that time considered the best in the world".

For a complete chronological list of the historical relationship between Spain and England see Appendix N.

# DON DIEGO DE GARDOQUI

Don Diego de Gardoqui attended the inauguration of George Washington as a special guest (together with the French Ambassador) because of all the help that both Spain and France provided to the American Revolution (and a great deal conveyed through the family business he represented, Joseph Gardoqui and Sons in Bilbao). Gardoqui sent clothes and blankets to George Washington during his ordeal at Valley Forge. The Gardoqui firm in Bilbao, Spain was the primary company sending arms, ammunition, military supplies, etc. to the Americans.

Don Diego de Gardoqui maintained a friendly relationship with George Washington. They exchanged letters throughout the years. He also supplied his good friend Washington with a prized royal Spanish stud work-donkey so Washington could breed his own mares and produce work mules. Washington named the donkey "Royal Gift." This became the beginning of the U.S. mule industry. The Spanish minister also presented George Washington with a four-volume edition of Cervantes by *Don Quixote*.

Gardoqui pronounced the inaugural address as "an eloquent and appropriate address." In honor of the inauguration, Gardoqui decorated the front of his house on Broadway in New York City, near Bowling Green, "with two magnificent transparent gardens, adorned with statues, natural size, imitating marble.... There were also various flower-pots, different arches with foliage and columns of imitation marble, and on the sky of these gardens were placed thirteen stars, representing the United States of America--two of which stars showed opaque, to designate the two states which had not adopted the Constitution."

Diego stood at the left side of George Washington (the French Ambassador to his right) during his inaugural parade in New York City, then our nation's capital. Ambassador Gardoqui positioned the Spanish brigantine, the *Gálveztown*, in New York Harbor. It served as Gálvez' flagship during the Gulf Coast campaign. It was the only foreign gunship thus honored.

In the early years after the Revolutionary War when congress and the president resided in New York City, Gardoqui's house was also the meeting place of the first Catholic dignitaries representing their respective countries. Mass was said there for the congregation composed of such men as representatives of France, Spain, and Portugal, as well as Charles Carroll, his cousin Daniel, and Thomas Fitzsimmons, Catholic members of Congress, officers and soldiers of the foreign contingent, merchants and others.

On October 5, 1785, Diego de Gardoqui laid the cornerstone of St. Peter's, the first permanent structure for a Catholic church erected in the State of New York. The church first opened on November 4, 1786. He was the first Spanish Ambassador to the United States.

**1889 oil painting by Ramon de Elorriaga entitled "The Inauguration of George Washington." It is an artistic rendition that depicts the first U.S. President taking his first oath of office on the balcony of Federal Hall April 30, 1789, surrounded by his cabinet and officials.**

# DON JUAN DE MIRALLES

Don Juan de Miralles was a wealthy Spanish merchant from Havana, Cuba. King Carlos III appointed him as a Royal Envoy to the United States in 1778. On his initial trip to present his credentials to the Continental Congress, he persuaded the captain of the ship transporting him to enter the United States at the port of Charleston, South Carolina, rather than proceed directly to Philadelphia.

He was traveling in company with his secretary, Don Francisco Rendo'n. While in Charleston, Miralles initiated a plan of direct shipment of arms, ammunition, and military supplies directly from Havana. As he and his secretary made their way to Philadelphia by stage, they made similar arrangement for direct shipment of military arms, ammunition and supplies from Cuba to Baltimore. Upon his arrival, he made a similar agreement with officials in Philadelphia.

Mirales became a correspondent with General George Washington during the war. Washington, in one of his letters to Mirales, discussed strategy of dealing with the British in Florida.[185]

---

[185] Letter from General George Washington to Don Juan de Mirales dated 27 February, 1780.

## OFFICIAL THANKS TO SPAIN AND TO GENERAL BERNARDO DE GÁLVEZ FROM THE UNITED STATES

In 1777, Benjamin Franklin officially thanked the Spanish authorities for the 12,000 muskets sent to Boston.

In October 1777, Patrick Henry wrote two letters to General Gálvez, thanking Spain for it's help and requesting more supplies. Henry suggested that the two Floridas which Spain lost to England, should revert back to Spain.

In January 1778, Patrick Henry wrote another letter to General Gálvez, thanking Spain for its help and requesting more supplies.

On 8 November 1779, Thomas Jefferson wrote to General Gálvez, expressing his thanks for Spain's assistance to the revolutionary cause. In George Washington's farewell to his officers, he toasted Spain for its assistance during the revolutionary war.

In August 1781 General George Washington drank a toast to the kings of France and Spain at the home of Robert Morris, in Philadelphia.

In 1783 Congress agreed to display a portrait of Gálvez "in the hall where Congress meets."

In 1784 the U.S. Congress formally cited General Bernardo de Gálvez and Spain for their aid during the American Revolutionary War.

On 23 July 1980, the United States issued a commemorative 15 cent stamp honoring General Bernardo de Gálvez for his victory at the Battle of Mobile. The stamp was issued on July 23, 1980 in New Orleans, Louisiana. The day of issue (July 23) represents Gálvez' birthday, the year (1980) represents the bicentennial of the Battle of Mobile, and the city of issue (New Orleans) represents where he was headquartered as Governor of Louisiana.

Joint Resolutions to make General Bernardo de Gálvez an honorary citizen of the United States were introduced into both the U.S. House of Representatives and the U.S. Senate. The House Resolution was adopted unanimously on 14 June 2014. The Senate Resolution was adopted without dissent on 4 December 2014. At the time of publication the resolutions needs only the signature of President Obama to become law.

On 9 December 2014 an oil painting of General Bernardo de Gálvez was hung in the committee room of the Senate Foreign Relations Committee, with both the SAR and DAR represented.

It should also be remembered that it was

a) Spanish craftsmen and workers who made the muskets, musket balls, bayonets, tents, etc. supplied to the Americans;
b) Spanish workers who transported the goods to Spanish harbors;
c) Spanish longshoremen who loaded the goods onto Spanish and other ships;
d) Spanish ships and crews who transported the goods from Spain to Havana or other Caribbean ports.
e) Spanish longshoremen who unloaded the cargo and placed it into Spanish warehouses.
f) Spanish ships and crews who transported the goods from Havana to New Orleans and other U.S, ports.
f) It was Spanish militia who transported some of the goods up the Mississippi and Ohio Rivers.

Both the city of Galveston, Texas, and Gálveston County, Texas, where it is located, were named in 1785, for Bernardo de Gálvez. The town Gálvez, Louisiana was also named for him. The Louisiana counties of East Feliciana and West Feliciana were both named in honor of Gálvez' wife, Marie Felicite' de St. Maxent d'Estre'han Gálvez.

Please join me in donating to the fund to erect a life size equine bronze statue of Gálvez in downtown Galveston, TX. The fund raising campaign is being operated by the Galveston, TX SAR Chapter with the cooperation of the Order of the Granaderos y Damas de Gálvez. Estimated cost of the statute, base, landscaping, lights and park benches is $400,000.00.

Please send your tax deductible contributions to SAR Gálvez Statute, PO Box 1, Galveston, TX .

# GÁLVEZ DECLARED A U.S. CITIZEN

On 9 January 2014, a Joint Resolution was filed in the U.S. House of Representatives and an identical Joint Resolution was filed in the U.S. Senate on 4 Jun 2014, both providing that U.S. Citizenship should be conferred on Bernardo de Gálvez, posthumously. The House resolution was passed on June 14, 2014, while the Senate resolution was passed on Dec. 4, 2014. The Resolutions read as follows:

### JOINT RESOLUTION

*Conferring honorary citizenship of the United States on Bernardo de Gálvez y Madrid, Viscount of Galveston and Count of Gálvez.*

*Whereas, the United States has conferred honorary citizenship on 7 other occasions during its history, and honorary citizenship is and should remain an extraordinary honor not lightly conferred nor frequently granted;*

*Whereas, Bernardo de Gálvez y Madrid, Viscount of Galveston and Count of Gálvez, was a hero of the Revolutionary War who risked his life for the freedom of the United States people and provided supplies, intelligence, and strong military support to the war effort;*

*Whereas, Bernardo de Gálvez recruited an army of 7,500 men made up of Spanish, French, African-American, Mexican, Cuban, and Anglo-American forces and led the effort of Spain to aid the United States' colonists against Great Britain;*

*Whereas, during the Revolutionary War, Bernardo de Gálvez and his troops seized the Port of New Orleans and successfully defeated the British at battles in Baton Rouge, Louisiana, Natchez, Mississippi, and Mobile, Alabama;*[186]

*Whereas, Bernardo de Gálvez led the successful 2-month Siege of Pensacola, Florida, where his troops captured the capital of British West Florida and left the British with no naval bases in the Gulf of México;*

*Whereas, Bernardo de Gálvez was wounded during the Siege of Pensacola, demonstrating bravery that forever endeared him to the United States soldiers;*

*Whereas, Bernardo de Gálvez' victories against the British were recognized by George Washington as a deciding factor in the outcome of the Revolutionary War;*

*Whereas, Bernardo de Gálvez helped draft the terms of treaty that ended the Revolutionary War;*

*Whereas, the United States Continental Congress declared, on October 31, 1778, their gratitude and favorable sentiments to Bernardo de Gálvez for his conduct towards the United States;*

*Whereas, after the war, Bernardo de Gálvez served as viceroy of New Spain and led the effort to chart the Gulf of México, including Galveston Bay, the largest bay on the Texas coast;*

*Whereas, several geographic locations, including Galveston Bay, Galveston, Texas, Galveston County, Texas, Gálvez, Louisiana, and St. Bernard Parish, Louisiana, are named after Bernardo de Gálvez;*

---

[186] This is incorrect as New Orleans became the property of Spain in 1763 by the terms of the Treaty of Paris ending the French and Indian Wars.

*Whereas, the State of Florida has honored Bernardo de Gálvez with the designation of Great Floridian; and*

*Whereas, Bernardo de Gálvez played an integral role in the Revolutionary War and helped secure the independence of the United States:*

*Now, therefore, be it resolved:*

*That Bernardo De Gálvez y Madrid, Viscount of Galveston and Count of Gálvez, is proclaimed posthumously to be an honorary citizen of the United States.*

## HONORARY U.S. CITIZENSHIP FOR BERNARDO DE GÁLVEZ

Your author served on an international committee to seek honorary U.S. Citizenship for Bernardo de Gálvez. The international committee formed included members of the SAR, DAR, the Texas Connection to the American Revolution (TCARA) in San Antonio, TX; The Gálvez Association, of Jacksonville, FL; Los Bexarenos Genealogical Society of San Antonio, TX; the Order of the Founders of North America 1492-1692; and the Order of the Granaderos y Damas de Gálvez in San Antonio, Houston, New Orleans and Jacksonville, FL. Mimi Lozano, webmistress of *Somos Primos*, an Hispanic newsletter included the campaign in her newsletter to some 8,000 subscribers and asked for their assistance. Some 1.2 Million people access her web site each month.

Following an extensive letter writing campaign by the committee in 2013 the U.S. Congress got involved. In 2014, Joint Resolutions were introduced in both the U.S. House of Representatives and the U.S. Senate to confer honorary American Citizenship on Bernardo de Gálvez posthumously.

At the 2014 Congress of the National Society Sons of the American Revolution, this author prepared and presented to the delegates, a proposed resolution to be adopted by the SAR Congress in assembly at its annual Congress in Greenville, S.C., with copies to be sent to each member of the U.S. House of Representative and the U.S. Senate requesting that they adopt the Joint Resolution.

The SAR delegates unanimously passed the proposed resolution favoring the passage of the joint resolution which would make Bernardo Gálvez an honorary citizen of the United States. A copy of the SAR Resolution is appended as Appendix E. A copy of the cover letter to Congressmen and Senators from SAR President General (2014-2015) Lindsey Cook Brock is attached as Appendix F.

The U.S. Senate adopted the Joint Resolution on Dec. 4, 2014. Soon it will be sent to President Obama for signature into law. At that time the SAR and DAR can pat themselves on the back for playing an instrumental role in this long overdue honor being bestowed upon Bernardo de Gálvez.

The passage of the Joint Resolution of the House and Senate conferring Honorary U.S. Citizenship on Gálvez is highly unusual for two reasons. For the past few years the U.S. Senate has been the place where House Bills go to die.

The U.S. House of Representatives has passed and sent over 300 bills to the Senate - where with very few exceptions, they have languished. So, we are very lucky that our resolution was even considered by the Senate.

Secondly, only seven people have previously been selected Honorary U.S. Citizens. Those selected, the year of their selection, and their position are as follows:

| | | |
|---|---|---|
| Sir Winston Churchill | 1963 | Prime Minister of England during World War II |
| Raoul Wallenberg | 1981 | Swedish Diplomat who rescued Jews from the Holocost |
| William Penn | 1981 | Founder of Pennsylvania |
| Hannah Callowhill Penn | 1984 | Second wife of Wm. Penn; administrator of the Province of PA |
| Mother Theresa | 1996 | Founder of the Missionaries of Charity of Calcutta |
| Gilbert du Motier Marquies de Lafayette | 2007 | French officer who assisted in the American Revolutionary War |

| Casamir Pulaski | 2009 | Polish officer who assisted in the American Revolutionary War |

# GÁLVEZ PORTRAIT

This writer was also a member of another international committee to get Congress to honor a promise it made 231 years ago. In 1783, Congress pledged to hang a portrait in the U.S. Capitol honoring Bernardo de Gálvez. During the war Gálvez had received letters of appreciation for the assistance being rendered to Americans by him from George Washington, Thomas Jefferson and Virginia Governor, Patrick Henry. General George Rogers Clark stated that his victories at Kaskaskia, Cahokia and Vincennes were possible only because of the supplies he received from Gálvez.

An unlikely civil servant in D.C., Teresa Valcarce Graciani found herself as Chairman of our committee to get Congress to honor a promise it made in 1783, following the signing of the Treaty of Paris, which concluded the American Revolutionary War.

In May 1783, Elias Boudinot, the president of the Continental Congress, wrote to an American revolutionary financier, Oliver Pollock. In the letter, Boudinot accepted Pollock's gift of a portrait of Gálvez. Pollock had worked with Gálvez in New Orleans as a representative of both the United States and the state of Virginia to acquire and distribute Spanish arms, ammunition and military supplies to the Americans.

The international committee formed included members of the SAR, DAR, the Texas Connection to the American Revolution (TCARA) in San Antonio, TX; The Gálvez Association, of Jacksonville, FL; Los Bexarenos Genealogical Society of San Antonio, TX; the Order of the

Founders of North America 1492-1692; and the Order of the Granaderos y Damas de Gálvez in San Antonio, Houston, New Orleans and Jacksonville, FL. Again, a letter writing campaign proved to be successful.

In 2013, the committee dug up a congressional resolution from 1783 ordering the portrait to be "placed in the room in which Congress meets." Congressman Chris Van Hollen (D-MD), got the ball rolling again in the House of Representatives, and Sen. Robert Menendez (D-NJ), a Cuban-American, Chairman of the Senate Foreign Relations Committee led the movement in the US Senate.

Recognition should also be given to Mimi Lozano for her assistance on both securing honorary U.S. Citizenship and getting the Gálvez portrait hung. Mrs. Lozano is the webmaster of *Somos Primos*, a newsletter for Hispanic Americans. She has about 8,000 subscribers to her free newsletter. Some 1.2 million people look at her web page each month. Mrs. Lozano encouraged Latinos to contact their congressmen.

Manuel Olmedo Checa, was the Gálvez association member in Malaga, Spain who unearthed the 1783 letter. He knew that a portrait with an impressive provenance was kept in a private collection in Malaga, Spain. That painting had reputedly been commissioned by Spanish King Carlos III to honor Gálvez after his return from the Americas. A well-known Spanish artist, Carlos Monserrate, offered to copy the portrait as a donation.

## Portrait of Gálvez Hanging in the U. S. Congress

And so it was that in June, 2014, committee chairman, Teresa Valcarce received a lushly brushed oil painting, roughly 3 feet by 4 feet, of Bernardo de Gálvez, posed in an elegantly embroidered suit with a medal pinned to his chest. Because of the intervention of President General Dooley, the Daughters of the American Revolution displayed it until the end of November, 2014, when a crew hung it on the west wall of the U.S, Capital, room S-116, a compact but ornate room used by the Senate Foreign Relations Committee uses to host official coffees with heads of state.

There was a small celebration on Tuesday, December 9, 2014 in the Hall of the Committee of affairs outside of the Senate of the United States.

Bernardo de Gálvez is well deserving of both honors in 2014. He was a highly intelligent, well trained and industrious military officer, who planned the defeat of the English up the Mississippi River, and uprooted them from their heavily fortified fortresses in Mobile, Pensacola and Nassau. He rose to become the king's primary representative in the Western Hemisphere - all before reaching age 46. "But for" Bernardo de Gálvez and the assistance of King Carlos III, those of us in America would still be flying the British Union Jack.

So, we should join with Benjamin Franklin, Patrick Henry, Thomas Jefferson and George Washington, and give our thanks to Spain for its assistance.

# THE FIRST AMERICAN DOLLAR WAS A SPANISH COIN

The first legal-tender coin to circulate in the American colonies was the Spanish gold half Escudo coin, so it was America's "First gold dollar." It was the backbone of America's economy before and during the American Revolutionary War. Except for some small mintage in Boston, coins from Spain were the coins most used both in colonial

**Spanish Gold Coins minted in México City were in circulation in the colonies before the American Revolutionary War.**

times and up until the first coins were minted by the US Mint in 1793. Spanish coins continued to be legal tender until 1849. Picture if you will that these coins jingled in the pockets of George Washington, Thomas Jefferson, and Benjamin Franklin.

The coins, used from colonial America until the mid-19th century came from all over the world: Spain, Portugal, France, and England. The vast majority of them were Spanish coins because during this period of time Spain controlled the world's supply of gold and silver.[187]

**General Bernardo de Gálvez, Governor of New Spain, funneled gold and silver coins, arms, ammunition, medical supplies, uniforms and tents to General George Rogers Clark at Ft. Nelson, and to George Washington via Ft. Pitt. One of the three originals of this portrait hangs in the office of the SAR President General. The second graces the grand lobby of the Gálvez Hotel in Galveston, TX. The location of the third is unknown.**

Most of the silver and gold coins in circulation in the colonies during the Revolutionary War were minted in México City. These coins were transported overland to Veracruz, and shipped to Havana.

Carlos III had millions of these coins delivered to Bernardo Gálvez in New Orleans. From him the Spanish government donated many of these coins to the Americans. These coins were in addition to those jointly donated by Spain and France through the dummy corporation in Paris.[188] From 1776, the number of

---

[187] *The Journal of the Colonial Williamsburg Foundation.*

[188] See "Spain's Involvement in the American Revolutionary War", by E. F. Butler, *SAR Magazine*, Summer 2009, Vol. 104, No. 1, pp. 20-25.

Spanish coins in circulation in the colonies increased dramatically.

The type of Spanish colonial silver coin design in the colonies was a milled coin. The great majority of these coins were struck at the México City mint. Others were minted in Santiago (very rare), Lima, Guatemala, Bogotá (very rare) and Potosi (México) mints in the time period of 1732 to 1772. Such silver coins were in common use before, during and after the American Revolutionary War. Virginia, Massachusetts and Connecticut each passed laws making Spanish coins a legal tender.[189] The first cent was minted in Massachusetts in 1787, and its stated value was 1/100$^{th}$ of Spanish "Dollar."[190]

**Spanish silver coin minted in México City.**

This silver coin, valued at 8 *Reales*, came to be known as a "piece of 8", which could be cut into 8 "bits". This coin has become famous in American history as the principal coin of the American colonists[191]. One "bit" was worth 12 ½ cents, so 25 cents became known as "two bits."[192]

---

[189] *A Guide Book of United States Coins*, R.S. Yeoman, 43$^{rd}$ ed., 1990, p. 6.

[190] *A Guide Book of United States Coins*, id at p. 9.

[191] *A Guide Book of United States Coins*, id at p.2.

In 1771 the México City mint began minting the final type of Spanish colonial silver coin design in the New World.

Each silver and gold coin carried the bust of Carlos III on the obverse. They were struck at the México, Lima, Bogotá, Guatemala, Potosi', Santiago, Popayan, and Cuzco mints in the time period of 1771 to 1825. Spain's coins started carrying the bust of Carlos III in 1771.

Around the world this coin was known as the "pillar dollar" because of the two pillars shown on the reverse of the coin. These pillars symbolize the two huge escarpments that border the entrance into the Mediterranean: Gibraltar, which was historically part of the Spanish mainland, and Ceuta, the other monolith off the Mediterranean coast of Morocco. Although Gibraltar has been in the hands of the

**America's First Gold Dollar, adopted as legal tender by the US Congress in 1788.**

British for over

---

[192] *Complete Encyclopedia of U.S. and Colonial Coins*, by Breen, Walter. New York, NY: Doubleday Publishing, 1987.

200 years, the Spaniards still consider it part of their homeland.

After the Treaty of Paris concluded the revolution, the US Congress in 1788 officially adopted as legal tender, the Spanish half Escudo of the series which commenced in 1771, with the profile of Carlos III, King of Spain. Thus Carlos III was depicted on the first US gold Dollar!

Since Congress could have just as easily selected a coin from France,[193] Portugal, Sweden or Holland, it is suggested that our founding fathers were very appreciative of the support given by Spain, which started even before the Declaration of Independence was signed. So, it can be argued that Carlos III was viewed by our founding fathers as our most important ally during the revolution.[194]

---

[193] Nothing in this article should be construed in such a way as to minimize the valuable contributions to the American Revolutionary War by France. The king of France was the nephew of Carlos III. Under the agreement between them in early 1776, they were to provide equal amounts of financial and logistical support through the dummy corporation in Paris. France also provided about 8,000 soldiers, who fought the English in the colonies, as well as providing many ships at the battle of Yorktown. Both Spain and France were indispensible allies, without the support from each, our cause would have failed. Some 17,000 Spanish troops fought in the American campaign.

[194] As a practical matter, one of the reasons this coin was selected as the official US currency was the fact that it was already so widely circulated. It was so widely circulated because of the sheer number of these coins provided to the colonists by our Spanish allies.

**Coins were** primarily used because of the loss of faith in the Continental Dollar of the US, which resulted in the expression "it's not worth a Continental." The primary exception was the common use of the Spanish Milled Dollar, which was backed by the Spanish coins.

A Forty Spanish Milled Dollar Certificate

# SAR TRIP TO SPAIN AND GIBRALTAR[195]

## Hosted by President General Ed Butler and First Lady, Robin

### May 9 – 21, 2010

Fantastic! Wonderful! Great! These were just a few of the words from SAR participants and their families at the conclusion of the SAR trip to Europe. Thirty-three SAR members and their families took part in the SAR 2010 Tour of Spain. During our week in Spain, we:

Laid a wreath at the tomb of Carlos III at the royal crypt in El Escorial;

Toured El Cid's Toledo;

Chartered the new Spain SAR Society and the Spanish SAR Ladies Auxiliary, and inducted new officers in both organizations;

Met with US Ambassador to Spain, Alan Solomont at the US Embassy;

Toured Madrid, including the Royal Palace, Royal Armory, Naval Museum and the Prado;

---

[195] This article is an edited version of my article published in the *SAR Magazine* in 2010.

Had an audience with HRH Crown Prince Filipe de Borbón;

Had an audience with the Mayor and city leaders of Marcharaviaya, the ancestral home of General Bernardo Gálvez, and participated in ceremonies dedicating a plaque on the museum wall of the city; and

Had an audience with the Mayor of Malaga.

The SAR trip to Spain was part of the theme of the author's year as SAR President General, which was "Honor Spain".

On our first evening in Spain, we enjoyed dinner with Steve and Joy Renouf at the Restaurant Botin (from 1715 A.D.) – the oldest restaurant in the world according to *Guinness Book of Records*, which Robin and I had enjoyed on our last visit. Steve, current Vice President General of the SAR, served as liaison with the travel agent and with the Spanish DAR to coordinate the tour and meetings.

On our second day we enjoyed a private car tour with Steve Renouf and his wife Joy. In our new Mercedes, we drove north to **Moncanares El Real Castle,** where we visited the magnificent castle where the movie "El Cid" was filmed. It was built in 1475, and was in perfect condition. This wonderful castle was appropriately decorated with period furniture, carpets over tile floors, statuary, and weapons. The interior walls were covered with lovely large ancient tapestries and enormous oil paintings.

The following day our entire group enjoyed a panoramic city tour of the third largest city in Europe, Madrid, Spain, during which we passed through over 300 acres of large public parks. These parks were originally royal hunting grounds. The city also boasts hundreds of small parks and planted areas, filled with blooming flowers and colorful hedges. Most streets in central

Madrid are tree lined. Early construction called for underground irrigation. Some of the things that make Madrid so beautiful are the numerous round-abouts which contain impressive fountains and monuments, many of which are covered in gold-leaf.

The Prado Museum is one of the finest museums in the world. On our visit to the Prado, we were divided into two groups. Our guide focused on the Spanish painters: Velasquez, Goya and El Greco. Robin and I loved the marble tables inlaid with semi-precious stones, with the large golden lions at each corner of the table base. Each lion was depicted with a paw on the world globe. The globes were made of lapis.

Robin and I had forgotten the magnificent beauty of the Royal Palace. It is no longer the residence of the royal family, but it is still used for state events. The Throne Room is just as it was when used by Carlos III, who built the palace in 1764. Carlos also built the Prado Museum and several of the magnificent fountains downtown. Additionally, it was he who started factories to make tapestries, carpets, porcelain, crystal, china, and furniture.

In the reconstructed dining room, which once was three separate rooms, 146 people can be served dinner at the same table! Several state rooms in the palace have floors of inlaid marble, and beautiful tapestries and oil paintings cover most walls. The furniture was elegant. Most of the men loved the armoury. It was filled with hundreds of suits of armour, some of which were made to protect horses and a few designed for children. At one time it was considered stylish for children to wear armour.

One of El Cid's large battle swords was in a case near the entry. Display cases were overflowing with ancient pistols, knives, swords, rifles, maces, lances, helmets, shields and breast plates. One of the more interesting pieces in the collection was a 7-foot long rifle. The Crown Jewels were no longer on display, although one of our group said he spotted an emerald encrusted crown in the armoury.

The following day we drove north to El Escorial, the burial site for ancient Spanish Royalty, including Carlos III. When the Monastery was built in the 1570s by King Philip II, El Escorial was in the center of Spain. Philip wanted to also make it the center of the Catholic Anti-Protestant Movement. At the time, Madrid was occupied by the Moors to defend against attack by Christians in the north.

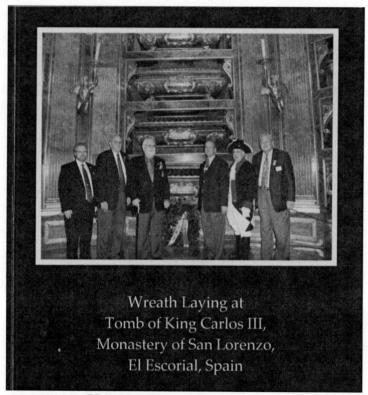

Wreath Laying at
Tomb of King Carlos III,
Monastery of San Lorenzo,
El Escorial, Spain

**Photo courtesy of Steve Renouf.**

After a wonderful five course lunch with wine at Las Viandas Restaurant, we were given a 2 ½ hour guided tour of the **San Lorenzo de Escorial Monastery**. It is the largest building in the Spanish empire.

Our visit took us to the **Basilica**, which was modelled after the Vatican. As King Philip aged, he could not get around very well. For this reason, he had apartments made for himself and the queen on the sides of the altar. That way, he could lie in bed and listen to mass. From the windows of King Philip's apartment, one could see the beautiful sculptured hedge gardens below.

The primary purpose of our visit was to lay a wreath at the tomb of Carlos III. The ceremony took place in the crypt beneath the Basilica. For a short period we had the crypt to ourselves. Although Philip II constructed the Basilica, it was Carlos III who established the royal crypt. Sarcophagi with royal remains were stacked four high in this circular tomb. The tomb of Carlos III was 2$^{nd}$ from the top in the above photo. In my remarks during the SAR wreath laying ceremony, I commented on the agreement between Carlos III and his young nephew, French King Louis XVI, to assist the Americans. Other members of the royal family were interred in tombs on the next level up from the crypt. The lids on each sarcophagus were intricately carved.

On Friday May 14, 2010, the SAR had its Royal Audience with Crown Prince Felipe. The week before we arrived, King Juan Carlos I had undergone lung surgery. The Madrid newspaper that day stated that Prince Felipe was serving as the "acting king" during Juan Carlos' period of recuperation. Our audience was not at the Royal Palace. It was at the beautiful Zarzuela Palace, where the Royal Family resides.

When we arrived at the gates, we underwent a passport check. It was about a 7 kilometer drive through the beautiful landscaped grounds to the palace. Robin and I both thought it resembled the Texas Hill Country. Dozens of deer calmly grazed in the shade of large oak trees. Just in front of the palace we went through a second security gate.

**Judge Ed Butler presents the SAR International Medal to Crown Prince Felipe (Photo courtesy of Palace photographer).**

As we alighted from our bus we were ushered into the palace and into a beautiful waiting room. The Major Domo took me into the large audience room and explained how the ceremony was to be conducted. Prince Felipe stood in the center of the room directly under the center chandelier. I entered the room first and was greeted by him. Robin followed and I introduced her to the Crown Prince.

Once everybody had shaken hands with the Prince, we posed for a group photo of the audience. At that time he gave us a formal greeting and welcome to the palace. Then Prince Felipe asked us to circle around him in the center of the room. At that time he asked me to deliver my remarks (which had been sent to the palace for review weeks earlier). Those remarks are attached as Appendix J.

When I presented him with the commemorative SAR Spain Medal, he asked me to pin it on his lapel. Lindsey Brock presented him with the Florida Society's Last Naval Battle Medal, and I also awarded him the Texas Society Gold Gálvez Medal. He then expressed his appreciation for the SAR informing the public about Spain's participation during the American Revolutionary War. He also expressed his appreciation for the medal and gifts.

Prince Felipe was very personable. Robin and I had a nice chat with him about my upcoming article about General George Rogers Clark and Clark's relationship with General Bernardo De Gálvez. Crown Prince Felipe again complimented me on my published articles about Spain. With a big smile on his face he asked me to write a book about Spain's help to America during the revolution. Then he said "I want you then to write a screen play so it can be made into a movie, and I want Antonio Banderas to play the part of Bernardo de Gálvez!" I told the prince that I could write the book, but we would have to leave it up to Hollywood about the movie.

I invited him to participate in the SAR Spain Society Charter Ceremony. Our audience lasted for an hour. As we departed, we presented him similar medals for the king, and extended our well wishes for his speedy recovery. In July I received a personal letter from King Juan Carlos, expressing his gratitude for the presents. See Appendix M. Late that afternoon, there was an official visit with US Ambassador Alan Solomont at the U.S. Embassy.

The following day was May 15th, San Isidro Day, and it was also the 150th anniversary of the opening in Madrid of the "Gran Via", a wide street in the center of the city. Saint Isidro is the patron saint of Madrid, and almost everything was closed except restaurants and museums. It was pure luxury to sleep late. After a late breakfast, Robin and I took a taxi to the Thyssen Museum for a delightful art lover's afternoon.

That evening our group was bussed to la **Gran Peña private club**, located on La Gran Via. It is the oldest private club in Spain. Our hosts were Martin Fernandez de Navarrete, **Marques De Santa Cruz** and his lovely wife. He was the Deputy Manager of the Rioja Winery. The Marques greeted us at the front door and ushered us into a large reception room. Waiters in white coats circulated among the group offering tempting appetizers and champagne. Once everybody was served he welcomed us to the club and introduced his wife, who was expecting their first son in two weeks. To our hosts and our members I offered the following toast:

*¡Salud, y dinero, y amor, y tiempo para disfrutarloes!*[196]

We were then invited into a large private dining room. At the center table were seated our hosts, the Butlers, Sympsons, and the Brocks. Robin sat on the Marquis' right. The Marquis and his wife both spoke excellent English. Years before he had worked in the US as a banker. At dinner, we were served three different wines – one from each of his vineyards.

---

[196] In English: Health, Wealth, and Love, and time to enjoy them all.

Photo courtesy of Steve Renouf.

Both the Marques and his wife were very personable. We learned that he is a direct descendant of El Cid, the famous Spanish warrior. There is an image of El Cid on his business card. After dinner we were given a private tour of this historic club. As we left the Marques, there were fireworks in the sky to celebrate, San Isidro Day, and the streets were crowded with revelers. It had been a wonderful evening.

On Sunday there was a full day excursion to Toledo, which was about an hour's drive south of the city. First, we circled this expansive fortress city to discover how impressive it was from afar. The city was started by the Romans in 200 BC. In the $5^{th}$ century AD the Moors invaded and remained until 1492 – the year Columbus discovered America. It is a typical medieval city which sits high over the river below.

Over the front door of the cathedral was a stone carving of the coat of arms of Ferdinand and Isabella (my ancestors) – the Catholic Kings. In 1492 Ferdinand and Isabella moved to Granada, where they are both now buried.

Monday morning we walked to the Spanish Naval Museum for a private visit for our group, arranged by the Madrid Navy League. It was very expansive, with large oil paintings, huge ship models, and interesting nautical memorabilia. We also got to visit the Spanish Naval Headquarters in the adjoining building, which was a beautiful palace.

That afternoon a bus took the group to **Iglesias San Jorge**, an Episcopal church. There we conducted the SAR Spain Society Charter Ceremony. First, each member, including the dual members, signed the charter application. It was my pleasure to induct several new members, and to present them their respective SAR certificates and rosettes. I inducted the new officers of the Spain Society, and then presented the SAR Spain Charter to Don Francisco Enrique de Borbón y Escasny, the Duke of Seville, who was the charter president of the Spain Society.

Founding of
SAR Spain Society
Madrid, Spain

**President General Butler Inducting Don Francisco Enrique de Borbón y Escasny, The Duke of Seville, as President of the Spain Society, Sons of the American Revolution in Madrid, Spain, in May, 2010. Photo courtesy of Steve Renouf.**

The main tour was over on Tuesday. About half our group headed home, but 16 of us flew to Malaga, Spain on Spanair for a three-day tour of the province of Andalucía on the southern

Mediterranean coast of Spain. When we arrived in Malaga, we went directly to the mountain village of Marcharaviaya – the birthplace of General Bernardo de Gálvez.

This scenic village was built upon the ruins of an ancient Arabic settlement and its name is derived from Arabic *Machxar Abu Yahya*, which means "Abu Yahya's Court." Macharaviaya was known as "Little Madrid" as a result of the prominence of the Gálvez family in the Spanish court.

The village's mayor, Antonio Campos Garin, and councilors greeted us at City Hall, where in Spanish, I thanked them for Spain's contribution to the American Revolution and presented the mayor with a SAR Spain Medal. A walking tour of the village followed with visits to General Gálvez' birthplace and the church of San Jacinto where the Gálvez family is buried.[197] Commemorative prayers were offered in *Plaza Bernardo De Gálvez* beneath the SAR plaque dedicated in 1997, which we rededicated.

This was followed by the dedication of a new bronze plaque at the **Museum de los Gálvez**, commemorating this visit. The plaque has the author's name on it as the leader of the visit. Our final event in Macharaviaya was an *al fresco* festive multiple-course luncheon that had been prepared and served by the ladies of the village. As we departed, each participant was given a box containing two bottles of the wine they produced in the village, and a box of grapes from which the wine is made.

The group returned to Málaga to visit the **Nereo shipyards** where an exact replica of the brig *Gálveztown* is under construction. The *Gálveztown* was commanded by Bernardo de

---

[197] Both Bernardo and his father are buried in México City.

Gálvez during the capture of Pensacola in 1781. We observed fitting of one of the oak frames in the keel of the ship, and each of us were privileged to sign our names on the frame.

We had some free time in Malaga due to the cancellation of the ferry to Tangier, Morocco. Strong winds and high seas prevented the ferry from operating. The old city was very romantic with colorful flowers growing from pots hanging in front of each building. When we stopped for refreshments, strolling musicians serenaded us.

We then proceeded to **Málaga's City Hall** where we ascended the imperial staircase to the Hall of Mirrors, where we were greeted by the Cultural Minister. The Hall of Mirrors is used when there are important presentations by the city. I expressed our thanks to the people of Malaga, who financially supported the Americans through their contributions to Gálvez.

Our final stop in Málaga was the unusual **cathedral** with a completed north tower and unfinished south tower. The money for the south tower was given by the church to Bernardo Gálvez to be used to help finance the war in the American colonies during revolution. The unfinished south tower gives the cathedral its nickname of *The Minutia* (the one arm woman). An SAR plaque at the base of the tower commemorates this contribution. There is also a DAR plaque on the church wall.

The following day we journeyed to **Gibraltar**,[198] the British overseas territory overlooking the Straits of Gibraltar. England

---

[198] During the American Revolutionary War, Gibraltar was a huge bone of contention between Spain, which claimed it, and England, which occupied it.

seized Gibraltar from Spain in 1704, and Gibraltar was given to England forever by the Treaty of Utrecht in 1713. Gibraltar is no longer a British naval base, but English warships do come in for maintenance, repairs and crew liberty. From Marbella, it was a 1 ½ hour ride. The main road into town took us across the airport runway!

Gibraltar played a huge role in the American Revolutionary War. The Siege of Gibraltar by Spain and France occupied scores of English ships and thousands of English troops, which could otherwise have been sent to America to fight the rebels.

Upon our arrival, we transferred to much smaller buses capable of negotiating the very narrow winding roads that lead to the top of "The rock." Although we didn't actually reach the top of the rock we visited "Europa Point" – the southernmost point of the Iberian Peninsula. We passed the Great Siege Tunnels that were constructed in 1779-83, when Spain laid siege on Gibraltar, to keep the English ships from the colonies.

A farewell dinner at the usual Spanish dinner hour of 10:00 p.m. was held at the Santiago Restaurant on the *Malecon* that overlooks the Mediterranean Sea. At midnight we said final goodbyes and returned to the hotel in time to pack for a very early morning flight.

As our flight departed Ma'laga the following day, I had a good feeling that the National Society Sons of the American Revolution had fulfilled our obligation to honor Spain for its assistance during the American Revolution.

# CONCLUSION

The American Revolution was a microcosm of a much larger world-wide conflict among three of the world's largest powers: England, France, and Spain; and to a lesser degree Holland (Netherlands) and Sweden. In addition to the conflict in the 13 colonies, Spain fought England up the Mississippi River, in the Northwest Territories, along the Gulf Coast, in the Caribbean, the Bahamas, India, and in Europe.

Far flung battles among the belligerents included the Philippines, Honduras, Nicaragua, Guatemala, Gala'pagos, Juan Ferna'ndez Islands, India, South Africa, Gibraltar and Menorca. The threat of invasion of the English homeland by France and Spain caused many warships and troops to be kept in England.

Captain John Paul Jones, who was being supplied by the Spanish firm of Joseph Gardoqui and Sons in Bilbao, Spain, kept that threat alive with his raids along the English coast, and his offshore sea battles with the English fleet. Spain captured 55 ships of the English fleet in British waters in one battle.

By creating a third front up the Mississippi River and along the Gulf Coast, Gálvez made it easier for Washington to defeat the British in the colonies. By keeping river traffic open up the Mississippi and Ohio Rivers, Washington's army received much needed food, arms, ammunition, supplies and more importantly, money. General George Rogers Clark, who commanded the second front west of the Allegheny Mountains also benefited from Spanish assistance.

To the list of foreign leaders to whom we owe our independence including Lafayette, Rochambeau, and de Grasse of France; Von Steuben and de Kalb of Prussia; Kosciuszko and Pulaski of Poland; we should add the name of Bernardo de Gálvez of Spain. His oil painting hangs in the lobby[199] of the SAR Headquarters in Louisville, KY.

The peace treaty signed on September 3, 1783, in Paris, gave Spain official control of the Floridas including all territory south of Natchez and east of the Mississippi River, and ended the American Revolutionary War. Only Canada remained in British control, as the new United States gained all territory east of the Mississippi River between Florida and Canada.

Reading between the lines, I hope I have shown that the hearts and minds of the typical Spanish soldier and Spanish militiamen were with the fight against the British. To assist the reader, I have documented centuries of warfare between Spain and England as an underlying cause for their fighting spirit.

Gálvez led at least 17,000 Spanish army and militia in North America in military action against the English during the American Revolutionary War. That number grows to over 20,000 if you include the attack on Nassau, and the Spanish military in California, who were at the ready. Add to that an equal number of Spanish military involved in the siege of Gibraltar and the thousands of casualties Spain incurred.

---

[199] During my term as President General of the National Society of the American Revolution, from July 2009 to July 2010, at my instruction, this painting hung in the President General's office.

Clearly, Spain was a valuable ally, and Galvez was the key player! Unmistakably, Galvez was the right man at the right time for the independence of the United States.

# BIBLIOGRAPHY

(Spanish) José Montero y Aróstegui. *Historia y descripción de la Ciudad y Departamento naval del Ferrol* (Google Ebook)

(Spanish) Rodríguez González, Agustín Ramón. *Victorias por mar de losEspañoles*. Biblioteca de Historia. Madrid 2006.

(Spanish) Fernández de Navarrete, Martín. *Biblioteca marítima española: obra póstuma del excmo: Vol. 2*

_____. "Texas and the American Revolution". *Southwestern Historical Quarterly*, vol. XCVIII, No. 4. Texas State Historical Society, Austin, 1995.

_____. "The El Paso Area in the Mexican Period, 1821-1848." *Southwestern Historical Quarterly 84* (July,1980).

_____. "The Population of the El Paso Area - A Census of 1784." *New México Historical Review 52* (October, 1977).

_____. *A Report on the Spanish Archives in San Antonio, Texas*. San Antonio: Yanaguana Society, 1937.

_____. *Bolton and the Spanish Borderlands*. Norman: University of Oklahoma Press, 1964.

_____. *Coronado, Knight of the Pueblos and Plains*. Albuquerque: University of New México Press, 1949.

_____. *Guide to Materials for the History of the United States in the Principal Archives of México*. New York: Kraus Reprint Corp., 1965.

_____. *Guide to Spanish and Mexican Land Grants in South Texas*. Austin: General Land Office, 1988.

_____. *Latin American Census Records*. Salt Lake City: *Instituto Genealogico e Historico Latinoamericano*, 1989.

_____. *Letters of an Early American Traveler, Mary Austin Holley; Her Life and Her Works, 1784-1846*. Dallas: Southwest Press, 1933.

_____. *Mexican Americans in Texas: A Brief History*. Arlington Heights, IL: H. Davidson, 1993.

_____. *Nacogdoches - Gateway to Texas: a Biographical Directory, 1773-1849*. Fort Worth: Arrow-Curtis Printing Co., 1974.

_____. *Nacogdoches County Cemetery Records*, Collected by Joel Barham Burk. Nacogdoches, Texas, 1974.

_____. *New Spain's Northern Frontier: Essays on Spain in the American West, 1540-1821*. Albuquerque: University of New México Press, 1979.

_____. *Spanish Exploration in the Southwest, 1542-1706*. New York: Barnes and Noble, 1959.

_____. *Texas in the Middle Eighteenth Century: Studies in Spanish Colonial History and Administration*. Austin: University of Texas Press, 1970.

_____. *The Colonization of North America*, 1492-1783. New York: MacMillan, 1923.

_____. *The Expedition of Don Domingo Teran de los Rios into Texas*. Austin, 1934.

_____. *The Opening of Texas to Foreign Settlement, 1801-1821*. Austin: University of Texas Press, 1927.

_____. *The San Saba Mission: Spanish Pivot in Texas*. Austin: University of Texas Press, 1964.

_____. The Spanish Abandonment and Reoccupation of East Texas, 1773-1779. Austin: s.n., 1906.

_____. *The Spanish Frontier in North America*. New Haven: Yale University Press, 1992.

_____. *The Texas Frontier., 1820-1825.* Harrisburg, PA: Harrisburg Publishing Co, 1900.

_____. *They Called them Greasers: Anglo Attitudes towards Mexicans in Texas, 1821-1900.* Austin: University of Texas Press, 1981.

_____. "Bernardo Gálvez's New Orleans Belle". *GUIDEPOST* [Madrid, Spain], July 5, 1996.

_____. *The Siege of Mobile, 1780, in Maps*. The Perdido Press, Pensacola, FL. 1982.

_____. "Diego Gardoqui: Spain's First Ambassador to the United States". *GUIDEPOST* [Madrid, Spain], July 5, 1996.

_____. *Coahuila y Texas, desde la consumación de la independencia hasta el trato de paz de Guadalupe Hidalgo*. México: n.p., 1945-1946.

_____. *El Fuerte del Cibola: Sentinel of the Bexar-La Bahia Ranches*. Eakin Press, Austin, 1992.

"American Independence: The Spanish Contribution", *Guidepost* [Madrid, Spain], July 1, 1994.

"Illinois in the American Revolution", *1890 Year Book, Illinois Society Sons of the American Revolution*, Wm. Johnson Printing Co., Chicago, 1896.

"The St. Joseph Mission" by Pare, George in *Mississippi Valley Historical Review, Vol. 17*, pp. 46-54.

1997 Map of México:
http://www.lib.utexas.edu/maps/americas/mexico_re197.jpg

Almaraz, Felix D. *Crossroad of Empire: The Church and State on the Rio Grande Frontier of Coahuila and Texas, 1700-1821.* San Antonio: University of Texas at San Antonio, Center for Archaeological Research, 1979.

Almaraz, Felix D. *Empty Echoes in a Howling Wind: Myths and Realities in the Tejano Community, from Cabeza de Vaca to Santa Anna.* El Paso, TX: University of Texas El Paso Press, 1986.

Archer, Christen I., *The Army in Bourbon México, 1760-1810*, Albuquerque, Univ. of NM Press, 1977.

Archives of the Indies, Seville Spain (New Spain soldier's records ).

Ashford, Gerald. *Spanish Texas: Yesterday and Today.* Austin: Jenkins Publishing Co., 1971.

Bancroft, Hubert H., *California Pioneer Register and Index Including Inhabitants of California, 1769-1800*, Bancroft Library, Univ. of California, Berkeley.

Bancroft, Hubert H., *History of California*, 7 vols., Bancroft Library, Univ. of California, Berkeley.

Bancroft, Hubert H.. *History of North Mexican States and Texas.* 2 vols. San Francisco: History Co., 1886-1889.

Bannon, John Francis. *The Spanish Borderlands Frontier, 1513-1821.* New York: Holt, Rinehart, and Winston, 1970.

Barker, Eugene Campbell. "Notes on the Colonization of Texas". *Texas State Historical Quarterly*, Austin, 1924.

Beer, William. "The Surrender of Fort Charlotte, Mobile, 1780." *American Historical Rev., Vol. I* (July 1896), pp. 696-99.

Beerman, Eric. *Espana y la Independencia de Estados Unidos*. Madrid Spain; Editorial MAPERE, 1992, (in Spanish).

Beers, Henry Patna. *Spanish and Mexican Records of the American Southwest*. Tucson: University of Arizona Press, 1979.

Benson, Nettie Lee. *Texas as Viewed from México, 1820-1834*, 1987.

Biblioteca Nacional de México: http://biblional.bibliog.unam.mx/bib01.html .

Bisset, Robert. *The History of the Reign of George III. to Which Is Prefixed, a View of the Progressive Improvement of England, in Prosperity and Strength, to the Accession of His Majesty.* Vol. III (1820).

Bolton, Herbert E. *The Beginnings of Mission Nuestra Senora del Refugio.*

Bolton, Herbert F. *Athanase de Mezieres and the Louisiana-Texas Frontier, 1768-1780.*

Bolton, Herbert. *Texas In The Middle Eighteenth Century: Studies in Spanish Colonial History and Administration*, 1970 [976.4 Bolton, San Antonio Pub. Lib.]

Botta, Carlo. *History of the war of the independence of the United States of America* New Haven : N. Whiting publishing (1837) ASIN B002XXBVAU

Bowden, Jocelyn J. *Spanish and Mexican Land Grants in the Chihuahuan Acquisition*. El Paso.

Brinckerhoff, Sidney B., and Faulk, Odie B., *Lancer For the King: A Study of the Frontier Military System of Northern New Spain, with a Translation of the Royal Regulations of 1772*, Phoenix, Arizona Historical Foundation, 1965.

Bugbee, Lester Gladstone. *Some Difficulties of a Texas Empresario*. Harrisburg, PA: Harrisburg Publishing Co., 1899.

Butler, Judge Edward F., SR. "The United States First Gold Dollar was a Spanish Coin". *SAR Magazine*, Winter 2010, Vol. 104, No. 3, pp.23.

Butler, Judge Edward F., SR. "Chronology of Events Surrounding Spain's Participation in the American Revolutionary War". *SAR Magazine*, Winter 2010, Vol. 104, No. 3, pp.20-22.

Butler, Judge Edward F., SR. "Spain's Involvement in the American Revolutionary War", *SAR Magazine*, Summer 2009, Vol. 104, No. 1, pp. 20-25; reprinted from *NGS Newsmagazine*, The Magazine of the National Genealogical Society, Vol. 28, No. 2, Mar/Apr 2002, pp. 122-125, and Vol. 28, No. 5, Sep/Oct 2002, pp. 304-307.

California Pioneers:
http://www.ancestry.com/search/rectype/inddbs/1040.htm

Canary Islanders website:
http://freepages.genealogy.rootsweb.com/~brasscannon/ .

Carlos, Alfonso de. "Bernardo Gálvez: Un General Espanol en la Independencia de los EE. UU." *YA*. Madrid, Spain, July 4, 1976 (in Spanish).

Castaneda, Carlos E. *Our Catholic Heritage in Texas, 1519-1936.* 7 vols. Austin: Von Boeckmann-Jones Co., 1936.

*Catfish and Crystal*, by Kirschten, Ernest, 1960, Doubleday & Co., Garden City, NY

Catholic Archives of Texas: http://www.onr.com/user/cat/

Catholic Church Records of the New Spain Missions.

Caughey, John Walton, *Bernardo Gálvez in Louisiana 1776-1783*, Berkley, Univ. of CA Press, 1934; repub, Gretna, LA: Pelican Pub. Co., 1972.

Céliz, Fray Francisco. *Diary of the Alarcón Expedition into Texas, 1718-1719.* Translated by Fritz L. Hoffman. 2 vols. Los Angeles: Quivera Society, 1935.

Chao, Jesus J. "Myth and Reality: The Legacy of Spain in America". Essay presented on February 12, 1992 at the Institute of Hispanic Culture of Houston as a part of the Commemoration of the 500th Anniversary of the Encounter of Two Worlds.

Chapa, Juan Bautista. *Texas and Northeastern México, 1630-1690.* Austin: University of Texas Press, 1997.

Chavez, Thomas E. *Spain and the Independence of the United States; An Intrinsic Gift*; U. of N.M. Press, Albuquerque, 2002.

Chipman, Donald. *Spanish Texas, 1519-1821*, Austin: University of Texas Press, 1992 [976.402 Chipman, San Antonio Pub. Lib.].

Christian, Jane MacNab. *Spanish in the Southwest: An Historical Survey.* 1963.

Churchill, Charles Robert. *Bernardo Gálvez, Services to the American Revolution*; Louisiana Society, SAR, March, 1925.

Clark, Robert Carlton. *The Beginnings of Texas, 1684-1718.* Philadelphia: Porcupine Press, 1976.

Cleveland: The Arthur H. Clark Co., 1914

Coker, William S., and Coker, Hazel P. *The Siege of Pensacola, 1781, in Maps.* The Perdido Bay Press, Pensacola, FL, 1981.

Coleman, Roger E. *The Arkansas Post Story.* Southwest Cultural Resources Center, Prof. Papers, No. 12. Eastern National, 1987. Repub. Div. of History, Southwest Cultural Resources Center, SW Reg., NPS, DOI, 2002.

Connor, Seymour V., *Texas In 1776/A historical Description*, Jenkins Pub. Co, Austin, 1975.

Crespi, Juan. *First Expedition into California, 1769-1770, A Description of Distant Roads.*

Cruz, Gilbert R. *Let There Be Towns; Spanish Municipal Origins in the American Southwest, 1610-1810.* College Station, TX: Texas A & M Univ. Press, 1988.

Cummins, Light Townsend. *Spanish Observers and the American Revolution, 1775-1783*; LSU Press, Baton Rouge, 1991.

Dart, Henry P., ed. "West Florida: The Capture of Baton Rouge by Gálvez, September 21st, 1779." *Louisiana State Historical Quarterly, Vol. 12* (April 1929), pp. 25-65.

De La Garza, Rodolfo 0. *Texas Land Grants and Chicano Mexican Relations: A Case Study.* Austin: University of Texas Press, 1986.

De La Teja, Jesús F. *San Antonio de Béxar: A Community on New Spain's Northern Frontier.* University of Texas at Austin, 1988.

De Leon, Arnoldo. *Apuntes tejanos*. Ann Arbor: University of Michigan Press, 1978.

De Leon, Arnoldo. *La cominidad tejana*. México City: Fondo de Cultura Econ6mica, 1988.

De Ville, Winston, *Louisiana Soldiers In The American Revolution*, Smith Books, Ville Platte, LA, 1991.

De Ville, Winston, *Settlers of Cabanocey and La Fourche in the Spanish Province of Louisiana During the American Revolution*, Ville Platte, LA, 1993.

Del Hoyo, Eugenio, and McLean. *Diario Y Derrotero (1777-1781) por Fray Juan Augustin de Morfi; Noticias Geograficas E Historicas Del Noreste De México; Instituto Technologico De Estudios Superiores De Monterrey*; Monterrey, MX, 1967 (in Spanish).

Derkum, Adam C., "Spanish Families of Southern California", Family History Library, Salt Lake City, UT, microfilm rolls 1597975 through 1597979.

DeVoe, Thomas. "The Spanish Regiment of Louisiana." *Bull Schott, Vol.2* (March 1979), pp. 45-47.

Dura, Juan. "Espana y la Independencia Norteamericana: 1776-1783 – La Ayuda Economica Fue Vital par alas Colonias". *YA*, Madrid, Spain, July 4, 1976. Edited and translated by Alan K. Brown. San Diego State University Press, 2002.

Edwards, Charles. *Texas and Coahuila*. New York: Osborn and Buckingham Printers, 1834.

Ericson, Carolyn R. and Joe E., *A Guide To Texas Research*. ISBN # 911317-55-4.

Ericson, Carolyn Reeves. *Citizens and Foreigners of the Nacogdoches District, 1809-1836.* Nacogdoches, Texas, 1981

Feldman, Lawrence H., *Anglo-Americans In Spanish Archives/Lists of Anglo-American Settlers in the Spanish Colonies of America*, General Pub. Co., Baltimore, ISBN # 0-8063-1313-7, 1991.

Fernandez y Fernandez, Enrique. *Spain's Contribution to the Independence of the United States*, Washington, DC: Embassy of Spain, 1985.

*Fort History, Fort St. Joseph Archaeological Project*, Western Michigan Historical Soc.

Gálvez, Bernardo de. "Diary of the Operations of the Expedition against the Place of Pensacola, Concluded by the Arms of H. Catholic M., under the Orders of the Field Marshall Don Bernardo Gálvez." Trans. by Gaspar Cusachs. *The Louisiana Historical Quarterly, Vol. 1* (January 1917), pp. 44-84.

Gamio, Manuel. *The Mexican Immigrant*. New York: New York Times/ Arno Press, 1969.

Garcia, Genero, ed. *Historia de Nuevo Leon: Con noticias sobre Coahuila, Texas, y Nuevo México*. México City: Libreria de la Vda. de Ch. Bouret, 1909.

Garcia, Richard A., comp. and ed. *The Chicanos in America, 1540-1974: A Chronology and Fact Book*. Dobbs Ferry, NY: Oceana Publications, 1977.

Gayarre, Charles. *History of Louisiana*. 4 vols. New Orleans: 1879.

Gomez Canedo, Lino. *Primeras exploraciones y poblaciones de Texas, 1686-1694*. Monterrey.

Gomez, Mardonio. *Compendio de historia antigua completa de Coahuila y Texas*. Saltillo:Gutierrez Ibarra, Celia. *Como México perdió Texas: analisis y transcripción del informe secreto de*

*Juan Nepomuceno Almonte*. México City: Instituto Nacional de Antropologia e Historia, 1987.

Gordon, William. *The history of the rise, progress, and establishment of the Independence of the United States of America*, Books for Libraries Press (1969) ISBN 978-0-8369-5024-3

Guthrie, William. *A New Geographical, Historical And Commercial Grammar And Present State Of The World, Complete With 30 Fold Out Maps - All Present.* J. Johnson Publishing. London (1808) ASIN B002N220JC

Haarmann, Albert W. "The Spanish Conquest of British West Florida, 1779-1781." *Florida Historical Quarterly, Vol. 39* (October 1960), pp. 107-134.

Habig, Marion Alphonse. *Spanish Texas Pilgrimage: The Old Franciscan Missions and other Spanish Settlements of Texas, 1632-1821.* Chicago: Franciscan Herald Press, 1990.

Haring, C.H. *The Spanish Empire in America.* New York City. Harcourt, Brace & World, Inc., 1947.

Hatcher, Mattie Austin. Captain Francisco Amangual's Diary, 1808 Expedition from San Antonio to Santa Fe. S.l.: s.n., 1934.

Haynes, Robert V., *The Natchez District and the American Revolution*, 1976.

Hinojosa, Gilberto Miguel. *A Borderlands Town in Transition: Laredo, 1755-1870.* College Station, TX: Texas A&M Press, 1983.

Hispanic Soldiers in California:
http://freepages.history.rootsweb.com/~havnar/ca-hispanic.html.

*Hispanic Texas: A Historical Guide*, 1922 [917.64046 Hispanic San Antonio Pub. Lib.

Holmes, Jack D. L., "Some Irish Officers in Spanish Louisiana." *The Irish Sword, The Journal of the Military History Society of Ireland, Vol. 6* (1963-1964), pp. 234-47.

Holmes, Jack D. L., *Honor and Fidelity: The Louisiana Infantry Regiment And The Louisiana Militia Companies, 1766-1821*, Birmingham, 1965.

Hough, Granville W. and N.C., *Spain's Arizona Patriots in its 1779-1783 War With England During the American Revolution, Part III*, Spanish Borderland Studies, 1999, Soc. of Hispanic & Ancestral Search Press, Midway City, CA.

Hough, Granville W. and N.C., *Spain's California Patriots in its 1779-1783 War With England During the American Revolution, Part I*, Spanish Borderland Studies, 1998, Soc. of Hispanic & Ancestral Search Press, Midway City, CA.

Hough, Granville W. and N.C., *Spain's California Patriots in its 1779-1783 War With England During the American Revolution, Part II*, Spanish Borderland Studies, 1999, Soc. of Hispanic & Ancestral Search Press, Midway City, CA.

Hough, Granville W. and N.C., *Spain's Louisiana Patriots in its 1779-1783 War With England During the American Revolution, Part VI*, Spanish Borderland Studies, 2000, Soc. of Hispanic & Ancestral Search Press, Midway City, CA.

Hough, Granville W. and N.C., *Spain's New* México *Patriots in its 1779-1783 War With England During the American Revolution, Part IV*, Spanish Borderland Studies, 1999, Soc. of Hispanic & Ancestral Search Press, Midway City, CA.

Hough, Granville W. and N.C., *Spain's Texas Patriots in its 1779-1783 War With England During the American Revolution,*

*Part V*, Spanish Borderland Studies, 2000, Soc. of Hispanic & Ancestral Search Press, Midway City, CA.

Hough, Granville W., "California In The Revolutionary War,", *SAR Magazine*, Winter 1999, Vol. XCIII, No. 3, reprinted at http://www.sar.org/sarmag/CRW.html.

Hughes, Arin E. *The Beginnings of Spanish Settlement in the El Paso District*. Berkeley: University of California Press, 1914.

Ielman, Chester V., *Guide to Microfilm of Bexar Archives 1717-1803*, Austin: University of Texas Archives, 1967.

Institute of Texan Cultures. *The Spanish Texans*. San Antonio: Institute of Texan Cultures, 1972.

Jackson, Jack. *Los Mestenos: Spanish Ranching in Texas*, Texas A & M. Univ. Press, College Station, TX, 1986.

James, James Alton. "Oliver Pollock, Financier of the Revolution in the West." *Mississippi Valley Historical Review* (1929), XVI.

Jones, Oakah L. *Los Paisanos, Spanish Settlers on the Northern Frontier of New Spain*. Norman: University of Oklahoma Press, 1979.

Knowlton, Clark S. "Spanish and Mexican Land Grants in the Southwest: A Symposium." Fort Collins, CO: *The Social Science Journal*, 1976.

Kuether, Allan J., *Military Reform and Society in New Granada, 1773-1808.* Gainesville: The Univ. Presses of Florida, 1978.

LaFarelle, Lorenzo G. *Bernardo Gálvez: Hero of the American Revolution*. Eakin Press, Austin, TX, 1992.

Land grants, deeds, sales, wills and estates, powers of attorney, contracts, military discharges, law suits, laws, proclamations, military reports and other records created by Spanish administrators. Texas State Archives, Austin, TX.

Lang, James. *Conquest and Commerce - Spain and England in the Americas*. New York: Academic Press, 1975.

Langley, Lester D., *Struggle for the American Mediterranean, United States-European Rivalry in the Gulf-Caribbean, 1776-1904*. Athens: The Univ. of Georgia Press, 1969.

Llull, Francisco Ferrer, and Hefter, Joseph. "The Spanish Louisiana Regiment in the Floridas, 1779-1781." *Military Collector & Historian, Vol. 16* (Fall 1964), pp. 79-80.

Louisiana Sons of the American Revolution, *Gálvez and Other Louisiana Patriots*.

Lund, Harry. Harry Lund Collection, 1594-1967. (manuscripts).

Marshall, Douglas W., and Peckham, Howard W. *Campaigns of the American Revolution: An Atlas of Manuscript Maps.* U. of Mich. Press, Ann Arbor, 1976.

Martinello, Marian L., and Robinson, Thomas H. *San Antonio: The First Civil Settlement in Texas: A Guide for Teachers K-12*; Canary Islands Descendants Assoc., San Antonio, TX, 1981.

Martinez, Antonio. *The Letters of Antonio Martinez, Last Spanish Governor of Texas*. Austin: Texas State Library, 1957.

Matovina, Timothy M. *Tejano Religion and Ethnicity*: San Antonio, 1821-1860. Austin: University of Texas Press, 1995.

McAllister, Lyle N. "The Reorganization of the Army of New Spain, 1763-1766." *Hispanic American Historical Review, Vol. 33* (February 1953), pp. 1-32.

McDermott, John Francis, ed. *The Spanish in the Mississippi Valley 1762-1804.* Urbana: Univ. of Illinois Press, 1974.

McWilliams, Carey. *North from México: The Spanish Speaking People of the United States*. Philadelphia: J.B. Lippincott Co., 1949.

Mechan, J.L. "Northern Expansion of New Spain, 1522-1822: A Selective Descriptive Bibliographical List." *Hispanic American Historical Review 1* (1927).

Meier, Matt S. and Feliciano Ribera. *Mexican Americans, American Mexicans: From Conquistadors to Chicanos*. New York: Hill and Wang, 1993.

Montejano, David. *Anglos and Mexicans in the Making of Texas, 1836-1986*. Austin: University of Texas Press, 1987.

Montemayor, E. A. and Beerman, Eric. *Yo Solo: The Battle Journal of Bernardo Gálvez during the American Revolution*. Polyanthos, New Orleans, 1978.

Mora, Carl. "Spain and the American Revolution; The Campaigns of Bernardo Gálvez." *Mankind: The Magazine of Popular History, Vol. 4* (August 1974), pp. 50-57.

Morfi, Juan Agustin. *History of Texas, 1673-1779*. Albuquerque: The Quivira Society, 1935.

Morrison, Richard. *Eyewitness Texana: A Bibliography of Firsthand Accounts of Texas Before 1860*. Austin: W. M. Morrison Books, 1992.

Mullen, Thomas, Jr.. "The Hibernia Regiment of the Spanish Army." *The Irish Sword: The Journal of the Military History Society of Ireland, Vol. 8* (1967-1968), pp. 218-25.

Mullins, Marion D. *The First Census of Texas, 1829-1836*. Washington, D.C.: National Genealogical Society, 1962.

Mundo Lo, Sara de. *Bibliography of Hispanic American Collective Biography*. Boston: G.K. Hall and Co., 1980.

Mundo Lo, Sara de. *Index to Spanish American Collective Biography*. Boston: G.K. Hall, 1981.

Murphy, W.S. "The Irish Brigade of Spain at the Capture of Pensacola, 1781." *Florida Historical Quarterly, Vol. 38* (January 1960), pp. 216-25.

Murry, Mildred L., *Spanish Mysteries And Missions During The American Revolution/A Resource Guide For Teachers* (California).

Nachbin, Jac, ed. "Spain's Report of the War with the British in Louisiana." *The Louisiana Historical Quarterly, Vol. 15* (1932), pp. 468-81.

Nachogdoches Archives, University of Texas Archives, Austin, TX.

National Society, Daughters of the American Revolution, *Louisiana Patriots, 1776-1783*, Washington, 1994.

*Nine Grants in Fee Simple of Eleven Leagues ... Located on the Rio Nueces*. Texas: n.p., 1935.

Nogales, Luis G. *The Mexican Americans: A Selected and Annotated Bibliography*. Stanford: Stanford University Press, 1971.

Northrop, Marie, *Spanish-Mexican Families of Early California 1769-1850, Vols. 1* (revised 1987) & *Vol. 2* (1984).

ÓConnor, Kathryn. *The Presidio La Bahia Del Espiritu (i.e. Espiritu) Santo De Zuniga, 1721 to 1846*, 1966. [976.4123 ÓConnor San Antonio Pub. Lib.]

ÓGorman, Edmundo. *Historia de las divisiones territoriales de México*. 4th ed. México City: Editorial Porrua, 1968.

*Old Fort St. Joseph, or Michigan Under Four Flags*, by McCoy, Daniel, pp. 5-8, Delivered before the Michigan Pioneer and Historical Soc. at its Thirty –Second Annual Meeting, June 7, 1906; Wynkoop Hallenbeck Crawford Co., State Printers, Lansing, 1907.

ÓRourke, Thomas P. *The Franciscan Missions in Texas, 1690-1793.* Washington, D.C.: Catholic University of America, 1927.

Osario, Alfred J. "Organization and Description of El Regimiento de la Luisiana, 1777-1783." *Military Notes, Vol. 3* (Spring 1978), pp. 218-224.

Parkinson N, C. *The Trade Winds: A Study of British Overseas Trade during the French wars, 1793–1815.* Routledge; Reprint edition. ISBN 978-0-415-38191-8

Parks, Virginia. *Pensacola: Spaniards to Space-Age*; Pensacola Historical Soc., 1986, rev. 1996.

Platt, Lyman D., *Census Records for Latin American and the Hispanic United States*, General Pub. Co., Baltimore.

Powell, Philip Wayne. *Tree of Hate: Propaganda and Prejudices Affecting United States Relations with the Hispanic World.* Ross House Books, Vallecioto, CA, 1985.

Poyo, Gerald F., ed. *Tejano Journey, 1770-1850.* Austin: University of Texas Press, 1996.

Primm, James Neal, *Lion of the Valley: St Louis*, 1981, Pruitt Pub. Co., Boulder.

Ramsay, David. *Universal History Americanized, or an Historical View of the World from the Earliest Records to the Nineteenth Century, with a Particular Reference to the State of*

*Society, Literature, Religion, and Form of Government of the United States of America*. Vol. VI (1819)

*Residents of Texas 1782-1836* (3 Vols.), Institute of Texan Cultures, San Antonio, TX   ISBN # 911317-33-3.

Richardson, Rupert N. *Texas: The Lone Star State*. Englewood Cliffs, NJ: Prentice Hall, 1988.

Robles, Vito Alessio. *Acapulco, Saltillo, y Monterrey en la historia y en la leyenda*. México City: Editoral Porida, 1978.

Rosenbaum, Robert J. *The History of Mexican Americans in Texas: A Preliminary Survey*. Boston: American Press, 1980.

Rubio, Abel G. *Stolen Heritage: A Mexican American's Rediscovery of his Family's Lost Land* Grant. Austin: Eakin Press, 1986.

Sanchez, Ramiro. *Frontier Odyssey: Early Life in a Texas Spanish Town*. Austin: Jenkins Publishing Co., 1981.

Scott, Florence, J. *Historical Heritage of the Lower Rio Grande*. *3rd ed.* Rio Grande City, Texas: La Retama Press, 1972.

*Secretaria de Gobernacion Indice del ramo de provincias internas*. 2 vols. México City: Archivo General de la Naciόόn, 1967.

Shayegan Special Collection, The University of Texas - Pan American Univ. Library, Edingburg, TX.

Sonnichsen, C.L. *Pass Of The North: Four Centuries On The Rio Grande*,  El Paso, Texas: Texas Western Press, 1968 [976.4 Sonnichsen San Antonio Pub. Lib.]

Syers, William Edward. *Texas, the Beginning, 1519-1834.* Waco, TX: Texian Press, 1978.

Syrett, David. *The Royal Navy in European Waters during the American Revolutionary War*. University of South Carolina Press. ISBN 978-1-57003-238-7

Taylor, Virginia, *Spanish Archives Of The [Texas] General Land Office*.

*Tejano Origins In Eighteenth-Century San Antonio*, 1991. [976.4351 Tejano San Antonio Pub. Lib.].

Temple, Thomas Workman, II, "Soldiers and Settlers of the Expedition of 1781," *Historical Society of Southern California Quarterly* (1931).

*Texas And The American Revolution*; The Univ. of Texas at San Antonio, Institute of Texan Cultures, 1975.

Texas Before the Republic: The Béxar Archives: http://www.cah.utexas.edu , by Don Pusch, November 2000.

Texas General Land Office. *An Abstract of the Original Titles of Records in the General Land Office of Texas*. Austin: Pemberton Press, 1964.

The Battle of Fort San Carlos, May 26, 1780, Commemoration Committee pub.

The London Encyclopedia.

*Universal Dictionary Of Science, Art, Literature And Practical Mechanics, Comprising A Popular View Of The Present State Of Knowledge*, Vol X. Thomas Tegg Publishing. London (1829).Campbell, Thomas. *Annals of Great Britain from the ascension of George III to the peace of Amiens,* Printed by Mundell and Co., for Silvester Doig and Andrew Stirling (1811).

*The Revolution in the Environs of St. Louis*, Parkin, Robert E., 82 pp. no date. lists 13 Prime Sources, plus maybe 50+ Bibliography (some 28 pages of unit rosters) and biós of some citizens at the time.

*The Battle of St. Louis, 26 May 1780*, McDermott, John Francis, MO Historical Society Bulletin, #36, #2. April 1980, pp 143-151. ALSO by McDermott as editor *The Spanish in the Mississippi Valley*, 1762-1804, pp 314-405. He indicates "thoroughly documented" in this.

*The Scots Magazine. MDCCLXXXIII. Volume XLV,* Edinburgh: Printed by Murray and Cochran.

Thomson, Buchannon Parker. *Spain: Forgotten Ally of the American Revolution*. North Quincy, Massachusetts: The Christopher Pub. House, 1976.

Thonhoff, Robert H. *The Texas Connection With The American Revolution*; Eakin Press, Burnet, TX, 1981.

Thonhoff, Robert H. *The Vital Contributions of Spain In the Winning of The American Revolution.* Self published in English and Spanish, undated.

Thonhoff, Robert H. . *The Vital Contributions of Texas In the Winning of The American Revolution.* Self published in English and Spanish, undated.

Timmons, Wilbert H. *The Anglo-Americans Advance into Texas, 1810-1830.* Boston: American Press, 1981.

Tinch, Helen Pearl. *Days of Colonial Texas*. Houston: American Museum Society of Houston Baptist College, n.d.

Twitchell, Ralph F. *The Spanish Archives of New México*. Cedar Rapids, IA: Torch Press, 1914.

Villere, Sidney Louis, *The Canary Island Migration To Louisiana, 1778-1783*, General Pub. Co., Baltimore, 1972.

Vito, Alessio Robles . *Coahuila y Texas en la epoca colonial.* México City: Editorial *Cultura*, 1938

Volo, M. James. *Blue Water Patriots: The American Revolution Afloat*, Rowman & Littlefield Publishers, Inc. (2008) ISBN 978-0-7425-6120-5

Weber, David J. *The Spanish Frontier in North America.* Yale U. Press, New Haven, 1992.

Weber, David J. *Foreigners in their Native Land: Historical Roots of the Mexican Americans*. Albuquerque: University of New México, 1973.

Weber, David J. *The Mexican Frontier, 1821-1846: The American Southwest under México*. Albuquerque: University of New México Press, 1982.

Weber, David J., ed. *Troubles in Texas, 1832: A Tejano Viewpoint from San Antonio*. Dallas: Wind River Press, 1983.

Weddle, Robert S. and Thonhoff, Robert H. *Drama & Conflict: The Texas Saga of 1776*. Madrona Press, Austin, 1976.

Weddle, Robert S. *San Juan Bautista: Gateway to Spanish Texas*. Austin: University of Texas Press, 1968.

Welsh, Agatha Maverick. *The First Explorers of Texas: 1527-1537.*

Whitaker, Arthur Preston, *The Spanish-American Frontier: 1783-1795: The Westward Movement and the Spanish Retreat in the Mississippi Valley*. Lincoln: University of Nebraska Press, 1969.

White, Gifford E. *The 1840 Census of the Republic of Texas.* Austin: Pemberton Press, 1966.

Woods, Richard D. *Reference Materials on Mexican Americans: An Annotated Bibliography.* Metuchen, NJ: Scarecrow Press, 1976.

Wright, J. Leitch, Jr. *Florida in the American Revolution.* Univ. of Florida Press, Gainsville, 1975.

Wright, J. Leitch, Jr. *Anglo-Spanish Rivalry in North America.* Athens: The University of Georgia Press, 1971.

Yoakum, Henderson K. *History of Texas from its First Settlement in 1685 to its Annexation to the United States in 1846.* Austin: Steck, 1953.

# APPENDICES

# APPENDIX A

CASA DE S. M. EL REY
EL JEFE DE LA SECRETARIA
DE S. A. R. EL PRINCIPE DE ASTURIAS

Palacio de la Zarzuela
Madrid, /₹ de marzo de 2010

MR. EDWARD F. BUTLER SR.
President General of The Sar Magazine
Sons of the American Revolution
8830 Cross Mountain Trail
SAN ANTONIO, TX 78255-2014
U.S.A.

Estimado amigo:

Su Alteza Real el Príncipe de Asturias me encarga acusar recibo y transmitirle Su agradecimiento por el ejemplar N° 3 de la revista *The SAR Magazine, Sons of the American Revolution* que tan amablemente Le ha hecho llegar y, asimismo, que le envíe Su saludo afectuoso.

Reciba un atento saludo,

JAIME ALFONSÍN

rb

# APPENDIX B

EL JEFE DE LA CASA DE
S. M. EL REY

Palacio de La Zarzuela
Madrid, 5 de abril de 2010

Señor
EDWARD F. BUTLER
President General "The Nacional Society
Sons of the American Revolution"
8830 Cross Mountain Trail
SAN ANTONIO, TX 78255-2014 (USA)

Estimado amigo:

Le escribo en relación con el ofrecimiento que había formulado a Su Majestad el Rey y a Su Alteza Real el Príncipe de Asturias del nombramiento de socios fundadores de la nueva «Sociedad de España de "Los Hijos de la Revolución Americana"».

A este respecto, deseo señalarle que, si bien Su Majestad y Su Alteza Real valoran y aprecian su amable ofrecimiento, lamentablemente no les será posible corresponderlo, habida cuenta de que ante las numerosas solicitudes que, en este mismo sentido, reciben los distintos Miembros de la Familia Real y la imposibilidad de atender a todas ellas como sería Su deseo, hace tiempo que esta Casa ha adoptado el criterio, con carácter general, de declinar los nombramientos de carácter permanente.

No obstante lo anterior, me complace comunicarle que Su Alteza Real el Príncipe de Asturias recibirá a sendas representaciones de "The Nacional Society Sons of the American Revolution" y de la "Asociación Granaderos de Gálvez" en el curso de una audiencia, que tendrá lugar en el Palacio de La Zarzuela el viernes día 14 del próximo mes de mayo, a las 11'00 horas.

Con esta misma fecha me dirijo al Cónsul General de España en Houston, informándole en este mismo sentido y concretando detalles para la celebración de la audiencia.

Reciba un cordial saludo

ALBERTO AZA ARIAS

js

# APPENDIX C

CASA DE S. M. EL REY
EL JEFE DE LA SECRETARIA
DE S. A. R. EL PRINCIPE DE ASTURIAS

Palacio de La Zarzuela
Madrid, 2 8 de abril de 2010

Señor
EDWARD F. BUTLER
President General "The Nacional Society
Sons of the American Revolution"
8830 Cross Mountain Trail
SAN ANTONIO, TX 78255-2014 (U.S.A.)

Estimado Presidente:

Le escribo como continuación de nuestra carta del pasado día 5 para comunicarle que debido a ajustes en la agenda de Su Alteza Real el Príncipe de Asturias, recibirá a sendas representaciones de "The National Society Sons of the American Revolution" y de la "Asociación Granaderos de Gálvez" en una audiencia, que tendrá lugar en el Palacio de La Zarzuela el viernes día 14 del próximo mes de mayo, a las 10'30 horas, en lugar de las 11'00 como le comunicaba en la referida carta.

Reciba un cordial saludo,

JAIME ALFONSÍN

vg

# APPENDIX D

CASA DE S. M. EL REY
EL JEFE DE PROTOCOLO

PALACIO DE LA ZARZUELA
31 de mayo de 2010

Señor
EDWARD F. BUTLER
President General the National Society Sons of the American Revolution
8830 Cross Mountain Trail
78255-2014 San Antonio (TX) (Estados Unidos de América)

Estimado Señor:

Su Majestad el Rey me encarga que le traslade su agradecimiento más sincero por los obsequios que le ha hecho llegar con ocasión de la Audiencia concedida por Su Alteza Real el Príncipe de Asturias a la Sociedad Nacional Hijos de la Revolución Americana, celebrada el pasado 14 de mayo en el Palacio de la Zarzuela.

Su Majestad, que ha apreciado mucho esta atención, le envía un saludo muy afectuoso junto con sus mejores deseos, extensivo a todos los miembros de la Sociedad.

Reciba un saludo muy cordial,

Alfonso Sanz Portolés

ag.

## APPENDIX E

## RESOLUTION

### National Society Sons of the American Revolution

### In Congress Assembled

### Greenville, South Carolina - July 22, 2014[200]

**WHEREAS**, Spain supported the American Colonists during the American Revolutionary War, and

**WHEREAS**, Spain's primary representative in North America was General Bernardo de Gálvez, and

**WHEREAS**, General Bernardo de Gálvez assisted the colonists by providing money, arms, ammunition, uniforms, tents, medical supplies and other materials, and

**WHEREAS**, General Bernardo de Gálvez protected our western frontier from the British and its Indian allies by leading his Spanish army troops, Spanish Militia and other volunteers in battles at Manchak, Baton Rouge, and Natchez, and

**WHEREAS**, General Bernardo de Gálvez protected our southern frontier from the British and its Indian allies by leading his Spanish army and navy troops, Spanish Militia and other volunteers in battles at Mobile, Pensacola and the Bahamas, and at the time the 1783 peace treaty was concluded, was along with

---

[200] This resolution was drafted by Judge Edward F. Butler, Sr.. He introduced it before the SAR Congress and spoke on behalf of its passage.

the French, preparing to attack the two forts in Jamaica, Britain's strongest point in the Western Hemisphere, and

**WHEREAS**, General Bernardo de Gálvez protected our northwestern frontier from the British and its Indian allies by making his Spanish army and navy troops, Spanish Militia and other volunteers in battles at Ft. San Carlos, Ft. St. Joseph, and Arkansas Post, and

**WHEREAS**, General Bernardo de Gálvez protected our northwestern frontier from the British and its Indian allies by providing arms, ammunition, and other military supplies to General George Rogers Clark, who defeated the British at Kaskaskia, Cahokia, and Vincennes, and

**WHEREAS**, General George Rogers Clark credited General Bernardo de Gálvez and the support he had received from Spain through General Clark,

**WHEREAS**, General Bernardo de Gálvez provided arms, ammunition and other supplies to General George Washington through Ft. Pitt, and

**WHEREAS**, during his lifetime he received personal letters of appreciation from George Washington, Thomas Jefferson, Patrick Henry, Benjamin Franklin, King Carlos III of Spain and the United States Congress, and

**WHEREAS**, The U.S. Congress has previously honored other foreign Revolutionary War heroes French Compte Gilbert de Motier, Marquis de Lafayette in 2002, and Polish Kasimir Pulaski in 2007, by granting each with honorary U.S. Citizenship, and

**WHEREAS,** there are now Joint Resolutions pending in both the U.S. House of Representatives and the U.S. Senate, to confer Honorary United States Citizenship posthumously to Bernardo de Gálvez y Madrid, Viscount of Galveston and Count of Gálvez, which Joint Resolutions are H. J. RES. 105 and S. J. RES. 38

**NOW, THEREFORE, BE IT UNANIMOUSLY RESOLVED BY The National Society Sons of the American Revolution,** assembled in Greenville, S.C. for its annual Congress on this the 22nd day of July, 2014 as follows:

1. That the NSSAR 2014 Congress Unanimously voted to endorse the passage of the Joint Resolutions pending in both houses of Congress to confer Honorary Citizenship to General Bernardo Gálvez y Madrid, Viscount of Galveston and Count of Gálvez
2. That a copy of this resolution be provided to members of the United States Senate and the United States House of Representatives, and
3. That a copy of this resolution be spread upon the minutes of the annual meeting of the society.

I, Lindsey Brock, President General of the National Society Sons of the American Revolution hereby certify that the above Resolution was unanimously adopted at the General Congress of the Society in Greenville, S.C. for its annual meeting on this the 22nd day of July, 2014.

S/ Lindsey C. Brock, President General 2014-2015

National Society Sons of the American Revolution

Attest:

S/ Thomas E. Lawrence, Secretary General

## Appendix F

## National Society Sons of the American Revolution

Aug. 1, 2014

The Honorable Jeff Miller

336 Cannon House Office Building

Washington D.C., 20515

Dear Congressman Miller,

By letter dated July 16, 2014 from then National Society Sons of the American Revolution (SAR) President General Joseph W. Dooley, you were advised that the SAR strongly supported H.J. Res. 105, granting honorary U.S. citizenship to General Bernardo Gálvez.

I am pleased to inform you that the enclosed Resolution in favor of Gálvez becoming an honorary citizen was **unanimously** adopted by annual Congress of the National Society on July 22, 2014. General Gálvez was the primary representative of Carlos III, King of Spain before and during the American Revolution.

King Carlos was the uncle of King Louis of France. By virtue of the "Bourbon family Compact" Spain and France agreed to provide equal sums of money to the cause for American Independence, which was forwarded through a French dummy corporation.

It was Gálvez who distributed much of the funds and who sent arms, ammunition, and supplies up the Mississippi and Ohio Rivers to George Washington through Fort Pitt, and to General George Rogers Clark at what is now Louisville. His Spanish army and militia forces drove the British out of the Mississippi River Valley and the Gulf of México, thereby preventing a British second front.

We strongly urge Congress to pass the joint resolutions.

Very truly yours,

Lindsey Cook Brock, President General 2014-2015

# Appendix G

## Cattle, Branded and *Orejano*, Exported from Texas under Governor Domingo Cabello, 1779–86

| Exporter | 1779 | 1780 | 1781 | 1782 | 1783 | 1784 | 1785 | 1786 | Total |
|---|---|---|---|---|---|---|---|---|---|
| Simón de Arocha | | 306 | {423<br>{419 | 186 | 330 | | 760 | 802 | 3,226 |
| Luis Mariano Menchaca | | | 300,<br>with Sambrano | 243 | {130<br>{427,<br>with A. Delgado | {144<br>{612 | 360 | | 2,216 |
| Felipe Flores | | | | 770 | | | 104 | 412 | 1,286 |
| Vizente Flores | | | 200 | | 75 | | 551 | 433 | 1,259 |
| Juan José Flores | | 440 | 120 | | {108<br>{229 | | | | 897 |
| Juan Barrera | | | | 84 | 274 | | | 373 | 731 |
| Julián de Arocha | 441 | | | | | | | 266 | 707 |
| Santiago Seguín | | | | | | 300 | | 281 | 581 |
| Manuel de Arocha | | | | 215 | | 119 | | 208,<br>with Calvillo | 542 |
| José Antonio Curbelo | | | | 414 | (308,<br>with M. Delgado) | | | | 414 |
| Marcos Hernández | | 1,234 | | | | | | | 1,234* |
| Antonio (le) Blanc | | | | 1,200 | | | | | 1,200* |
| José Andrés Hernández | 19 | | | | | | 160 | | 179 |
| Francisco de Arocha | 281 | | | | | | | | 281 |
| Sebastián Monjarás | 170 | | | | (330,<br>with F. Flores) | | | | 170 |
| Joaquín Flores y Zendeja | 138 | | | | | | | | 138 |
| Manuel Gonzáles | 30 | | | | 80 | | | | 110 |
| Mission Espada | | | 208 | | | | | | 208 |
| Manuel Delgado | | | | 308,<br>with Curbelo | | | | | 308 |
| Juan Monjarás | | | | 188 | | | | | 188 |
| Ignacio Calvillo | | | | | 50 | {55<br>{35 | 35 | (208,<br>with M. de Arocha) | 175 |
| Francisco Flores | | | | | 330,<br>with S. Monjarás | | | | 330 |
| Francisco Péres | | | | | 118 | | | 70 | 188 |
| José de Cárdenas | | | | | | 143 | | | 143 |
| Francisco X. Rodríguez | | | | | | 139 | | 165 | 304 |
| Juan José Pacheco | | | | | | 369 | | | 369 |
| Amador Delgado | | | | | (427,<br>with Menchaca) | | | 140 | 140 |
| Carlos Martinez | | | | | | 50 | | | 50 |
| Félix Gutiérrez | | | | | | 16 | | | 16 |
| Macario Sambrano | | | (300,<br>with Menchaca) | | | 150 | 103 | | 253 |
| Various | | | | | | | 50 | 224 | 274 |
| Total | 1,079 | 1,980 | 2,084 | 3,194 | 2,151 | 2,132 | 2,123 | 3,374 | 18,117ᵇ |

Source: BA.

Note: Some rancheros made more than one drive in a given year; this is noted by dual figures for that year, joined by a brace. Some made occasional joint drives with other rancheros; this is noted by giving the joint figure both places and the name of the partner. For one partner the information is given in parentheses, and these parenthetical numbers are not figured into the totals. Thus, joint drives contribute only once to the column and row totals.

* To Louisiana.

ᵇ Cabello's total was 18,449, an addition error of 332.

## Appendix H, p. 1

### Compañia Presidial de la Bahia

Noticia de las cantidades con que voluntariamente han contribuido los individuos de dicha compañia á S.M. para gastos de la presente Guerra contra Ynglaterra

**Nombres** — **P[eso]s.**

| | |
|---|---|
| Capitan.. Vacante | |
| Teniente.. D. Sebastian Rodriguez | 3.0.0. |
| Alferez 1.º D. Francisco Vasquez | 5.0. |
| Idem 2.º D. Jose Antonio Cadena | 2.5. |
| Capellan B.r D.n Jose Miguel Martinez | 2.5. |
| Armero. Pedro Arrambide | " 8. |
| Sargento Francisco Rios | 1.5. |
| Juan Chirino | " 5. |
| Mario Maldonado | 1.0. |
| Tambor Jose Encarnacion Bocanegra | " 5. |
| Cavos... Ermenegildo Gomez | 1.0. |
| Miguel Bezerra | 1.0. |
| Fernando Galan | 1.0. |
| Tomas de la Garza | 1.0. |
| Agustin de la Garza | 1.0. |
| Jose Maria Ramon | 1.0. |
| Francisco de la Garza | 1.0. |
| Diego Cadona | 1.0. |
| Soldados. Alexo de Leon | 1.0. |
| Francisco Venitez | " 8. |
| Diego Menchaca | " 8. |
| Antonio del Rio | " 8. |
| Juan Andres Contreras | " 8. |
| Jose de la Garza | " 8. |
| Juan Maria Flores | " 8. |
| Carlos Delgado | 1.0. |
| Francisco Villafranca | " 8. |
| D. Andres Benito Courbiere | " 5. |
| Lorenzo Treviño | " 8. |
| Antonio Vela | " 8. |
| Pam. à la Buelta | 42.0. |

## Appendix H, p. 2

Suma de la Buelta 420.
Gerardo Arellano............. " " 0.
Juan Jose Estrada............ " " 8.
Jose de Luna................. " " 0.
Pantaleon de la Garza........ " " 8.
Antonio Aldrete.............. " " 8.
Tomas Ullan.º de la Garza.... " " 8.
Dionicio Lienon.............. " " 0.
Pedro Grane.................. " " 0.
Francisco Vasquez............ " " 7.
Refugio Vela................. " " 8.
Ygnacio Cruz................. " " 8.
D. Jose de Jesus Alderete.... " " 0.
Jose Trexo................... " " 0.
Domingo Trexo................ " " 8.
Juan Franc.º Chirino......... " " 8.
Bernabé del Rio.............. " " 8.
Fran.co Ant.º Urrutia........ " " 7.
Bernabé de la Garza.......... " " 8.
Nepomuceno de la Garza....... " " 7.
Jose M.ª de la Garza 2º...... " " 8.
Julian de Soto............... " " 8.
Juan Jose Ernandez........... " " 8.
Juan Jose Ortis.............. " " 7.
Antonio Aguirre.............. " " 8.
Bernabé Treviño.............. " " 6.
Trinidad Ramon............... " " 8.
Jose M.ª Arrañaga............ " " 8.
Pedro Cevallos............... " " 8.
Jose Maria Riosas............ " " 6.
Loreto Becerra............... " " 8.
Sacramento Vasquez........... " " 8.
Jose M.ª de la Garza 2º...... " " 0.
Luiz Mendoza................. " " 8.
Francisco Peña............... " " 4.
Antonio de Leon.............. " " 0.
Pedro Castañeda.............. " " 8.
Diego Chirino................ " " 8.
Faustino de Luna............. " " 2.
Para à enfrente 720.

## Appendix H, p. 3

Suma de enfrente ... 720.
Xavier de los Santos .... „ „ „ 8.
Lorenzo de la Garza ....... „ „ „ 8.
Jose M.ª Cortinas 1º ... „ „ „ 9.
Francisco Gutierrez ..... „ „ „ 8.
Juan Jose Manzolo ..... „ „ „ 8.
Pedro Ernandez .... „ „ 9.
Antonio Vasquez ..... „ „ „ 7.
Jose Maria de Luna .... „ „ „ 8.
Manuel Florez ....... „ „ 8.
Zaragoza Rios ........ „ „ 8.
Juan Jose Gamez ...... „ „ 6.
Tomas Marias ...... „ „ 8.
Blaz Esparza ... ..... „ „ 8.
Francisco Albarado ... „ „ 9.
Jose Lazo .......... „ „ 3.
D. Ant.º de Mezieres ... „ „ 9.
Jose Antonio Martinez „ „ 9.
Juan Jose Cevallos ..... „ „ 9.
Ermeregildo de la Cruz ... „ „ 8.
Jose Maria Valdez .... „ „ 8.
Manuel de la Garza .... „ „ 8.
Valentin de la Roza ..... „ „ 8.
Vizente Duran ...... „ „ 8.
Lorenzo Cortes ........ „ „ 8.
Jose M.ª Cortinas 2º ..... „ „ 9.
Total ... „ 900.

Bahia del Espiritu Santo 31. de Diziembre de 1798.

Jose Miguel del Moral

# Appendix I, p. 1

# Donativo Report From Alta, CA[201]

### MISSION CHART
### ALTA CALIFORNIA MISSIONS, PRESIDIOS, PUEBLO –
### THEIR LOCATION, FOUNDING DATES AND DONATIONS
### TO COMPLY WITH KING CARLOS III'S 1780 ROYAL ORDER

| Missions, Presidios, Pueblo and Location Today | Date of Founding | Amount of Donation |
|---|---|---|
| San Diego de Alcala – San Diego (See Mission San Juan Capistrano) | 1769 | |
| • Presidio | 1769 | $515.00 |
| San Carlos Borromeo de Carmelo – Carmel | 1770 | 106.00 |
| • Royal Presidio at Monterey | 1770 | 833.00 |
| San Antonio de Padua de los Robles –Jolon | 1771 | 122.00 |
| San Gabriel Archangel (of the Earthquakes) – San Gabriel | 1771 | 134.00 |
| San Luis Obispo (of the Pichos Fixlini) de Toloso – San Luis Obispo | 1772 | 107.00 |
| Our Lady of San Francisco de Asis (Dolores) – San Francisco (Includes Mission, Presidio and Mission Santa Clara) | 1776 | |
| • Presidio | 1776 | 373.00 |
| San Juan Capistrano – San Juan Capistrano (Includes Mission San Diego) | 1775, 1776 | 229.00 |
| Santa Clara de Asis – Santa Clara (See Mission San Francisco, Presidio) | 1777 | |
| Pueblo de Los Angeles – Los Angeles | 1781 | 15.00 |
| Santa Barbara Presidio – Santa Barbara | 1782 | 249.00 |
| San Buenaventura – Ventura | 1782 | |
| Santa Barbara – Santa Barbara | 1786 | |
| La Purisima Concepcion – Lompoc | 1787 | |
| Santa Cruz – Santa Cruz | 1791 | |
| Nuestras Senora de la Soledad – Soledad | 1791 | |
| San Jose – San Jose | 1797 | |
| San Juan Bautista – San Juan Bautista | 1797 | |
| San Miguel Archangel – San Miguel | 1797 | |
| San Fernando Rey de Espana – San Fernando | 1797 | |

# Appendix I, p. 2

| Mission Founding Dates and Compliance with 1780 Royal Order (continued) | |
|---|---|
| San Luis Rey de Francia - San Luis Rey | 1798 |
| Santa Ines - Solvang | 1804 |
| San Rafael Arcangel - San Rafael | 1817 |
| San Francisco Solano - Sonoma | 1823 |

Total donations from missions; $2,683 Spanish Silver dollars

Compiled by Dr. Mildred L. Murry, California State Society Daughters of the American Revolution

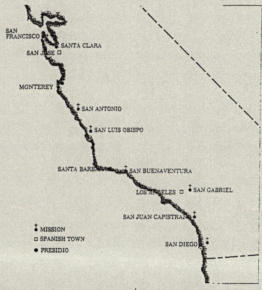

The above map shows Alta California at the time of Fr Junípero Serra's death in 1784. There were nine missions, four presidios and two pueblos -- all built in just fifteen years. *James L. Copley Library.*

Appendix J, p. 1

# REMARKS OF JUDGE EDWARD F. BUTLER, SR., 106TH PRESIDENT GENERAL NATIONAL SOCIETY SONS OF THE AMERICAN REVOLUTION TO HIS ROYAL HIGHNESS CROWN PRINCE FELIPE DE BORBÓN AT THE ROYAL AUDIENCE IN THE ROYAL PALACE IN MADRID - May 14, 2010

*Your Royal Highness, distinguished guests, ladies and gentlemen:*

*When I was inducted as the President General of the National Society Sons of the American Revolution last July, I delivered a short acceptance speech. In that speech I stated that the theme of my administration would be to honor Spain for its assistance to our revolutionary fathers, which enabled us to become free.*

*This year I have spent dozens of hours researching the relationship between Virginia Militia General George Rogers Clark; General Bernardo Gálvez Spanish Governor of Louisiana; and Fernando de Leyba, Governor of North Louisiana. General Clark was the senior American military officer west of the Allegheny Mountains. After the war he credited his success to the wonderful assistance he received from Spain in the war, including arms, ammunition, money, food and supplies. He described in detail the time and effort expended by Governors Gálvez and Leyba. King Carlos III, promoted both, and granted a coat of arms to Gálvez, with the motto "Yo Solo" for his personal victory at the siege of Pensacola.*

*In the first three editions of the SAR Magazine this year there have been four feature articles about Spain's assistance to the*

## Appendix J, p. 2

*colonists during the American Revolutionary War. Hopefully, next year, I will submit another article for publication in the SAR Magazine.*

*It was decided this year that on the middle week-end of June, 2014, the Topic for the **SAR Conference on the American Revolutionary War**, will be "Spain's Assistance during the American Revolutionary War". Ten history scholars will present their respective professional papers in historic San Antonio, Texas – my home. Once fully vetted, the SAR will publish a book each year with copies of each of these papers, with perhaps others.*

*With the helpful assistance of one of our SAR members in Madrid, and the hard work of one of our DAR ladies here, I will be allowed to present a charter to the Spain SAR Society, and I understand that the Duke of Seville has agreed to serve as the charter president of the society.*

*The SAR Spain Charter Ceremony will be on May 17, 2010 at 4:15 p.m. at Iglesia St. Jorge's. Your Royal Highness, since you will be a charter member of this new society, and if your busy schedule would permit, we would be extremely honored and delighted to entertain you and your family at that ceremony.*

*The thirty-one SAR members and wives from the U.S. are here to pay honor to the wisdom and courage of your ancestor, Carlos III, who provided money, arms, ammunition, tents, uniforms and supplies to the American colonists. "But for" the support of Spain, the English flag might still be flying over our nation*

## Appendix J, p. 3

today. To honor Carlos III, we are placing a wreath at his tomb in El Escorial yesterday.

On behalf of the National Society Sons of the American Revolution it is my pleasure and honor to present to you the **SAR INTERNATIONAL MEDAL** with an accompanying certificate. Thank you for your very honorable public service and your support of the efforts of our SAR Society.

Now, Secretary General, J. David Sympson, the uncontested nominee for President General, 2010-2011 would like to make a present to you of, the **TEXAS GOLD GÁLVEZ MEDAL,** from our Texas SAR Society, of which both Mr. Sympson and I are members.

Next, Historian General Lindsay Brock, upon behalf of the Florida SAR Society will present to you **THE LAST NAVAL BATTLE MEDAL**.

If I may, I would also like to present you with one of my personal **SAR Recognition Coins**, to express my personal best wishes to you, the Royal Family, and the citizens of Spain.

We wish your father, King Juan Carlos, a speedy recovery and would like to leave with you similar awards for him.

Thank you very much for this audience.

## Appendix K[202]

**Money Paid by the Spanish Treasury in Havana to French Officials,
1779–1783
(All money in pesos unless stated otherwise)**

| DIRECT PAYMENTS | LOANS BETWEEN THE TWO GOVERNMENTS | LOANS ARRANGED BY FRANCISCO DE CABARRUS |
|---|---|---|
| 1. Nov. 1780—Given for assistance to hospitalized Spanish soldiers at Cape François—152,190 (livres) | 1. Nov. 1780—151,300. | 1. April, 1782—1,000,000 (650,000 to Cape François) (350,000 to Martinique) |
| 2. Nov. 1780—Turned over at Cape François for French troops stationed in Spanish Santo Domingo—60,000 | 2. June, 1781—To French fleet under Caballero de Monteil—68,656 | 2. Dec. 1782—1,000,000 (510,000 to Martinique) (490,000 to ?) |
| 3. June, 1781—Paid at Cape François for aid to Spanish soldiers—23,568 (livres) | 3. June, 1781—To Officials at Cape François—200,000 | 3. June, 1783—1,000,000 (? to Cape François) (? to Martinique) |
| 4. August, 1781—Payment for French troops stationed in Spanish Santo Domingo—100,000 | 4. August, 1781—To Officials at Cape François—100,000 | 4. 1785—1,000,000 (Royal Order issued to make above payment for loan made during the war, but it is not clear whether the funds were turned over to Cabarrus) |
|  | 5. August, 1781—To Admiral de Grasse—500,000 |  |
|  | 6. Sept, 1781—To Caballero Villegas for Martinique—1,000,000 |  |

Sources: For direct payments, see: Archivo General de Simancas (hereafter AGS), Secretaría de Marina (hereafter Marina), 420. Juan Bautista Bonet to Marqués González de Castejón, Havana, 26 Nov., 1780. AGN, Int., 56. Urriza a Mayorga, Havana, 3 Nov., 1780. AGI, SD, 1849, exp. 191. Caja cuenta de 1781, Ignacio de Peñalver y Cárdenas, Havana, 30 June, 1782. For the direct loans between Spain and France, see: AGN, Marina, 12, exp. 5, fojas (hereafter f. or ff.) 139–41. Urriza to Mayorga, Havana, 16 Oct., 1781. AGS, Secretaría y Superintendencia de Hacienda (hereafter Hac.), 2350. Estado . . . de Exército y Marina . . . de Junio, Ignacio Peñalver y Cardenas, Havana, 30 June, 1781. AGS, Hac., 998, f. A-5. Marqués de Zambrano to Miguel de Múzquiz, Madrid, 29 March, 1782. AGI, IG, 1578. Saavedra to J. Gálvez, Havana, 18 August, 1781. AGI, SD, 1668-A, exp. 1954. Urriza to J. Gálvez, Havana, 16 Jan., 1787. For loans from Cabarrus, see: AGI, SD, 1659, exp. 98. Urriza to J. Gálvez, Havana, 4 May, 1782. AGI, IG, 1583, exp. 1552. Urriza to J. Gálvez, Havana, 23 Feb., 1785. AGI, IG, 1583, exp. 933. Matias de Gálvez to J. Gálvez, México, 27 August, 1784. AGI, IG, 1583. Royal order to audiencia of Mexico, El Pardo, 19 Jan., 1785. The negotiations between Cabarrus and the Spanish government are contained in AGS, Hac., 997, folio 5.

---

[202] *Las Damas de la Havana, el Precursor, and Francisco de Saavedra: A Note on Spanish Participation in the Battle of Yorktown*, James A. Lewis, p. 99, citing *The Americas*, Vol. 37, No. 1 (July 1980, pp.83-89.

# Appendix L[203]

## Havana Residents Who Loaned Money for Admiral de Grasse's Expedition to Yorktown, August 16, 1781

| NAME | AMOUNT IN REALES | INTEREST (ALL LOANS WERE TO BE REPAID FROM THE FIRST SHIPMENT OF SPECIE FROM MEXICO) | AMOUNT REPAID IN REALES (SEPT. 24–OCT. 2, 1781) |
|---|---|---|---|
| 1. José Olzaval | 160,000 | 2% | 800,000 (plus 3,200 interest) |
| 2. Francisco del Corral | 200,000 | 2% | 248,000 (plus 4,960 interest) |
| 3. José Manuel López | 310,000 | 2% | 720,000 (plus 6,480 interest on 120,0 |
| 4. Juan Dias de Muñoz | 48,000 | 2% | 48,000 (plus 960 interest) |
| 5. Tomás de Evia[a] | 264,000 | none | 264,000 |
| 6. Lorenzo Quintana | 200,000 | 2% | 200,000 |
| 7. Manuel Quintanilla | 600,000 | 2% | 720,000 (plus 12,000 interest on 600, |
| 8. Pedro Valverde[b] | 160,000 | none | 160,000 |
| 9. Rafael Medina | 160,000 | 2% | 160,000 (plus 3,200 interest) |
| 10. Juan Paitcor | 608,000 | 1% | 816,000 (plus 12,160 interest on 608, |
| 11. Juan Uregué[c] | 240,000 | none | 240,000 |
| 12. Manuel Esteban[d] | 200,000 | none | 200,000 |
| 13. Carlos Tectorua[e] | 168,000 | 2% | 289,000 (plus 5,972 interest on 280,0 |
| 14. Ferrero Brothers | 160,000 | 2% | 240,000 (plus 3,200 interest on 160,0 |
| 15. Bartolome de Castro | 48,000 | 2% | 48,000 (plus 960 interest)8 |
| 16. Nicolás Varela | 48,000 | 2% | 144,000 (plus 960 interest on 48,000 |
| 17. Cristobal de Nis | 24,000 | 2% | 88,000 (plus 480 interest on 24,000 |
| 18. Pablo Sera | 160,000 | 2% | 320,000 (plus 3,200 interest) |
| 19. José Feu | 160,000 | 2% | 160,000 (plus 3,200 interest) |
| 20. Pedro Figueroa | 80,000 | 2% | 80,000 (plus 1,600 interest) |
| 21. Miguel Núñez | 112,000 | 2% | 112,000 (plus 2,240 interest) |
| 22. Doña Bárbara Santa Cruz[f] | 80,000 | none | 80,000 |
| 23. Jaime Boloix | 80,000 | 2% | 240,000 (plus 1,600 interest on 80,0 |
| 24. Francisco Asbert | 48,000 | 2% | 144,000 (plus 960 interest on 48,000 |
| 25. Pedro Peraza | 64,000 | 2% | 144,000 (plus 1,280 interest on 64,0 |
| 26. Pedro Martin de Leiba | 64,000 | 2% | 184,000 (plus 1,280 interest on 64,0 |
| 27. Cristoval Murillo | 16,000 | 2% | 16,000 (plus 320 interest) |
| 28. Francisco del Corral | 48,000 | 2% | (See second name above) |
| | 4,520,000 | | 6,865,000    70,132 int |

Source: AGI, SD, 1869, exp. 191. Caja Cuenta de 1781. Ignacio Peñalver y Cárdenas, Havana, 30 June, 1782.

Notes: a) Paymaster, Regiment of Guadalajara. b) Paymaster, Infantry Regiment of Havana. c) Paymaster, Regiment of Yberina. d) Paymaster, Regi of Soria. e) Festona? f) Marquesa de Cárdenas. g) Paid to Andrés Ferraris.

Note: The Exchequer turned over to the French 4,000,000 reales (500,000 pesos), evidently keeping the rest. Military unit's loaned approximately on of the total, and the treasury secured one-fourth of the total at no interest. It is quite possible that not all the creditors on this list were Spanish ci (See nos. 17, 19, 23, and 24). (Only one contributor was female. (See no. 21).

# Appendix M

HOUSEHOLD OF HIS MAJESTY THE KING
THE CHIEF OF PROTOCOL

PALACE OF ZARZUELA
31 May 2010

Mister
EDWARD F. BUTLER
President General the National Society Sons of the American Revolution
8830 Cross Mountain Trail
San Antonio, TX 78255-2014 (United States of America)

Esteemed Sir:

His Majesty the King entrusted to me transcribing his most sincere gratitude for the token gifts that were given to him on the occasion of the Audience granted by His Royal Highness the Prince of Asturias to the National Society Sons of the American Revolution, celebrated the past $14^{th}$ of May in the Palace of Zarzuela.

His Majesty, who very much appreciates this courtesy, sends a very affectionate greeting together with his best wishes, extended to all the members of the Society.

Receive a very warm greeting,

Alfonso Sanz Portolés

ag.

*TRANSLATION of original document in Castilian Spanish.*

## Appendix N

## CHRONOLOGY OF EVENTS SURROUNDING SPAIN'S PARTICIPATION IN THE AMERICAN REVOLUTIONARY WAR; NOTING OTHER IMPORTANT DATES BETWEEN SPAIN AND ENGLAND LEADING UP TO THE WAR

To better understand Spain's participation in the American Revolutionary War, the following list of significant events in chronological order is presented:

1337-1453   100 Year War. Aragon, Castile and Majorca were allied with France against England, which was allied with Aquitaine and Navarre.

1381-1382   3rd Ferdinand War. England was allied with Portugal against Castile.

1492   Ferdinand and Isabella financially provided Christopher Columbus with ships, crews, food and supplies on his search that led to the discovery of America.

1526-1530   War of the League of Cognac. England vs. Spain.

1540   A party led by two Spaniards, Francisco de Silvera and Juan de Villalobos were sent by Hernando de Soto to what is now Lee County, VA to search for gold.

1585-1604   First Anglo Spanish War

1586   British ships and soldiers attack the Spanish town of St. Augustine, FL

1588   The sinking of the Spanish Armada by Admiral Sir Francis Drake and Admiral Sir. Robert

| | |
|---|---|
| | Cross, was the main cause of Spanish hatred of the English. |
| 1589 | The destruction of the remainder of the Spanish fleet and the capture of Cádiz by Admiral Sir. Robert Cross, was the crowning blow of Spanish hatred of the English, which lasted well over 200 years. |
| 1598 | Vicente de Zaldivar led a Spanish expedition into the Buffalo Plains of Texas. |
| 1625-1630 | Second Anglo-Spanish War. |
| 1654-1660 | Third Anglo-Spanish War started by Oliver Cromwell. English forces attacked Spanish holdings in the Caribbean, Spanish Netherlands, Canary Islands and Spain. Spain lost Jamaica to the English in the 1670 Treaty of Madrid. |
| 1683 | Fernando del Bosque led a Spanish expedition into Texas. |
| 1689 | Alonzo de Leon led a second Spanish expedition into Texas. |
| 1690 | Alonzo de Leon led a third Spanish expedition into Texas. |
| 1691-1692 | Domingo Teran de los Rios led a fourth Spanish expedition into Texas. |
| 1693 | Gregorio de Salinas Verona led a fifth Spanish expedition into Texas. |
| 1709 | Father Isidro de Espinosa, Father Antonio de Olivares, and Captain Pedro de Aguirre led a sixth expedition into Texas. |

| | |
|---|---|
| 1713 | Spain was divested of its possessions in Europe at the conclusion of the War of the Spanish Succession. |
| 1716 | Domingo Ramon explored the missions and presidios in Texas. |
| 1718-1719 | Martin de Alarcon led a seventh Spanish expedition into Texas. |
| 1721-1722 | Marques de San Miguel De Aguayo led an eighth Spanish expedition in to Texas. |
| 1727 | Pedro de Rivera led the Spanish on the Rivera and Rubi's ninth expedition into Texas. |
| 1761 | The "Borbón Family[204] Compact", between France and Spain, provided that any nation which attacked one nation, attacked both; and that when one of the countries was at war, it could call upon the other for military or naval aid. |
| 1763 | End of the "Seven Years War" (also known as the "French and Indian War") between England and the Spanish-French Alliance. Spain lost Havana and Manila to the English. To get these forts back, Spain traded East Florida and West Florida to England. Spain received New Orleans from the French. |
| 1767 | Pedro de Rivera and Marques de Rubi led the Spanish military's tenth expedition into Texas. |

---

[204] The kings of Spain and France were both members of the Borbon family, and were cousins.

| | |
|---|---|
| 1768 | Caspar Jose' de Solis led the eleventh Spanish expedition into Texas. |
| 1 Dec. 1774 | The First Continental Congress forbade the importation of any British goods. |
| 1 Jan. 1775 | British Parliament forbade American colonies from importing guns and ammunition from any country. |
| 1 Sep. 1775 | The First Continental Congress forbade exports to Britain. |
| Bef. 4 Jul 1776 | Spain and France entered into a secret agreement with the colonists to support them in their rebellion against England.[205] |
| 1776-1779 | During the three years before Spain declared war on England, it provided credit to the colonists totaling 8 million *reales*, for military and medical supplies and food. |
| Aug. 1776 | General Charles Henry Lee, second in command to General George Washington, sent Captain George Gibson, with a group of 16 colonists, from Ft. Pitt to New Orleans, to obtain supplies from Spain. |
| Sept. 1776 | Spain sent 9,000 pounds of gunpowder to the colonists up the Mississippi River, and an additional 1,000 pounds by ship to Philadelphia. |

---

[205] The promise of secret support from both Spain and France surely gave confidence to the colonists prior to the signing of the Declaration of Independence.

| | |
|---|---|
| 25 Nov. 1776 | Carlos III ordered Gálvez to secretly collect intelligence about the British. Later, Gálvez was ordered to render secret help to the colonies. |
| 24 Dec. 1776 | Order issued by Minister of the Indies, Jose' Gálvez, to Luis de Unzaga y Amezaga, the Governor of Louisiana, instructing him to support the Americans. |
| Bef. July 1777 | Spain sent another 2,000 barrels of gunpowder, lead and clothing up the Mississippi to assist the colonists. King Carlos III made secret loans of 1,000,000 *livres*. Additional arms, ammunition and provisions were sent by the Spanish to General George Rogers Clark's posts along the Mississippi; and to George Washington's Continental Army. |
| 1777 | American Representative in France, Benjamin Franklin,[206] arranged for the secret transport from Spain to the colonies of 215 bronze cannon; 4,000 tents; 13,000 grenades; 30,000 muskets, bayonets and uniforms; 50,000 musket balls; and 300,000 pounds of gunpowder. |
| Sep. 1777 | By this time, Spain had already furnished 1,870,000 *livres tournaises* to the Americans. Much of this was contributed through a dummy |

---

[206] Since the colonies had not obtained their independence from England yet, France could not accept an Ambassador. Yet, Franklin, the "Representative" was afforded all the courtesies normally extended to other Ambassadors.

|  |  |
|---|---|
|  | corporation,[207] for which France mistakenly received total credit. |
| Oct. 1777 | Patrick Henry, as Governor of Virginia, wrote two letters to General Gálvez, thanking Spain for its help and requesting more supplies. Henry suggested that the two Floridas that Spain lost to England, should revert back to Spain. |
| 1778-1779 | American General George Rogers Clark obtained a considerable amount of his supplies from General Gálvez in New Orleans. These supplies were used in his victories over the British at Kaskaskia, Cahokia and Vincennes. |
| Jan.1778 | Governor Patrick Henry wrote another letter to General Gálvez, thanking Spain for its help and requesting more supplies. |
| Feb.1778 | The "Treaty of Alliance" between France and The United States, obligated Spain to assist France against the English. General Gálvez began to recruit an army, under the guise that it was for the defense of New Orleans. |
| Mar.1778 | U.S. Captain James Willing left Ft. Pitt with an expedition of 30 men, bound for New Orleans to obtain supplies for the war. They plundered the British settlements along the Ohio and |

---

[207] The famous "Rodrigue Hortalez and Company" served as the conduit for Spanish assistance. Its main director was the French playwright and statesman, Pierre Augustin Caron de Beaumarchais.

|  |  |
|---|---|
|  | Mississippi Rivers. General Gálvez welcomed them to New Orleans and assisted them in auctioning off of their British plunder. Gálvez sold them military arms and ammunition for their return trip to Ft. Pitt. |
| 1779-1782 | Spanish Ranchers along the San Antonio River between San Antonio and Goliad, sent between 9,000 to 15,000 head of cattle, several hundred horses, mules, bulls and feed to General Bernardo de Gálvez in New Orleans. The cattle were used to feed his troops and to provision George Washington's Continental Army at Valley Forge. |
| 1779 | All males, including Indians, over 18 in New Spain were required to become a member of the Militia in their respective areas. |
| Apr. 1779 | A secret treaty was entered into between the French Ambassador in Madrid, and Count Floridablanca, Spanish Secretary of State, which drew Spain into the conflict between the American Colonies and England. |
| 21 Jun. 1779 | Spain declared war on England. Carlos III, King of Spain, ordered Spanish subjects around the world to fight the English wherever they were to be found. General Bernardo Gálvez in New Orleans was ready for battle. French officials were ordered by the French Crown to cooperate with their Spanish neighbors in every way possible. Even de Grasse himself had orders to be of service to the Spaniards in operations against the British. The French and Spanish navies formed an armada of 104 ships to invade England. While waiting many crew members |

developed scurvy, typhus and smallpox, and thousands of them died. Britain took notice of the threat to their homeland. As a result, hundreds of British gunships that could have been deployed to the Americas, were kept at home; and thousands of soldiers were held at home in the event of an invasion. The action of Spain and France was an important element in our victory over England.

27 August - 7 Sep. 1779   General Bernardo de Gálvez led the Spanish Army at New Orleans up the Mississippi River 90 miles to attack Ft. Bute, in Manchak, Louisiana. Ft. Bute was surrendered by the English on 7 September 1779.

29 Aug. 1779   Carlos III, King of Spain, issued a proclamation that the main objective of the Spanish troops in America was to drive the British out of the Gulf of México and the Mississippi River.

20 Sep. 1779   General Gálvez' army captured Baton Rouge, and negotiated the surrender of the British fort at Natchez. By clearing the Mississippi River of British forces, Gálvez allowed Captain William Pickles to bring an American Schooner onto Lake Pontchartrain. Pickles seized the British privateer, *West Florida*, which had dominated the lake for two years.

8 Nov. 1779   Thomas Jefferson wrote to General Gálvez, expressing his thanks for Spain's assistance during the revolutionary cause.

1780   Carlos III issued a Royal Order requesting a one-time voluntary donation of two *pesos* per Spaniard and one *peso* per Indian in each

| | |
|---|---|
| | provincial site in Spain's New World Empire, to defray the expense of the war with England. This request for a "*donativo*" was viewed as a crown order, followed by a high level of participation. |
| 15 Jan. 1780 | John Adams visited Bilbao, Spain and met with Diego Gardoqui of Joseph Gardoqui and Sons. In one of the two letters sent by him from his Inn in Bilbao, John Adams wrote the following: "We have had the pleasure of finding Mr. Gardoqui and sons friends willing to collaborate with us in all aspects." Through the Bilbao merchant "Joseph Gardoqui e hixos,[208]" Spain sent 120,000 *reales* to the United States in pieces of eight in cash and payment amounting to 50,000 *reales* on other orders. These coins were used to support the U.S. public debt and gave rise to its own currency, the dollar. Through Joseph Gardoqui and Sons, Spain also provided 215 bronze cannon, 30,000 muskets, 30,000 bayonets, 51,314 musket bullets, 300,000 pounds of gunpowder, 12,868 grenades, 30,000 uniforms and 4,000 tents, with a total value of 946,906 *reales* to the United States. |
| 28 Jan. - 9 Mar. 1780 | Gálvez led the attack on Mobile. The siege lasted from 10 February to 9 March 1779, when the British surrendered. Gálvez was promoted to Field Marshall and was given command of all Spanish operations in America. |

---

[208] "hixos" is the same as "hijos" the current Spanish name for sons.

| | |
|---|---|
| Apr. 1780 | The Spanish fleet sailed from Cádiz, Spain to America to reinforce the army of General Bernardo de Gálvez. |
| 24 Jun. 1780 | Carlos III by royal order to the Governor of Havana, appointed Francisco de Saavedra as a Special Emissary to represent the Crown, giving him authority to make decisions regarding transfer of funds from the Royal Treasury in Havana. |
| 16 Oct.1780 | Field Marshall Gálvez led a Spanish fleet of 15 warships and 59 transport ships from Havana to attack Pensacola. Embarked were 164 officers and 3,829 men. |
| 18 Oct. 1780 | A hurricane hit the Spanish flotilla. Many were lost. The survivors retreated to Havana. For fear that the British might seek to retake Mobile before he could take Pensacola; Gálvez dispatched two gunships and 500 soldiers to reinforce Mobile. |
| Nov. 1780 | Spanish Treasury in Havana paid 152,190 *livres* to France in payment for hospitalization of Spanish soldiers in Cape Francois. Spain loaned the French government 151,300 *pesos*. Spain also paid 60,000 *pesos* to French officials at Cape Francois for the benefit of French troops stationed in Spanish Santo Domingo. |
| 28 Feb.1781 | A second (and smaller) Spanish flotilla, with 1,315 soldiers, sailed from Havana, Cuba to assist Field Marshall Bernardo de Gálvez in his attack on Pensacola. |
| 9 Mar.1781 | A two month Spanish siege on Pensacola began. Gálvez had previously ordered troops stationed |

|  |  |
|---|---|
|  | in New Orleans and Mobile to join in the attack on Pensacola. Mobile sent 500 men, and 1,400 arrived from New Orleans. |
| 19 Apr. 1781 | 1,600 reinforcements from Havana arrived in Pensacola. |
| 8 May 1781 | The British surrendered at Pensacola. This removed the British threat from both the Gulf of México and the Mississippi River. Gálvez was assisted by four French frigates. He gave them 500,000 *pesos* to repair and reprovision their ships. King Carlos III renamed Pensacola Bay to Bahia Santa Maria de Gálvez; promoted Gálvez to Lieutenant General; named his "Count of Gálvez; and granted him his own coat of arms with the motto, "Yo Solo."[209] |
| Jun. 1781 | The Spanish Treasury in Havana paid 23,568 *livres* to France for aid to Spanish soldiers. Spain loaned 68,656 *pesos* to the French fleet, and loaned an additional 200,000 *pesos* to French officials at Cape Francois. |
| Jul. 17, 1781 | French Admiral de Grasse met with Francisco de Saavedra, Special Emissary of the King of Spain at Cape Francois concerning delaying the attack on Jamaica until after the French fleet is sent to Yorktown. De Grasse was concerned about leaving French colonies in the Caribbean unprotected should he take the entire French fleet to Yorktown. Saavedra convinced de Grasse not to divide the French fleet, |

---

[209] Spanish for "I alone."

| | |
|---|---|
| | promising to protect French colonies with the Spanish warships from Havana. |
| Jul. - Aug. 1781 | The French had no silver or gold with which to pay their soldiers money to become involved in the siege of Yorktown.[210] |
| Jul. 29, 1781 | When de Grasse wrote to Rochambeau by letter dated July 29, 1781 that Rochambeau could count on de Grasse delivering 1,200,000 *livres* that he had been requested to bring, although de Grasse did not yet have those funds. |
| Jul. 31, 1781 | De Grasse's request for loans from wealthy French merchants at Cape Francois fell on deaf ears. |
| Aug. 1, 1781 | The following day de Grasse requested financial help from Spain through Saavedra. Saavedra immediately agreed. |
| Aug. 3, 1781 | Saavedra sailed from Cape Francois on August 3rd, bound for Havana to obtain silver and gold to pay the French soldier's salaries, and to provide food and military supplies for their troops. |
| Aug. 15, 1781 | Saavedra reached Havana on August 15th, only to find the Spanish treasury empty. Jose' Ignaci de Urizza, Intendant of Havana and Juan Manuel de Cagigal, Governor of Cuba, received instructions from Saavedra to deliver 1,000,000 *pesos* to French officials. It took them six hours to secure necessary loans from Spanish |

---

[210] It should be remembered at this time that the U.S. paper money was "not worth a Continental".

merchants, and from the military garrison of Havana, who were promised repayment shortly when the ships ladened with silver coins from the Mexican mint arrived within a few weeks. From Saint-Dominique, French Admiral de Grass sent a frigate to Havana, Cuba to secure the silver coins from Spain. Not only did Spanish officials provide the needed specie, many women of Havana offered their diamonds for the cause. Merchants and four Spanish Army Regiments loaned a total of 4,520,000 *reales*, from which the Exchequer delivered 4,000,000 *reales*, which at the time equaled 500,000 *pesos*. The merchants charged 2% interest, but the Spanish Army Regiments made interest free loans. For a list of the Spanish merchants who made the emergency loan to France, see Appendix L.

Aug.16, 1781  General Bernardo de Gálvez arrived in Havana on August 16$^{th}$, and gave his approval of the loan and transfer. The frigate *Aygrette*, ladened with gold and silver from the Spanish merchants in Havana, departed Havana on the night of August 16.

Aug.17, 1781  The *Aygrette* rendezvoused with de Grasse off the coast of Cuba the next day. The French ships then proceeded to join the French blockade of Yorktown, which led to the British surrender.

| | |
|---|---|
| Aug. 1781 | General George Washington drank a toast to the kings of France and Spain[211] at the home of Robert Morris, in Philadelphia. |
| Aug. 1781 | The Spanish treasury at Havana paid France 100,000 *pesos* for French troops stationed in Spanish Santo Domingo and loaned 100,000 *pesos* to French officials at Cape Francois. |
| Aug. – Sep. 1781 | French officials loaned money (received from Spain in Havana) to the 13 colonies with which to pay one month's salary to the Continental Army. The French Army also used money from Spain to purchase supplies in Virginia. |
| Sep. 1781 | The Spanish treasury at Havana loaned 1,000,000 *pesos* to France to be used in Martinique. |
| 19 Oct. 1781 | General Cornwallis surrendered at Yorktown. |
| 6 May 1782 | General Gálvez' forces attacked the Bahamas, which surrendered. |
| 4 Feb. 1783 | King George III declared a formal cessation of hostilities in the American Revolutionary War. By Feb. 1783, England was confronted with the possibility of losing its holdings in the Caribbean. Bernardo de Gálvez was waiting to |

---

[211] It should be noted that to a lesser degree, the colonists received aid and assistance from Holland (now the Netherlands) and Sweden. Each allowed American ships the use of their ports. The current king of Sweden has been offered membership in the Sons of the American Revolution

invade Jamaica with 10,000 Spanish troops in Guarico, Haiti. Additional Spanish troops were being marshaled in Cádiz, Spain awaiting orders to sail to the West Indies. Gálvez had already been named as the overall commander of the invading forces. It was the imminent threat of the loss of the British holdings in the West Indies that secured the victory at Yorktown.

3 Sep.1783   With the signing of the Paris Peace Treaty, peace was declared between England, the United States, Spain and France.[212]

## Interesting Events That Followed The 1783 Peace Treaty:

1784   The U.S. Congress formally cited General Bernardo Gálvez and Spain for their aid during the American Revolutionary War.

1784   Both the United States and New Spain (especially New Orleans) were suffering from a depression. England had set up an embargo on the import of American goods to both England and her Caribbean colonies. Spain now possessed both East Florida and West Florida, and blocked commerce on the lower

---

[212] Both the Daughters of the American Revolution and the Sons of the American Revolution recognize service between the period 19 October 1781 and 3 September 1783 as "qualified" patriotic service.

|  |  |
|---|---|
|  | Mississippi. The cost to Spain for its involvement in the American Revolutionary War was devastating. In late 1793, Carlos III had ordered a shipment of Mexican Gold to New Orleans to bolster its economy. |
| Jan. 1784 | The Spanish Galleon *El Cazador* set sail from Vera Cruz, México ladened with silver and gold coins from the Mexican mint in México City. This ship was lost at sea. Its cargo was discovered in 1993 by fishermen on the *Mistake* in the Gulf of México about 50 miles from the Louisiana coast. The ship's remains were found in about 300 feet of water. |
| 1785 | Upon his father's death, General Bernardo de Gálvez was named Viceroy of New Spain. |
| 30 Nov. 1785 | General Bernardo Gálvez died in México City, México. |
| 1 Oct. 1800 | The Treaty of San Ildefonso. Spain's economy was so bad that in 1800 it sold Louisiana to France. Only three years later, Napoleon sold Louisiana to the US for pennies an acre. |

**Questions**:

1) If the *Cazador* had reached New Orleans with its treasure, would Spain have still been forced to sell Louisiana to France?

2) If the *Cazador* had reached New Orleans with its treasure, what would have happened to the desire of the U.S. to expand westward?

3) After Conwallis' defeat, the British still had several large concentrations of troops at St. Augustine, Florida: Charleston, South Carolina; Newburgh, New York; and Detroit. Why didn't Britain use these troops to reinvade? It has been suggested that they were about to lose Jamaica with the massing of Spanish and French ships and troops and that it was better to negotiate than to lose all its Caribbean possessions.

## INDEX

Admiral de Grasse, 174, 175

Admiral Jose Solano, xv, xvi

Ally, xxxv, l, lii

ammunition, xxxvi, xxxix, xl, 10, 18, 19, 20, 25, 26, 27, 30, 33, 34, 86, 95, 97, 98, 103, 105, 108, 117, 147, 157, 164, 167, 179, 183, 195, 201, 221

Ann Patten of Pennsylvania, lvii

Antonio Banderas, xxxiii, lvi, 212

Antonio Campos Garin, 217

Antonio Gil Ybarbo, xxix, 149

Arkansas Post, xxiii, xliv, 116, 133, 134

Arkansas River, 117, 133

arms, xxviii, xxxvi, xxxix, xl, xlv, 11, 18, 20, 23, 25, 26, 27, 30, 33, 34, 59, 86, 95, 97, 103, 108, 109, 117, 157, 161, 164, 167, 179, 183, 195, 201, 215, 221

Arms of Bernardo de Gálvez, 59

Arthur Lee, xxxviii, 32, 33, 34

artillery, 24, 72, 81, 85, 86, 112, 119, 161

audience, xxxiii, 207, 210, 211, 212

Bahamas, xliv, 89, 151

Barcelona, Spain, 24

Baron Grantham, British Ambassador to Spain, 18

Baton Rouge, xviii, xxi, xxxviii, xliv, 12, 57, 58, 69, 71, 116, 169, 190

Battle of Fort Jefferson, 114

Battle of Fort San Carlos, 123, 124

Battle of Mobile, 186

Battle of Pensacola, xxii, 79

Benjamin Franklin, xxxvii, 17, 19, 20, 31, 32, 40, 45, 166, 185, 198, 200

Bermuda, 3, 48

Bilbao, Spain, xl, 11, 20, 21, 25, 28, 32, 33, 34, 45, 164, 169, 179, 221

Black Legend, xxxi

Borbón Family Compact, 5

Brazil, 9

brig *Benjamin*, 32

Brig *Northampton*, 34

Brigadier General Nathanael Greene, 11

British fleet, 21, 152, 163

British intelligence, 23

by Admiral Luis de Córdova y Córdova, 139

California Presidios, xxiii

Canada, 3, 54, 57, 145, 163, 222

Canary Islanders, 1, 55, 68, 70, 116, 147

Canary Islands, 5, 54, 67, 116, 149

cannon, xvii, 23, 45, 47, 73, 75, 79, 81, 86, 105, 121, 122, 161, 166, 170

cannon balls, 23, 161

Captain Elias Durnford, 72

Captain Emanuel Hesse, 120

Captain General of Havana, 58

Captain George Gibson, xxviii, 28, 165

Captain John Paul Jones, xxxviii, xli, 42, 45, 46, 164, 221

Captain José Calvo de Irazabal, 79

Captain William Pickles, 51, 70, 71, 169

Captain-General of Louisiana, 59

casualties, 86, 121, 222

cattle, xxx, xlviii, 143, 147, 149, 155, 156, 167

cattle drive, 143, 149, 156

Chapultepec Castle, 58

Chronology Of Events, xlix

Citizenship, 189, 191, 192, 196

clothing, 20, 26, 30, 32, 37, 165

cod fish, 32

commemorative 15 cent stamp honoring General Bernardo de Gálvez, 185

Committee of Safety, 23, 29, 55

Conde D' Aranda, 40

Continental Congress, 17, 18, 23, 25, 63, 64, 65, 99, 102, 112, 183, 190, 195

Continental Congress Committee on Secret Correspondence, 17

cordage, 32, 33, 37

Corn Island, 101, 129

Count de Grasse, xxix

Count de Vergennes, xxix, 39

Count of Floridablanca, xviii, xxvi

Count of Gálvez, 57, 59, 86, 189, 191

Crown Prince Felipe, xxxii, xxxiii, xxxiv, xliv, xlvi, xlviii, xlix, 210, 211, 212

DAR, xxx, xxxiii, xxxvi, lii, 110, 137, 155, 156, 187, 191, 192, 195, 207, 218

Daughters of the American Revolution, xxx, lii, lvi, 155, 156, 160, 177, 197

Declaration of Independence, 10, 20, 21, 22, 26, 28, 164, 204

DeGrasse, xxxvi, 152

Diego de Gardoqui, xxiii, 180

Dollars, 160

Don Diego de Gardoqui, 179

Don Fernando de Leyba, xxvii, 95, 115, 117, 118

Don Francisco Cruzat, 124

Don Francisco de Saavedra, xxvii

Don Francisco Enrique de Borbón y Escasny, 157, 215, 216

Don Juan de Miralles, xxvii, 183

Don Juan De Miralles, xxiii

*Donativo*, xxiii, 137, 169

Dr. Granville W. Hough, li

drugs, 32

Duke of Seville, xlvi, 157, 215, 216

East Florida, 3, 6, 48

El Cid, 206, 207, 208, 214

Elbridge Gerry, 12, 22, 23, 25, 36

English fleet, 4, 221

Falls at Louisville, 110

Felipe VI de Borbón, xxvi, lvi, 157

Ferdinand and Isabella,, xxx

First American Dollar, xxiv

fish, 32, 33

Fort Cahokia, Illinois, xxii

Fort Concordia, 134

Fort Crescent redoubt, 85

Fort Jefferson, Kentucky, xxii

Fort Kaskaskia, Illinois, xxii

Fort Massac, 102

Fort Nelson, KY, xxiii

Fort Sackville at Vincennes, 105, 168

Fort San Carlos, Missouri, xxii

Fort San Juan, Nicaragua, 48

Fort St. Joseph, Michigan, 116

Fort Vincennes, Indiana, xxii

France, xi, xxiii, xxvi, xxviii, xxix, xxxi, xxxvi, xxxvii, xxxviii, xxxix, xl, xli, xlix, li, 2, 3, 4, 5, 6, 9, 10, 11, 17, 18, 19, 20, 23, 24, 25, 26, 27, 31, 35, 38, 40, 42, 43, 45, 48, 49, 55, 56, 97, 107, 151, 152, 153, 164, 166, 167, 172, 173, 176, 177, 179, 180, 185, 200, 201, 204, 219, 221, 222

Francisco Garcia, 143

French fleet, 83, 91, 152, 174

French frigate, the *Aygrette.*, 175

French ships, 22, 55, 152, 170, 176

Frenchmen, 107, 121, 125, 126, 149

frigates, 23, 40, 43, 76, 77, 83, 89, 140, 141, 171, 173

Ft. Carlos, 133, 134

Ft. Charlotte, xxi, 71, 72

Ft. George, xxii

Ft. New Richmond, xxi

Ft. Panmure, xxi

Ft. Pitt, xliv, 28, 35, 63, 95, 98, 129, 165, 167, 173, 201

Galveston, TX, xv, 188, 201

*Gálveztown*, xxix, 51, 68, 70, 80, 180, 217

General Bernardo de Gálvez, xv, xxi, xxvi, xxx, xxxviii, xliv, liii, 38, 39, 66, 82, 116, 117, 155, 162, 165, 167, 168, 175, 178, 185, 187, 201, 217

General Charles Henry Lee, 28, 165

General George Rogers Clark, xxxviii, 63, 91, 95, 98, 99, 108, 122, 128, 129, 166, 167, 195, 201, 212, 221

General John Campbell, 72, 80

George Washington, xii, xvi, xxxix, lii, 28, 30, 128, 153, 165, 167, 176, 179, 180, 181, 183, 185, 190, 195, 198, 200, 201

Gerald Burkland of Michigan, lvii

Gibraltar, xxiv, xxxvii, xli, 7, 9, 43, 50, 162, 163, 203, 218, 219, 221, 222

Governor of the Kingdom of Guatemala,, 54

Governor Rocheblave, 103

Governor, Lord William Campbell, 14

Gran Peña private club,, 213

Great Britain, xxi, xxxviii, xliv, l, 24, 38, 39, 42, 54, 67, 93, 97, 121, 162, 171, 189

grenades, 31, 166, 170

Gulf Coast Campaign, xlv, 61

gunpowder, xxviii, 11, 12, 19, 21, 22, 23, 25, 29, 30, 31, 32, 55, 56, 94, 98, 107, 129, 161, 165, 166, 170

gunships, xvii, 25, 45, 49, 50, 76, 77, 140, 172

*hats*, 33, 37

Havana, Cuba, xv, xxvii, 39, 82, 173, 175, 183

*HMS Gatton*, 142, 171

*HMS Godfrey*, 142, 171

*HMS Hillsborough*, 140, 141, 142, 171

*HMS Mountstuart*, 142, 171

*HMS Port Royal*, 51, 86

*HMS Ramillies*, 140, 171

*HMS Royal George*, 142, 171

*HMS Saint Fermin*, 51

*HMS Tamen*, 14, 16

*HMS West Florida*, 51

Holland, 11, 19, 23, 27, 36, 176, 204, 221

honorary citizenship, 189

Hurricane, xv, xxi, xlv, 84

Iglesias San Jorge, 215

Illinois County, Virginia, 95

in *Plaza Bernardo De Gálvez*, 217

information, l, 14, 21, 30, 56, 133, 156

Inquisition, xxxi

Inspector General of New Spain, 53

Jack Vance Cowan, lvi

Jamaica, xv, xxiii, xliv, 3, 5, 40, 48, 49, 151, 152, 174

James Warren, Speaker of the Massachusetts House of Representatives, 22

Jeremiah Lee, 11

Joe Perez, lvii

John Adams, 19, 169

Joseph Gardoqui & Sons, xxvii, 11, 12, 21, 25, 32, 33, 35, 36, 37

Juan Carlos de Borbón, xxvi

Juan Manuel de Cagigal, Governor of Cuba, 175

Judge Robert Thonhoff, lii

Kentucky County, Virginia, 129

*kettles*, 33, 37

King Ferdinand, liii

King George III, 12, 119, 177

King Philip II, 209

Lafayette, xxxvi, 193, 222

Larry D. McClanahan, x, lvii

lead, 10, 19, 30, 99, 165, 219

Lieutenant Governor Henry Hamilton, 105, 108

Lieutenant Governor of the Texas Province, 149

Lieutenant William Linn, xxviii

Light Townsend Cummins, 12

Lila Guzman, lvii

Lindsey Brock, 212

Livres, xxxviii, 30, 161, 165

Lord Viscount Weymouth, 17

Lord Weymouth, 34

Los Bexarenos Genealogical Society of San Antonio, TX, 191, 195

Louis XVI of France, xxxix

Louisville, xxii, 36, 63, 93, 101, 122, 129, 130, 173, 222

Luis De Unzaga y Amezaga, xxvi

Madrid, Spain, 207, 216

Majorca, xli, xliv, 4, 55, 162

Malaga, Spain, 196, 216

Manchac, xviii, xxi, xxxviii, xliv, 57, 58, 67, 68, 116, 169

Marie Felicite' de St. Maxent d'Estre'han Gálvez., 187

Marques De Santa Cruz, 213

Martin Fernandez de Navarrete, 213

Martin Station, 130

Martinique, 26, 48, 177

Massachusetts Board of War, 32, 36

Massachusetts Committee of Supplies, 12

Matias de Gálvez, xxvi

medical supplies, 10, 37, 161, 165, 201

medications, 32

men-of-war, 23, 24

México City, 58, 178, 201, 202, 203

military supplies, xxxviii, 26, 28, 34, 36, 86, 98, 120, 124, 164, 179, 183, 195

Mimi Lozano, l, liii, 196

Minorca, xli, xliv, 7, 9, 44

Missions, xliv, xlvi, 136

Mississippi River, xxi, xxxviii, xl, xliv, xlv, 3, 28, 29, 31, 35, 36, 40, 41, 43, 48, 55, 57, 59, 65, 69, 71, 92, 101, 102, 111, 115, 116, 117, 119, 120, 123, 124, 126, 128, 133, 134, 153, 163, 165, 167, 168, 169, 173, 198, 221, 222

Mississippi Valley, xii, xxii, 95, 128, 129

Mobile, xviii, xxi, xxxviii, xliv, 57, 59, 70, 71, 72, 73, 75, 77, 82, 123, 170, 172, 173, 186, 190, 198

Moncanares El Real Castle, 207

Money, xlix

Most Favored Nation, 28

musket balls, 31, 161, 166, 187

muskets, 11, 18, 19, 21, 31, 56, 161, 164, 166, 170, 185, 187

N.C. Hough, lii, 56, 98, 116, 122, 130, 155

Natchez, xviii, xxi, xxxviii, xliv, 57, 59, 69, 71, 116, 169, 190, 222

National Society Sons of the American Revolution, x, lvii, 130, 192, 219

naval blockade of the American coastline, 12

naval capture, 139, 171

Nereo shipyards, 217

New England Restraining Act of March 1775, 13

New Orleans, xv, xxviii, xli, xliv, 26, 27, 28, 29, 30, 32, 35, 38, 41, 43, 54, 55, 57, 58, 63, 65, 67, 71, 73, 75, 77, 82, 94, 95, 97, 98, 101, 111, 115, 116, 117, 120, 126, 129, 133, 143, 149, 163, 164, 165, 166, 167, 168, 173, 186, 187, 189, 190, 191, 195, 196, 201

New Spain, xlii, xliv, 1, 3, 28, 48, 98, 144, 145, 149, 150, 167, 190, 201

Nicholas Brown, 23

NSSAR Congress in Paris, xxxvi

Observers, 12

Ohio River, xli, 29, 30, 43, 55, 91, 93, 97, 101, 106, 110, 113, 115, 118, 122, 124, 128, 129, 162, 187, 221

Oliver Pollock, xxi, xlv, 29, 36, 55, 63, 64, 65, 67, 195

Order of the Granaderos y Damas de Gálvez, x, xiii, xxxiii, lvi, lvii, 188, 191, 196

Patrick Henry, 35, 93, 95, 104, 166, 167, 185, 195, 198

Patriotic Lineage Societies, xxiii

Pensacola, xv, xvii, xviii, xxi, xxii, xxxviii, xliv, xlv, 3, 40, 51, 55, 57, 59, 67, 70, 71, 72, 73, 75, 76, 77, 79, 80, 81, 82, 83, 84, 86, 87, 91, 123, 172, 173, 175, 190, 198, 218

Perdido Key, 79, 81, 86

Pesos, 65

Philadelphia, 12, 19, 20, 26, 27, 28, 29, 64, 165, 176, 183, 185

Philip II, 210

pieces of eight, 170

Pierre Beaumarchais, xxix

portrait of Gálvez, 185, 195

Portugal, 4, 9, 18, 180, 200, 204

Pounds, 33, 109, 171

President of the Council of the Indies,, 53

Presidio de Alta, CA, xlviii

Presidio de la Bahia, TX, xlviii

Prime Minister, José Moñino y Redondo, xviii

Prince Gabriel Antonio de Borbón of Spain, 18

Prince Masserano, the Spanish Ambassador to Britain, 13

Professor Thomas E. Chavez, lvi

provisions, 15, 30, 40, 90, 107, 126

Puerto Rico, 3, 24, 39, 48, 54, 55

Queen Isabella, 7

Ranchos, 147

Raven duck, 32

Reales, 165, 170, 202

Red Cliff Fort, 81

rifles, 56, 208

Robert Morris, xxviii, 29, 55, 157, 176, 185

Rochambeau, xxxvi, 174, 222

*Rockingham*,, 25

Roderigue Hortalez & Cie, xxxviii

Royal Audience, xlix, 210

Royal Presidio at Monterey, 135

Russian duck, 32

sail cloth, 23

saltpeter, 21, 23

San Antonio de Bexar, 144, 145, 149

San Antonio River, 143, 146, 147, 149, 167

San Antonio, TX, liii, 191, 195

San Diego de Alcala, 135

San Fernando Church, 58

*San Juan Nepomuceno*, xvi, xliv

Santa Domingo, 172, 176

Santa Rosa Island, 79, 81, 82, 86

SAR, x, xi, xxiv, xxx, xxxiii, xxxvi, xliv, xlv, xlvi, xlviii, lii, 43, 109, 110, 115, 137, 156, 157, 187, 188, 191, 192, 195, 201, 206, 207, 210, 211, 212, 215, 217, 218, 222

*SAR plaque*, 217, 218

SAR Spain Society, 212, 215

SAR Trip to Spain, xxiv

schooner *Glover*, 33, 34

schooner *Marblehead*, 37

schooner *Tabby*, 36

Seven Years War, xl, 133

SHHAR, li, liv

*shirts*, 33, 36

*shoes*, 33, 36, 37, 161

siege, 43, 55, 72, 82, 84, 87, 90, 113, 163, 170, 173, 174, 219, 222

Silas Deane, 18, 20, 25, 32

sloops, 24, 81

*Somos Primos*, lii, liii, liv, lvii, 191, 196

Sons of the American Revolution, x, xi, xxx, xxxvi, l, lii, lvi, 150, 156, 157, 160, 176, 177, 216

Spain, x, xi, xviii, xx, xxi, xxii, xxiii, xxvi, xxvii, xxviii, xxix, xxx, xxxi, xxxii, xxxiii, xxxv, xxxvi, xxxvii, xxxviii, xxxix, xl, xli, xliv, xlvi, xlix, l, li, lii, lvi, lviii, 1, 2, 3, 4, 5, 6, 7, 8, 9, 10, 11, 12, 13, 16, 17, 18, 19, 20, 21, 22, 23, 25, 26, 27, 28, 29, 30, 31, 32, 34, 35, 36, 37, 38, 39, 40, 41, 42, 43, 44, 48, 49, 53, 54, 55, 56, 58, 63, 64, 66, 67, 68, 70, 71, 75, 77, 80, 82, 86, 91, 95, 97, 98, 101, 102, 103, 115, 116, 117, 120, 122, 126, 127, 129, 130, 133, 134, 139, 140, 145, 153, 155, 156, 157, 159, 161, 162, 163, 164, 165, 166, 167, 168, 169, 170, 172, 173, 174, 175, 176, 177, 178, 179, 180, 185, 187, 189, 190, 196, 198, 200, 201, 203, 204, 206, 207, 209, 212, 213, 215, 216, 217, 218, 219, 221, 222, 223

Spanish army, 43, 54, 119, 150, 156, 222

Spanish fleet, xxxviii, 9, 24, 39, 50, 71, 79, 83, 86, 139, 140, 163, 170, 172

Spanish half Escudo, 204

Spanish Lieutenant Governor, 95

Spanish militia, 121, 126, 172, 187, 222

Spanish Milled Dollar, 205

*Spanish Patriots of the American Revolution*, li

Spanish privateers, xxxviii, 47

Spanish silver coin, 202

spy, 22

St. Augustine, 90, 177

St. Louis, 3, 43, 57, 91, 95, 96, 97, 101, 111, 112, 114, 115, 116, 118, 119, 120, 121, 123, 133, 170, 173

St. Louis, Missouri, 91, 101, 111, 173

Steve Renouf, 207, 209, 214, 216

*stockings*, 33, 36, 37

Stone Tower at Ft. San Carlos, xlvi

supplies, xxviii, xxxvi, xxxviii, 9, 10, 12, 17, 26, 27, 28, 32, 33, 35, 36, 37, 55, 56, 63, 64, 65, 66, 68, 85, 90, 95, 96, 97, 102, 103, 105, 107, 108, 109, 117, 120, 122, 125, 126, 157, 163, 164, 165, 166, 167, 173, 176, 183, 185, 189, 195, 221

Sweden, 176, 204, 221

swivel guns, 23, 105

tents, 24, 31, 32, 36, 68, 161, 166, 170, 187, 201

*the Alexander*, 36

the Bahamas, xxii, xxxviii, xlv, 3, 48, 57, 87, 90, 91, 151, 161, 163, 177, 221

*the Charlotte*, 37

The Gálvez Association, of Jacksonville, FL, 191, 195

the *Lydia*, 37

the Society of Hispanic Historical and Ancestral Research, li, liii, liv

*the St. John the Baptist*, 17

the *Success*, 33, 37

*The Texas Connection to the American Revolution*, lii

Theresa de Leyba, 120

Thomas Jefferson, xxxix, 95, 113, 169, 185, 195, 198, 200

Thomas Robinson, 2nd Baron Grantham, 13

U.S. Commemorative Stamp issued in 1929 to honor Clark, 106

U.S. Congress, xxiv, xlvi, xlviii, 178, 185, 192

U.S. House of Representatives, 187, 192, 193

U.S. Senate, 187, 189, 192

uniforms, 31, 109, 161, 166, 170, 201

USS *Bonhomme Richard*, 45, 47

USS *Ranger*, 45

vaqueros, 1, 144, 155

Veracruz, Mexico, 98

Viceroy of New Spain, 58, 178

Viscount of Gálveztown., 59, 86

Wabash River, 106, 107, 108

West Florida, xv, xviii, 3, 7, 48, 57, 70, 71, 86, 87, 169, 190

Wheeling, 29, 56, 63, 98

Whitehaven, England, 45

Wickliffe, Kentucky, 113

wreath laying ceremony, 109, 110, 210

Xebeck, 24

*Yo Solo*, xlv, 59

Zarzuela Palace, 210